M000023163

Transference Neurosis and Psychoanalytic Experience

GAIL S. REED

Transference Neurosis and Psychoanalytic Experience

Perspectives on Contemporary Clinical Practice

Yale University Press New Haven and London

Portions of this text incorporate work that originally appeared in the following journals and is reproduced with their permission:

"Scientific and Polemical Aspects of the Term 'Transference Neurosis' in Psychoanalysis." *Psychoanalytic Inquiry* (1987): 7:465–484.

"The Transference Neurosis in Freud's Writings." *Journal of the American Psychoanalytic Association* (1990): 38:423–450.

"A Reconsideration of the Concept of Tranference Neurosis." *International Journal of Psychoanalysis* (1990): 71:205–217.

Designed by Sonia L. Scanlon.
Set in Times Roman type by Marathon Typography Service, Durham, North Carolina.
Printed in the United States of America by Edwards Brothers, Inc., Ann Arbor, Michigan.

Library of Congress Cataloging-in-Publication Data
Reed, Gail S.
Transference neurosis and psychoanalytic experience : perspectives on contemporary clinical practice / Gail S. Reed.
p. c.m.
Includes bibliographical references and index.
ISBN 0-300-05957-4
1. Transference (Psychology) 2. Psychoanalysts—Interviews. I. Title.
RC489.T73R44 1994
616.89'17—dc20 94-1406
CIP

A catalogue record for this book is available from the British Library.

The paper in this book meets the guidelines for permanence and durability of the Committee on Production Guidelines for Book Longevity of the Council on Library Resources.

10 9 8 7 6 5 4 3 2 1

To my mother and my father

Contents

Acknowledgments

My husband, Tom, has been inestimably understanding, supportive, and patient. My children, Bill and Danielle, willingly and generously gave of their time and energy. I benefited from all of their intelligent comments and assistance.

To my colleagues in the Group for the Study of the Psychoanalytic Process, Inc., with whom I have shared many hours of intense intellectual excitement in the context of profound friendship, I owe collective discoveries about psychoanalysis that are surely reflected in my thinking in these pages. Colleagues in a group engaged in a study of various aspects of the history of psychoanalysis, especially a clinical reassessment of ego psychology, under the chairmanship of Martin Bergmann, also contributed helpfully to my thinking. The Psychoanalytic Investigative Group at the Institute for Psychoanalytic Training and Research cochaired by Norbert Freedman and Doris Silverman devoted two stimulating meetings to a discussion of my interviews and their methodology from which I greatly profited.

Stanley Olinick, Alan Skolnikoff, Joseph Reppen, Ros Goldner, and Marc Rubenstein generously took the time to read and comment helpfully on earlier versions of this manuscript. Jacob Arlow generously did the same for several chapters. Francis Baudry, Warren Poland, Sherwood Waldron, Graciela Abelin, Conrad Stein, Marion Oliner, Gerald Fogel, Donald M. Kaplan, and the late Nathaniel London commented equally helpfully on specific portions. Candidates at the San Francisco Psychoanalytic Institute usefully reacted to a crucial part of an earlier draft of the manuscript. Many other colleagues who have exchanged ideas and friendship with me directly or indirectly have helped in the writing of this book. My gratitude is not diminished although I have not the space to thank them publicly.

Above all, this book could not have taken shape without the twenty-one analysts who gave of their time and experience remarkably openly and honestly, chose anonymity, and overcame the shock of reading verbatim transcriptions of their interviews sufficiently to allow me to reproduce their words.

Needless to say, I alone am responsible for the result.

Transference Neurosis and Psychoanalytic Experience

CHAPTER ONE

Transference Neurosis and Psychoanalytic Experience

Freud used the term *transference neurosis* in two ways. One was nosological and designated hysteria, phobia, and obsessional neurosis (Freud, 1917). When intended this way, the term usually appeared in the plural. The transference neuros*es* were opposed to the narcissistic neuroses and were deemed treatable by psychoanalysis because patients could develop transferences to the psychoanalyst. More precisely, each patient troubled by one of the transference neuroses would develop a transference neuros*is*. As Freud (1914) wrote when he first used the term:

> We admit [the patient's compulsion] into the transference as a playground in which it is allowed to expand in almost complete freedom and in which it is expected to display to us everything in the way of pathogenic instincts that is hidden in the patient's mind. . . . We regularly succeed in giving all the symptoms of the illness a new transference meaning and in replacing his ordinary neurosis by a "transference-neurosis" of which he can be cured by the therapeutic work. The transference thus creates an intermediate region between illness and real life through which the transition from the one to the other is made. The new condition has taken over all the features of the illness; but it represents an artificial illness which is at every point accessible to our intervention. (p. 154)

This use of the term in the singular, designating an "intermediate region between illness and real life," thus pertained to a particular and organized development of the transference in the course of psychoanalytic treatment. The transference neurosis was seen as an illness centered uniquely on the psychoanalyst. The treatment became a situation in which the repressed libidinal impulses and related hurts and frustrations originating in the soil of childhood oedipal conflicts could flower. Once they emerged from repression, inevitably attracted by the presence of the analyst as a substitute object representation for loved and frustrating oedipal objects, their energy could be liberated for a healthier deployment in reality. The transference neurosis represented an illness necessary to cure. The focus of my inquiry is the contemporary meaning of this second entity.[1]

Much in psychoanalytic theory and practice has changed since Freud described and elaborated on the concept of transference neurosis. Although the classical description continues to be useful for many analysts, the transferences of many patients do not obviously fit that description. Moreover, we see oedipal conflict as having preoedipal precursors; we consider more thoroughly the roles of character and aggression; and we organize according to the structural and newer theories as well as or instead of the topographic. Not surprisingly, discrepancies and inconsistencies in what clinical constellations the concept refers to and consequent differences of opinion about the very usefulness of the concept have gradually become evident. The concept today is confused and confusing.

The goal of my inquiry is accordingly twofold: first, to delineate the inconsistencies, discrepancies, and differences of opinion about the usefulness of the concept that exist today; second, to attempt to synthesize a contemporary description of the transference neurosis that clarifies as many of the discrepancies as possible, that is true to contemporary clinical practice as I understand it, and that retains whatever remains valuable in Freud's concept. This endeavor cannot be objective. My trying to conserve what I deem valuable in the concept already involves a position in the dispute about its validity, and deciding on what is true to clinical practice depends on my personal clinical assessment. Moreover, the discrepancies and inconsistencies that appear today are also products of internal subjective conflicts in analysts, and I shall spend some time on the nature of the conflicts the concept of transference neurosis evokes in psychoanalysts that have shaped its current position.

In the course of this book I shall formulate a contemporary definition that is an attempt to make sense of my own clinical experience, my understanding of the concept from the literature, and the accounts of twenty-one practicing analysts who generously described their concept of the transference neurosis to me in the specific terms of their clinical work. These conversations—taped, transcribed, and partly reproduced in this book—make available a needed range of evidence from cases and from contemporary analysts grappling with the concept.

1. I shall not discuss questions related to the transference neurosis in the treatment of children.

The transference neurosis, I shall conclude, can be understood as a new organization that may arise in the course of a psychoanalysis, the transference reflection of an ego and superego sufficiently integrated and developed to give rise to neurotic conflict. This requisite psychic structure shapes the construction of the object representations of the analyst and their interweaving with an inner network of core, determinative, unconscious fantasies and related memories after the more self-enhancing, pain-reducing, distancing, and narcissistically protective versions of these fantasies are no longer needed by the analysand in his or her relationship with the analyst.

When the new organization arises one can say partly metaphorically that the series of variably constructed object representations of the analyst has become *entwined* with the network of core organizing, experience-near, perceptually influential fantasies and memories from childhood. The word *entwined* connotes the presence of a strong libidinal component as well as the greater proximity of core fantasies to moment-to-moment experience. The libidinal component allows the expression not only of itself but of hostile and humiliating aspects of conflicts. The patient's engagement also reflects the increasingly liberated capacities of the adult ego: he or she puts transference experience in the service of psychoanalytic work. The experience is one of immediate and intimate engagement for both parties to the dyad so that the analyst's conflicts are more likely to be activated than at other times. The difference in stages is not dependent on absolute external manifestations but is relative to an earlier stage of a particular analysis.

The necessary presence of capacities associated with a sufficiently developed ego and superego is the sign that the individual has traversed the organizing stage of the infantile neurosis. The latter is not synonymous with a symptomatic illness of childhood or with isolated oedipal conflict; rather, it is an attempted solution to frequently interrelated oedipal and preoedipal conflicts. Open to still later reorganizations through latency and adolescence, it results in a structure capable of some measure of impulse control, reality testing, symbolization, object constancy and related qualities of object relations, signal anxiety, the accepting of responsibility, and affect regulation.

I further employ a distinction between transference and transference neurosis that I believe Freud implied by describing transference as a process and transference neurosis as a mutable, evolving result. The transference or transferring process is that process which constructs the figure of the analyst through the shaping agency of the ego and out of the central unconscious fantasy/memory complexes that regulate the patient's perception.

The first, and original, description of the transference neurosis elaborates on the fate of impulses. They are attracted to the person of the analyst, as to a magnet, in a process necessary for cure. The object representation of the analyst is not primarily thought of as being subjectively constructed by the patient. Rather, the analyst is an objective recipient of urges, and the transference neurosis is a precipitate of illness made up of those urges, their displacements, and their condensations, a middle term between the patient's subjectivity and the analyst's material reality. In accordance with the topographic theory, the motives underlying the symptomatic transference illness must be made conscious in order to be resolved.

The second description speaks of an unconscious network of fantasies and memories in which the object representation of the analyst becomes entwined and which reflects a relatively integrated ego and superego. The object representation of the analyst is inevitably the patient's subjective construction, but it becomes more immediately experienced in the specific network of organizing fantasies and memories as more distancing and defensive fantasies are worked through. The intertwining of this representation with the web of core unconscious fantasies and memories originally from the past but continuing to exist in the present comprises a new core organization in the patient. That entity no longer needs to be the constant focus of discussion, however. Although it is a possible, and often desirable, conscious content of the psychoanalytic process, it is also the stimulus for making conscious the fantasies, conflicts, and memories from the past that compose it. The transference neurosis is always a means to an end: analysis of the critical compromise formations—that is, of the network of core organizing fantasies and memories that constitute that which has been transferred.

Such a contemporary modification of the concept of transference neurosis, however close it remains to the Freudian original, is not easily arrived at, either individually or collectively. The reasons for this difficulty are multiple, interrelated, and in some measure intrinsic to psychoanalysis. They are partly attributable to the nature of learning in the discipline and partly to the specific history and connotations of the concept.

First, when extraclinical factors mitigate against acknowledging a contradiction between clinical observation and the received understanding of a technical concept, strains are often collectively and unknowingly covered up. The term that designates the concept is used as though it still denoted an agreed-upon clinical phenomenon, when the term actually refers to diverse phenomena. Thus, exploration of the current concept of the transference neurosis will shed some light on the way change occurs in psychoanalytic discourse and the way technical language can disguise change.

Second, this inquiry into the current concept of the transference neurosis will touch on the contribution of the psychoanalytic history of a concept to those of its meanings that influence practicing analysts and affect their subsequent modifications of the concept. By virtue of its role in cure, the transference neurosis came to occupy a strategically important position that made analysts hesitant to modify it despite theoretical and technical change that logically dictated modifications.

Its strategic position included its standing at the important intersection of science and technique. When Freud (1905b, 1917) used the concept of transference to explain the uncanny effects of hypnosis, psychoanalysis became an account of mental events that could utilize the discoveries generated by its own procedures to explain apparently mysterious phenomena scientifically (see chap. 2). Then, when Freud conceived of the transformation of the patient's symptomatic illness into a transference illness that could be cured through interpretation, he utilized his scientific knowledge to shape psychoanalytic technique. Transference neurosis both conferred upon psychoanalysis and became imbued with scientific status. An examination of the current concept thus sheds light on a third area—how assumptions about the scientific nature of psychoanalysis and the nature of psychoanalytic science affect the field of psychoanalysis.

Fourth, it will shed light on the transference pressures involved in integrating clinical data with clinical theory. The position of the transference neurosis as the representative of scientific cure placed it at the intersection of science as inductive observation and science as protective status. The analyst who thought about the concept in doing clinical work risked being caught up in these contradictory functions. Such inevitable extraclinical functions and connotations placed a burden on psychoanalysts as practitioners and as the observers and integrators of clinical data and theory.

Finally, the influences of transferences, to Freud, to supervisors, to teachers, and to one's own analyst(s), are particularly strong in psychoanalysis because so much learning on the subject of the relations between self and others occurs through the immediacy of personal encounters. That is, transferences are inextricably involved with learning through the important place psychoanalysis gives to its oral tradition. This examination of the current concept of the transference neurosis will afford a view of the role of that oral tradition in the collective modification and development of concepts by using that tradition as the major vehicle of inquiry.

Technical Language in Psychoanalysis

Understanding psychoanalysis to be a science analogous to a natural science, many psychoanalysts have assumed that the technical language in which their concepts were couched was or should be purely denotative—that is, that it named things just as *femur* names a particular bone. Useful technical language in psychoanalysis functions differently because it must accommodate personal experience in general and personal *clinical* experience in particular. It is, therefore, connotative as well as denotative, fluid and ambiguous within a range, highly dependent on links between personal experience and collective understanding (Reed, 1984).

Technical concepts and the terms that represent them can be thought of as conventions in the literary sense. They are condensations of collective understanding, which itself is a result both of communally shared unconscious fantasy and of communally shared clinical experience and training. A technical concept in psychoanalysis thus functions as a stimulus for the reexperiencing of these commonly held fantasies, beliefs, and experience, all the while retaining its denotative meaning. In addition, the technical concept evokes private, idiosyncratic associations that can create additional individual variations in understanding.

If technical concepts represent combinations of personal and communal meaning, it follows that there will inevitably be ambiguities and uncertainties in usage and understanding that go beyond denotation. Provided that these ambiguities do not overwhelm denotative meaning, they facilitate clarification and discovery because they facilitate the posing of questions. That is, it is the very fact of integration of these different strata of comprehension that makes of any psychoanalytic concept the beginning of a dialogue—a system not closed but open to another person's subjective inquiry. Too idiosyncratic a use of a particular concept, however, will ultimately create confusion rather than communication and will not continue to be admitted by the community. Instead, it may be collectively discarded, or a schism may develop.

This need for the technical concept and its representative term to have a range of meaning that accommodates individual differences and permits creative insights without losing the unifying power of a consistent denotation cannot be overemphasized. Provided always that the range of meaning is limited, ambiguity in technical psychoanalytic concepts is not a failing but a fact. The dictionary compiled by Laplanche and Pontalis (1973) that traces the historical development of psychoanalytic concepts and terminology makes clear the constant presence of this range.

The source of these historical transformations is the experience of the individuals who use the concepts. Psychoanalytic clinical theory and its relevant concepts, however shrouded in polysyllables, is a discourse about the passions of our lives, about our fundamental loves, hates, longings, sorrows, disappointments, and uncertainties, about our childhood creation of explanations out of the coincidences, incidents, and stresses of everyday life, about how those childhood explanations became building blocks for subsequent endeavors and understanding, about the indirect and layered way they continue to shape adult character and perception. Psychoanalysts experience those sets of phenomena that our technical concepts designate because we are human beings and also because we become analysands in order to become analysts. We bring all this personal experience, conscious and unconscious, to our use of concepts and transmit it by the figurative language in which we express them.

While integrating these concepts, we also fashion them anew. Our own experience determines that we shall ignore certain connotations and discard certain denotations. Each of us individually and each generation collectively remakes to some degree our conceptual landscape. The present study focuses on the personal and collective remaking of the concept of transference neurosis in such a conceptual landscape. It looks at collective psychoanalytic conservation and change.

Transference Neurosis and Conceptions of Cure

From its inception, the concept of transference neurosis was associated with the occurrence of particular clinical phenomena centrally important to cure. Moreover, it designated an extended clinical phenomenon that was not only unique in *form* and, broadly, in content to each individual analysis but unique to a psychoanalytic treatment.[2] Since each patient's transference neurosis is unique, yet the general concept was central to Freud's psychoanalytic theory of cure, the variations among psychoanalysts in interpreting and applying the theoretical concept always occur in the context of variations in their concept of cure.

A standard theoretical definition was synthesized by Weinshel (1971): the transference neurosis constitutes not only "a revival" of the infantile neurosis within the analytic situation but also a "*transformation*." "It is not a simple replication of the old infantile neurosis in a new setting; it involves . . . , as Freud (1917) puts it, 'new editions of the old conflicts.'"

Clinical descriptions of the transference neurosis that aspire to generalization are highly elusive, however. If we read Glover's brilliant chapters struggling to convey the ineffable, this elusiveness will strike us immediately.[3]

2. It differs in these properties from a concept such as "isolation," which describes a recurring *formal* constellation recognizable in varying situations. (By formal, I mean properties recognizable without specific ideational content.) By virtue of its association to psychoanalytic cure, transference neurosis also differs from concepts such as "unconscious fantasy," which also vary in content with each individual.

3. Uncertainty, however, came to Glover with experience. In his original lectures on technique delivered in 1927, he was more certain about the appearance of the transference neurosis. One notes, he wrote there, that "the whole analytic situation has taken on an entirely fresh complexion and will maintain this complexion with varying degrees of exaggeration throughout the second phase of the analysis. *The transference neurosis has commenced*" (1928, p. 67). He had been describing a hysterical patient beginning to talk only about current matters in her life and then falling silent. *"We are driven to the conclusion that the patient has been caught up in a forward sweep of libidinal interest, and whilst it is certainly a defense in that it is a sweep forward . . . it ends in an almost complete jam in the process of thinking because its logical goal is preoccupation with the most immediate of all events, viz. life in the analytic room and the immediate relations*

> You will no doubt become aware of a seeming contradiction. . . . many of the indications of an oncoming transference-neurosis are abvious. . . . The analyst may nevertheless miss the indications. . . . The answer is . . . not all anxiety types manifest classical transference-neuroses. . . . A good general policy [is] . . . to look for [signs of the transference-neurosis] precisely when they appear to be absent. . . . The view that a typical transference-neurosis develops in all cases is not only theoretically improbable, but contrary to actual experience. . . . Although we might argue that . . . the sign of a transference-neurosis is the continuance of a prolonged analysis without any sign of a transference-neurosis, this would be a conclusion to be arrived at only sparingly. . . . So many problems and uncertainties beset this subject that it is often difficult even for experienced analysts to avoid developing garbled ideas on the matter or, still more unfortunate, seeking to gloss over manifest difficulties by clinging dogmatically to a few theoretical generalisations and some practical rules of thumb. (Glover, 1955, p. 113–114, 123)

This tentative approach evokes contemporary clinical attitudes extremely well.

But such tentativeness, however well founded in observation, may be taken as undermining the "scientific" account of psychoanalytic cure, especially if the absence of a transference neurosis does not preclude significant improvement in the patient. Despite Glover's tentativeness and his observation that "cases of character" do not always develop a "classical transference neurosis," a controversy involving the transference neurosis arose in the 1950s in response to the challenges of Franz Alexander. Nominally this controversy was over the question of altering the frame of a psychoanalysis to counteract patients' dependent needs. Less overtly, the controversy inevitably involved the whole psychoanalytic method and its theory of cure because Alexander and his followers had depicted the transference neurosis as potentially morbid and to be avoided (see chap. 2).

This assertion had significant repercussions. In the United States, the existence of a transference neurosis began to be used to measure whether or not a treatment was a psychoanalysis. The demonstration of a transference neurosis became a requirement for certification by the American Psychoan-

---

with the analyst" (p. 68). Even in 1927, he underlined the difficulty of recognizing the transference neurosis: *"It differs from the more explosive indications of positive and negative transference as seen in early phases of analysis in that it is liable to pass unnoticed certainly by the patient and in some cases by the analyst. . . . The main part of the analyst's work is to make this unconscious set of attitudes conscious"* (p. 68). By the time he revised these chapters in 1955, however, Glover had added important qualifications.

alytic Association. For instance, *The Revision of the Standards of Training* published by the Board of Professional Standards in 1984 stated: "Psychoanalysis as a treatment procedure depends decisively on the understanding and analysis of the phenomena of transference and resistance in the psychoanalytic situation. This requires the re-experiencing and analysis within the analytic transference of fundamental aspects of the infantile neurosis, of childhood events and fantasy in relation to the important figures of that period" (p. 3). Valenstein (letter, 1993) commented that the 1984 version was not "significantly different" from a draft of standards he collaborated on that was printed in 1971. "Within the discussions of the Membership Committee (now the Certification Committee) on which I served in the early 1970s, the expectation was that an analyzable transference neurosis should be implicitly, or better still, explicitly demonstrable in one or another of the case write-ups submitted by applicants for active membership."[4]

The striking contrast between Glover's caution and these requirements raises questions about whether polemic and scientific aspects of the concept may have become confused and if so what effect such confusion might have had on the way analysts understood and integrated the concept. Definitions of the transference neurosis could be too rigidly held, eliminating potential patients from analytic treatment. Alternately, the concept could be broadened to the point of vagueness, thereby including phenomena that would not logically belong with it. Such conceptual confusion might well affect technique and lend itself to a collective rationalizing of certain countertransferences.

To complicate matters further, it became clear that Freud's original definition, conceptualized in terms of the topographic theory, does not square easily with our current use of structural theory and other more contemporary paradigms. Were *transference neurosis* just another term, it might have been dropped entirely. Its centrality to the theory of cure in Freud, however, meant that the theory of cure itself had to be updated. Adapting the definition to contemporary practice was undoubtedly one of the motives informing the extraordinary panel on the subject at the 1968 American Psy-

4. Valenstein's letter adds important qualifications: "I should add, however, that the concept of transference neurosis that we shared in the committee was far broader than Freud's original description/definition of it. . . . It encompassed the spectrum and hierarchical variability of the set of transferences that might materialize during an analysis, and certainly was not limited to symptom reactivation as such, in a singular transference, as it might materialize during an analysis.

"As for the resolution of the . . . transference neurosis, . . . it was looked for in evaluating applications, at least to the extent that it should be understood as an aim in the termination phase. That it might not be resolvable, or at least only limitedly resolvable . . . might be acceptable for some cases that were part of the application, but then the applicant would have been expected to be aware of and discuss the reasons for such a state of affairs or their outcome" (Letter to the author, September 3, 1993).

choanalytic meetings (Blum, 1971; Calef, 1971; Harley, 1971; Loewald, 1971; Weinshel, 1971). Attempts there were made both to broaden it, retaining its centrality to cure, and to narrow it, reducing its connection to cure.

Today the term no longer designates a recognized unitary clinical phenomenon. Further, what Calef said at that time still holds true: even when the definition of the transference neurosis does not "differ widely from one analyst to another, there is nevertheless a considerable variety of opinion as to its clinical constitution" (1971, pp. 22–23).

In fact, there has recently been disagreement about the very value of the transference neurosis as a clinical concept, with some analysts today holding that the concept has outlived its usefulness, and others arguing the contrary (London, 1987; Rosenblatt, 1987; Cooper, 1987; Shaw, 1991). This debate is further confused by those who find the term unwieldy, contradictory, or tautological, but in practice respect the concept in some form, and those who flatly discard the concept as outmoded. Yet, as Weinshel (1971) noted, despite the centrality of the concept and the controversy accruing to it, surprisingly little has been written on it. These contradictions contribute to my wish to explore its contemporary appearance to see whether a reasonable contemporary account can be constructed.

The Nature of Psychoanalytic Science and the Scientific Nature of Psychoanalysis

Transference neurosis assumed a role as the conveyor of scientific status because the idea of transference neurosis as an intermediate illness that fosters the cure of the original illness permitted the analogy of psychoanalytic treatment to a medical cure in which the description of cure actually specified the stages in the transformation of a disease. This formulation in turn linked the concept of psychoanalysis to the natural sciences on which so much physical medical therapy is based.

Freud's discovery of transference was an important step in the process by which psychoanalysis laid claim to the status of science because it permitted the demystification of hypnosis. If the transference were suppressed or ignored rather than analyzed, "whatever else had been done in the treatment, it would not deserve the name of psychoanalysis," he wrote (1926b, p. 227). Psychoanalysis came to be seen as a procedure that utilized suggestion only to destroy the patient's suggestibility (see chap. 2). Yet the scientific status that Freud claimed for the discipline he discovered is a fragile one. Awareness of that fragility may well interfere with analysts' explicit reexamination of the transference neurosis.

Before returning to the transference neurosis, some fuller discussion of psychoanalysis as a science is in order because the scientific status of psychoanalysis is so often questioned (see Grunbaum, 1984). Although an idea of science based on a popular and overly narrow natural science model is the basis of many polemical attacks, an underlying misapplication of the concept of science often remains unspoken even in more serious considerations (Wurmser, 1989).

Moreover, in the context of the popular debate, calls for more research unwittingly tend to endorse rigid attitudes about what constitutes science. Well-meaning efforts to defend psychoanalysis from the accusation that it is not a science frequently result in claims that it is the wrong kind of science.[5] Indeed, what is often envisioned by the idea of psychoanalysis as a science is a concretistic natural science model updated to the computer age. Consequently, research that isolates and quantifies is designed: computer studies arranged around a series of binomial, yes/no alternatives.

But the effort to fit psychoanalysis into a particular nineteenth-century version of natural science ignoring unconscious processes hampers exploration. For instance, the assumption that technical language is or should be purely denotative, an outgrowth of such an expectation, has probably prevented inquiries into how psychoanalysts integrate a concept arising from received clinical theory with their own clinical experience.

Of course, those who would locate psychoanalysis among the natural sciences and who have in mind a concretistic concept of natural science are often only trying to define their vision of the science of psychoanalysis. Which natural scientific properties of psychoanalysis they emphasize depends on which properties of natural science they choose to analogize; but, by using natural science as an analogy, they unwittingly import extraneous and damaging expectations and connotations that then influence the development of concepts. For instance, many psychoanalysts analogize their objective observation of the patient's conflict to objective observation in the natural sciences. They describe listening to the contiguity of and breaks in the patient's associations after an intervention for signs of validation of the intervention. In fact, such inductive procedures are a very important aspect of good psychoanalytic technique and of clinical theory building, as they are of scientific observation and reasoning in general, but they are not the same as looking through a microscope.

Despite the somewhat naive assertions of Freud (1940, p. 195) and the optimistic efforts of the Hartmann era with its "conflict-free sphere," psychoanalysis has another, contradictory version of objective observation: it

5. I am characterizing an often ill-informed position. I do not, for the sake of polemic, want to downplay the heroic efforts of those who are looking to define the science of psychoanalysis appropriately and find research appropriate to it. A comprehensive monograph of *serious* efficacy studies is in preparation by R. Galatzer-Levy, H. Bachrach, A. Skolnikoff, and S. Waldron, *On the Efficacy of Psychoanalysis*. See also, H. Dahl, H. Kachele, and H. Thoma, eds., 1988; Bachrach, 1989; Meissner, 1989.

does not exist in pure form; there are only relative degrees of unconscious "contamination." As Loewald (1988) wrote: "With the psychoanalytic conception of the unconscious and of psychic reality psychoanalysis is stepping outside the bounds of nineteenth-century natural science and its interpretation (a hermeneutic construction) of nature as objective material reality."

It follows that all human understanding, including psychoanalytic understanding, is a product of conflict and compromise that includes unconscious motivations. I am not suggesting a consequent capitulation to postmodern thought by which we should sacrifice our clinical authority on the altar of relativity, but rather that our authority is limited by the circumstances of our being human. Within that framework, we strive toward objectivity sufficient to interpret to patients those unconscious fantasies and memories of which they apprise us through their associations and actions but of which they themselves remain unaware.

Our objectivity, however, is unavoidably relative. With patients, we find ourselves in a field of double forces, constantly trying to disengage ourselves from their pull. We must contend with our own character as well as those of our own more specific conflicts evoked by the patient at the same time that we endeavor to help the patient understand the unconscious forces motivating his or her behavior. The limits of our objectivity should not be banished from awareness in pursuit of an unrealizable ideal. Moreover, if we wrest clinical objectivity from subjective conflict only with effort, the same is true in attenuated fashion for our understanding and integration of clinical concepts.

Le Guen (1989) distinguished between sciences that observe nature and psychoanalysis as a human science that observes the human psyche. The former not only isolate phenomena before they are studied, but isolate the experimenter from the phenomena he or she observes. Nature is treated as fundamentally atemporal and objective as well. The psychoanalytic study of the psyche, in contrast, does not isolate the observer from the observed. Nature, moreover, Le Guen continued, is conceived as historical. By making free association, evenly hovering attention, and the mistaken ideas of truth that characterize the patient's transference neurosis the tools of his research, Freud understood that the isolation of the experimenter from his subject had to be reversed.

Our elevation of objective science is probably another way to repress the discovery of the unconscious. Freud noted that for human beings used to distinguishing themselves from animals by emphasizing their rationality, his discovery would represent a terrible narcissistic wound. "Scientific research" in psychoanalysis that does not take the unconscious into account may be seen as an attempt to dress this wound. Joel Dor (1988, 1:15) underlined the fundamental incongruity of expecting a model that admits only conscious, observable rationality to verify a model that takes unconscious motives into account by addressing himself to the disparity in the way we anticipate that meaning will be expressed in scientific and in psychoanalytic discourse: "le discours de la science, qui exige dans le principe même de sa production une négation de la Spaltung (incarnée par le sujet-de-la-science, le sujet-non-divisé) n'est aucunement opératoire à exprimer adéquatement quelque chose du champ psychanalytique, lequel, par définition, se soutient de cette division."[6]

Jean Laplanche (1987) has shown that the neurological concept of the reflex arc, profoundly important in the development of the topographic theory, was derived from a physiology that was already recognized as false in Freud's day (Laplanche, 1987, p. 6). The conclusions that Freud drew from his recourse to this analogy were not less fruitful for psychoanalysis because they came from a false physiology. Rather, the phenomenon of their fruitfulness in the context of their falseness makes clear the different nature of psychoanalysis as science and its different relations with neighboring disciplines: "The model borrowed from 'biology' or from psychophysiology is a *false* model. It is as though it signalled a *twofold* heterogeneity; not only is psychoanalysis *unlike* the other sciences in that it does not develop *in the same way* that they develop; its relationship *with* the other sciences may not be comparable to mutual relations between other sciences" (Laplanche, 1987, p. 7).

Grossman (1992a) has connected this uniqueness to the nature of the latent theoretical model of mental organization in Freud's writings. That model is a hierarchical and recursive one in which both boundaries and transformations in function across boundaries are necessary and prominent features. When Freud addressed the issue of psychoanalysis as science, suggested Grossman (1992a, p. 46), he "placed scientific thinking and science into the model of thought constructed of hierarchies and boundaries alongside psychoanalysis," effectively extending his model beyond psychoanalysis to its reciprocal relations with the way scientists construct theories out of data.

"For Freud, theory construction in both physical science and in psychoanalysis, on the one side, and the activities of the clinician on the other, all involved the forming and testing of hypotheses about reality" (Grossman, 1992a, p. 51). Thus, both psychoanalytic theory and method address the issue of "the effort to describe the analyst's use of self-observation as a tool

6. "Scientific discourse that demands by the very principle of its creation a negation of Spaltung (exemplified by the undivided subject of science) is not in any way functionally capable of explaining adequately something from the psychoanalytic field that assumes that division by definition" (my translation). "Spaltung" refers to the splitting of the subject, i.e., "the I," into conscious and unconscious.

in the study of his patients and their self-observations. Clinical interpretation tests the picture of the mind that is created. Psychoanalysis, in this sense, is about the way people try to understand one another in ordinary interaction as distinguished from laboratory experiments" (p. 58). That incorporation of self-analysis as a constituent of understanding another makes psychoanalysis different from other sciences:

> Freud's development of a method that systematically treated one's own mental life as one treated that of others was unique. . . . Therefore, there is also something unique in the way we as analysts learn about this picture of mind and go about modifying it, so long as we use the same method. This method and the picture of mental organization it presents (our theory) find their special relevance in relation to the processes involved in self-exploration through analytic dialogue. . . . The issues of its integration with other models and its close connection with self reflection in the foundations of psychoanalytic theory may contribute to some problems within and at the boundaries of psychoanalysis. These factors may account for some of the difficulty of formulating hypotheses for testing outside analysis, and for the special ways analysts use data outside their field. (pp. 58–59)

Psychoanalysis might be conceptualized as a science of the way humans make meaning and the kind of meaning they make. Such a conceptualization would inevitably include as objects of scrutiny psychoanalytic concepts and the terms that refer to them, such as *transference neurosis*, rather than erroneously relegating those terms to an objective sphere. Closest to my view, Barratt (1984) argued for the distinct nature of psychoanalysis as a science of representation, "a semiotics of the split subject" (p. 87). Psychoanalysis, he contended, starts with the "decision of common consciousness to treat itself as false" (p. 257). It "focusses on aberrations and impairments in the text of conscious and preconscious meaning" (p. 258). Psychoanalysis "places the immediacy and familiarity of ordinary mentation under suspicion and dispossesses its priority and authority" (p. 258). It thus "discloses the complicity of an entire network of meanings" (p. 260). Meaning, for Barratt, "is determined by the interrelationship of representations" (p. 264). Since neurosis implies that in pathological formations what is desired and repressed returns to disturb the conscious sense of self, there is a consequent division between conscious and unconscious in the subject. This split subjectivity is reflected in the representations a subject makes of self and world. Psychoanalysis as the science of representation addresses this split interrelationship of representations, attends to the consequent formation of psychic reality, and succeeds in transforming it.

Although submission of psychoanalysis to an incompatible system, as the popular version of natural science is, is neither the way to make it scientific nor the way to relieve the transference neurosis of its burden of upholding the natural science analogy, placing ordinary (nonlinear) psychoanalytic discourse about the transference neurosis under self-reflective observation may disclose a network of meanings bearing on the clinical situation and its interrelation with theory making.

Psychoanalytic Learning

Perhaps because as psychoanalysts we have been busy with what we thought we were supposed to be like, we have given very little thought to how we actually utilize what we are taught and how we change ourselves, our minds, and our ways of practicing. Examination of the progressively changing meaning to clinicians of the transference neurosis may shed light on this process.

Few of us would say that we practice as Freud practiced in 1914. Moreover, we can document changes in technique from the written literature (Bergmann, 1976). What is far less clear is how those changes actually came about. Although we sometimes cling to terms derived early in the history of psychoanalysis and by silent consensus redefine them to make them acceptable to our current views, we also sometimes behave as though we progress from discovery to discovery in a linear fashion, each discovery presented as a scientific paper. Yet what kind of *collective* internal system is at work through which we review clinical data, integrate deviant but valuable points of view, correct errors of technique, or as it sometimes unfortunately seems to happen, repress valuable aspects of our theory and decide that a particular written suggestion is pertinent?

To stay with the example of useful correctives rather than the less valuable modifications of theory that in actuality represent the repression of valuable concepts, let us take the issue of the analyst's silence. In the 1940s and 1950s, especially, many classical analysts clinging to a technique based on an outmoded topographic theory (e.g., Menninger, 1958) were rigidly silent with patients. This approach was buttressed by the widespread belief that the transference neurosis would develop on its own if the analyst did not interfere.[7] Arlow described the approach in 1987:

> In a strikingly reductionistic manner, some analysts maintain that, if the patient were really associating freely, his productions would take on the nature indicative of primary process functioning, that is to say, communication would become disjointed, fragmented, incoherent,

7. Orgel described a teacher of his advising candidates in a class just to wait, not to say or do anything, and that then the transference neurosis would emerge (personal communication).

> and symbolic, and thought would be experienced in terms of the primary sensory modalities, particularly vision. . . . Therapeutically this translates into the technical maxim of "helping the patient to regress" primarily by having the analyst assume an extraordinarily passive stance. (p. 73)

Arlow went on to dispute this stance:

> The analyst is not a passive witness to the patient's self revelations. . . . His presence . . . is a constant dynamic factor in the psychoanalytic situation. . . . he presides over the contest of forces arrayed in the patient's mind. He intervenes from time to time to delineate the nature of the forces involved and to explain the purpose they serve. He provides the opportunity . . . for each of the forces participating in the inner debate to have its say. (p. 74)

Arlow's paper elegantly and authoritatively codified something working analysts already knew. Passivity in the face of unconscious resistance may or may not lead to regression, but it does not resolve the patient's problems because it does not grapple with character structure and defense. Nor does the transference neurosis leap, full-blown, into the silent analyst's lap.

Although adoption of the structural theory made greater activity a technical imperative, such a realization did not immediately modify the traditional view of the ideal analyst as silent. The movement away from the passive stance proceeded rather as an empirical corrective process not necessarily consciously linked to the structural theory so much as to individual clinical observation. Such a process had been at work for years, so that, by the time of Arlow's paper, mercifully few analysts conducted themselves in so aloof a manner. The interdiction of activity remained so strong, however, that many may have minimized their activity in public reports of their clinical interventions.[8] Arlow's paper, by giving a theoretical reason for increased activity, may have encouraged the current trend in favor of examining aspects of the analyst's conflictual and nonconflictual activity.

Transferences of all kinds play a role in this process.[9] The weight of authority in psychoanalysis is substantial, especially if that authority is, accurately or inaccurately, associated with Freud. Freudian analysts were supposed to be silent so as not to jeopardize the organic growth of the transference neurosis. The transference neurosis was the key linking psychoanalysis to scientific cure. No matter that the theory justifying the pas-

8. Baudry (1993) notes that analysts tend to reduce the number of their interventions in reporting verbatim material.

9. One can infer these forces at work in the text of the Controversial Discussions at the British Society during World War II (King and Steiner, 1991).

sive technique had changed, necessitating a change in the concept of the transference neurosis as well. Such authority may often color empirical observations to the contrary, making them seem heretical when they may not be so, or it may give rise to a rebellious revisionism when a wholesale assault is not warranted.

On the other hand, radical changes in psychoanalytic theory and, eventually, technique may be accepted quite readily if they are presented in words that do apparently conserve rather than challenge major tenets and from a position within the mainstream. Few realized that the innovations of Hartmann (1939, 1950) and his collaborators (Hartmann, Kris, and Loewenstein, 1946) in the 1940s and 1950s were radical. By and large they spoke and wrote in the language of classical psychoanalysis and thought of themselves as adding to an existing body of knowledge, not substantially changing it; nevertheless, their emphasis on ego development led to a significant change in psychoanalytic perspective, and one incidentally that has had an impact on conceptualizations of the transference neurosis. By pointing out that conflict resolutions at one stage of development become the building blocks for conflict resolutions at the next stage, they enabled us to see the immensely complicated edifice that slowly forms throughout childhood and adolescence, not only obscuring memory and impulse but changing them, using them as changed, and rechanging them. They changed conceptions of cure in psychoanalysis from a relatively simple idea involving the excavation of conflicts associated with particular psychosexual levels of childhood to a therapy concerned with the transformation of conflicts into structures to be utilized for conflict resolution throughout an individual's development. It was no longer possible to think of *the infantile neurosis* emerging as *the transference neurosis* in any simple one-to-one way.

Their advocacy of the conflict-free sphere, however, was considerably less integrative. Their wish for psychoanalysis to become a general psychology led them to formulate development in terms of adaptation, the conflict-free sphere, and secondary autonomy so that these concepts could function as bridges to "normal" development and to general science. In the service of fitting into science, psychoanalysis became less focused on the work of the unconscious and no longer exclusively clinical and conflict-based. With a focus on reality and the patient's adaptation to it, clinicians' way of listening changed. No longer was listening to unconscious content seen as paramount. Concepts such as the therapeutic alliance divorced from the unconscious transference meaning of the patient-therapist relationship began to appear. And once a wedge between unconscious and reality aspects of the analytic situation was in place in analysts' minds, the way was opened to the importation of nonpsychoanalytically derived and, more important, nonpsychoanalytically informed data into psychoanalytic theory (Shaw, 1989).

Quinn's (1987) account of Karen Horney's battles with the psychoanalytic establishment in the late 1930s makes it clear that the legitimacy of technical changes based on clinical observation and concern will be overlooked if these technical changes are advanced and consequently perceived as part of an attack on fundamental theoretical tenets. Instead, a destructive, emotional battle will explode.

In perspective we can understand the upheaval around Horney's original *technical* (not her subsequent theoretical) changes as part of an untidy growth process, a rebellion preceding partial acceptance, and the organic transformation around the work of Hartmann, Kris and Loewenstein and their colleagues, for good and ill, as a tidier version of the same.[10] That growth process is more or less untidy because it evokes unconscious conflicts in individual participants. If we can see the relative value and drawbacks to controversial concepts more clearly at a distance, it is because the transferential elements that connected the theoretical and technical issues to unconscious conflicts have receded. The transference neurosis became embedded in such a transferential field.

The Oral Tradition in Psychoanalysis

Such transferential pressures are no doubt intensified by the emphasis in psychoanalysis on one-to-one contact. The substantial body of written work notwithstanding, psychoanalysis has a vitally important and often minimized oral tradition. The spoken word has a special status for us. It is perhaps a principal medium of our trade as well as of our personal enlightenment. Consider the well-known facts about our training: we undergo an extensive training analysis, we present to our supervisors verbatim accounts of sessions in the supervised analyses we conduct, we take part in case conferences and classes. Consider too the less talked about postgraduate experience: we may go on to more supervision, we take part in peer clinical groups, sometimes we reenter analysis, we join and form small study groups and seminars. Much of this postgraduate activity is informal. In much of it the groups and the individuals in them wrestle with technical problems, reconsider technical rules, and weigh theoretical formulations in the context of ongoing clinical work at the same time that they engage in the formal writing, presentation, reading, and discussion of papers. Unseen, this transferential network of the spoken word both informs the written work and provides the context in which papers are read. Papers probably strike us as valuable not only because they present discoveries on the model of the natural sciences but because they say something we have been

10. W. I. Grossman (1986) makes clear the underlying theoretical difference implicit in Horney's formulations.

thinking of or struggling with more cogently, authoritatively, or from a slightly different and therefore generative perspective.

This network of the spoken word is all the more necessary when one considers that the degree of apprenticeship involved in the system of training affords great weight to authority. Considering the intricacies of psychoanalytic practice, years of experience required, and personal pitfalls possible, deference to authority is reasonable. But it can have its drawbacks. One of its less welcome consequences is a rather uneasy relation between the theory of practice and the practice of practice that in turn influences the relation between the written and spoken sharing of clinical material. What people do clinically and what they think they ought to do according to the codified rules of technique are not always the same. Part of our personal learning involves learning to decide what is right for a particular patient and trying to separate out from a tentative decision the element that may be contributing to a countertransference enactment. Part of our learning may also be that some degree of subtle enactment and/or of countertransference is transiently inevitable. If this were true, the process of discovery would not necessarily sit well with our analytic superegos. The most interesting variations on the rules are often reserved for intimate groups and enter written discourse only gradually or enter it in the form of more general revisions of technical rules.

I am not suggesting some sinister collusion. Rather, conventions we use to discuss our work are compromises. We constantly struggle with how to encode what we experience and observe clinically. Conventions of writing about psychoanalysis in particular do not always allow what may be most interesting to a particular analyst in a colleague's approach to be elaborated. In contrast, what would be excluded from articles can be subtly transmitted in personal encounters between analysts. Since much of what happens between patient and analyst occurs outside of the verbal sphere, the less structured form of oral discourse between two or among a small number of analysts permits the re-creation of a clinical field fraught with affect. Oral discourse is closer to what we do than is technical writing.

This disjunction between our spoken and written communications is an inevitable result of many factors, some intrinsic to the gap between experience and expressing that experience in language, some intrinsic to the relation of the written to the spoken word. In addition, we must not forget that the need to maintain patient confidentiality is especially acute in public, written communication.

The frequent hesitation about public modification of central concepts, the indirect way in which change often occurs, most particularly the frequency and significance of oral encounter and its inevitable saturation with transferences—all of these characteristics of the field of psychoanalysis influenced the form of my inquiry into the current concept of the transference neurosis: I decided to ask other analysts to *tell* me about their idea of transference neurosis by *describing* their subjective experience and clinical case material.

A Note on Method

I spoke to twenty-two analysts of whom twenty-one ultimately allowed me to make use of what they had to say. To ensure geographical diversity and theoretical consistency within the context of a relatively stable set of standards for training, I limited my respondents to certified members of the American Psychoanalytic Association. Consistency was provided, to the extent possible, by the existence of the Board of Professional Standards, which assesses and must approve written case reports from all graduates of member institutes who request certification. I tape-recorded and transcribed my respondents' generally informal remarks about the transference neurosis.

For the interviews, I chose analysts who generally utilized a conflict model and considered themselves in the Freudian mainstream. It made sense to explore the current meaning of the concept with clinicians schooled in its importance, to limit variations in the concept stemming from theory in order to emphasize those more likely to arise from clinical observation and other experiential factors, and to introduce some consistency in regard to what is identified as clinical data and how the data are transformed into meaning. That is, since the *relation* among theory, technique, and clinical understanding in modern conflict theory pivots on the role assigned to the patient's words, free association and enactments transformed into verbal associations were the major method of psychoanalytic data gathering, and thus the method by which unconscious conflicts and transformatory processes were uncovered in the treatment situation.

Respondents were chosen because of their excellent reputation as clinicians and in certain cases their contributions to the psychoanalytic literature. I tried to choose reflective and independent-minded individuals who were diverse in gender, years of experience, and, within the limits of my budget, geographical location.[11] The interviews took place over a two-year period. Although many respondents had made substantial contributions to the general psychoanalytic literature, none had, at the time of the interviews, written on the transference neurosis.

11. At the time of the interviews, the youngest respondent had been practicing analysis for approximately ten years, the most senior for forty. Eighteen are or were training analysts. Four were women. The disproportion in gender among my respondents mirrored the general situation in the American Psychoanalytic Association at the time of the interviews where the pool of experienced analysts was predominantly male and many of the larger number of female analysts who practice today were still candidates or recent graduates.

The interviews were informal. To the extent that there was no questionnaire, they were also relatively unstructured. I asked the analysts to "tell me about the transference neurosis," as they understood the concept, to describe their clinical experience of it, and to give clinical illustrations. To assure myself that I was tapping into more than one line of what the French call "filiation"—that is, a tradition issuing from one teacher—I frequently began by asking respondents to mention teachers who had influenced their way of working.[12]

Even this minimal structuring probably influenced the material. The two-person setting, open-ended inquiry about what constituted a transference neurosis, and implicit two-analyst sharing of analytic experiences were factors that probably shaped the respondents' discourse into informal, unguarded, and atheoretical patterns. One analyst described the response he intended to give as an "analyst in the street" interview, and the attitude the phrase denotes both characterizes the spontaneity of the responses and at least partly explains the frequent evidence of theoretical inconsistency.

Another explanation concerns the possibility that certain unconscious conflicts, encouraged by the interview situation and its partial duplication of analytic dialogue, organized themselves around the concept of the transference neurosis and at times directed respondents' discourse in less than logical fashion. At least sometimes, the need and/or opportunity to talk about personal experience seemed to take over, leaving a less than optimal space for theoretical rigor. Indeed, it was my impression that powerful transferences shaped several of the interviews. Besides the circumstances —one-to-one free-form interviews between individuals who by their training and work were accessible to the reawakening of central unconscious conflicts—and the freighted subject matter, transference reactions may have been elicited more strongly by my question about teachers. When psychoanalysts are interviewed on a subject so central to their training, the formation of their professional identity, and particularly their own psychoanalysis, intense and immediate transferential evocations may be inevitable. Recent studies have shown that the transference neurosis is not, as Freud originally thought, eradicated (Oremland et al. 1975; Pfeffer, 1961, 1963, 1993) with its therapeutic resolution. It is, rather, capable of being revived, though the capacity for dealing with it when it is revived is more developed. It is possible that such a revival occasionally played a role.

Analysts work clinically with a combination of intuition and intellect. These interviews accentuate the intuitive side and often do not give an ade-

12. Here, too, there was a predictable diversity, with Lewin, Spitz, Arlow, W. Grossman, Loewald, Gardner, Zilboorg, and Calef some of those mentioned. Arlow's name came up most frequently (four times) and was mentioned by analysts from three different cities. Negative influences were also cited with some frequency, though usually without naming.

quate sense of the intellectual factors. Had these analysts been in a less unguarded, less dynamically reactivating situation, their responses would probably have been more carefully thought out. Crafted with paper and pen, or their modern computer equivalents, many of their discussions of the transference neurosis might have been different in content as well as in style. Oral discourse, even about a psychoanalytic concept, is closer to active, not necessarily reasoned, transient conflict solution than is written discourse.

Because of the probability of the intense affective field in which the words were generated, it is difficult to specify particular shaping influences on the interviews. For example, the question of teachers may have encouraged the respondents to speak of the transference neurosis in the context of training, but they might have spoken of it in that context in any event. The transference neurosis has played such a large role in the certification process that connotations of "measuring up" arise inevitably in its wake. Indeed, one analyst spoke of a particular case he was discussing as "passing muster with anyone" as a transference neurosis.

The transferential field generated by the interviews and/or their subject matter may also have been enhanced by my request to talk of clinical cases because talking about clinical cases sometimes stimulates the parallelism phenomenon (Arlow, 1963; Gediman and Wolkenfeld, 1980; Reed, 1982). That is, analysts may have reenacted some of the patient's conflicts in talking about the case. In one instance an analyst talking about a patient he found difficult to understand was himself difficult to understand. He was much more cogent when discussing his next case.

Another factor contributing to the subjective and theoretically inconsistent quality of the interviews was that, at least some of the time, respondents chose cases in which they seemed to be struggling with countertransferences (e.g., Dr. Z, chap. 3). When they were unaware of this fact, the struggle may have shaped their definition of the transference neurosis according to some element in their countertransference reaction; when they were aware, it seemed to shape it in the direction of defining transference neurosis in terms of intense countertransference reactions (see chap. 8).

To protect confidentiality and encourage spontaneity, I offered my respondents anonymity. All of them chose it despite the number of rich observations they were offering. Although I had hoped that anonymity would eliminate the need for disguise of clinical material, I also offered my respondents the opportunity to disguise their transcribed clinical material if, after reading the interview, they felt a further need to protect the confidentiality of their analysands. Some of them did.[13] The factor of anonymity may have been an additional stimulus for the off-the-cuff quality of many responses.

13. Disguise and anonymity did not preclude omission. A few analysts requested that specific, detailed, inevitably interesting material such as reenactments of specific

All this speculating about psychological causes, however, should not obscure a practical observation. Many analysts were unsure of the clinical definition of the transference neurosis. Their lack of clarity underlies much of the conceptual confusion. For instance, where respondents endorsed the concept, they were puzzled, whether they said so or not, about the difference between it and transference more generally.

These reports, then, emphasize the intuitive, experiential, countertransferential, inconsistently theoretical aspects of analytic experience. These tend to be part of oral rather than of written tradition. Although many might wish for more intellectually consistent formulations, the lack of clarity and the impressionism exist and must be taken into account both with regard to this particular concept and with regard to weighing the development and clinical application of abstract concepts more generally. Moreover, the confusions emphasize the necessity for complementarily more reasoned, experience-distant perspectives such as those supplied by written literature and theoretical critique.[14]

This inquiry took place in a field that in several respects reproduced a field characteristic of psychoanalytic work. Such a duplication is unfortunate inasmuch as it downplays reasoned reworking of concepts and material that is an ongoing necessary aspect of that work. But it is beneficial inasmuch as it emphasizes the affective intensity with which analysts contend from both within and without. If that emphasis encourages us to take into account more consistently in research the effects of the subjectivity that is the mark of the unconscious we study, it will be worthwhile to me even if clarification of the concept of the transference neurosis is not a result. Nevertheless, with regard to that concept, I shall attempt to supply some of the consistent theoretical perspective missing from the interviews, culling insights, commenting upon confusions, and attempting to bring some order to the concept. The concept of the transference neurosis that I shall delineate will ultimately be my own, subject to the same distorting that I have described and that all of us interminably struggle with.

---

childhood memories in the analysts' offices be omitted. Some withdrew whole cases; one, the entire interview. Less extensive specific material was also removed. Some specific material was disguised to prevent its removal, so that it is appropriate to warn readers that the clinical material reported should not be used for research purposes out of the context of the ideas it illustrates.

14. Because lack of clarity is data, I have deviated from the usual practice of presenting condensed vignettes and have retained as much as possible the language and syntax of my respondents. I have, of necessity, edited those portions of the transcriptions quoted to make them intelligible, to reduce repetition, and to clarify where the transcribed text is unclear but the meaning in the interview was not.

CHAPTER TWO

Some Historical Origins

Although the transference neurosis evolved under the aegis of the topographic theory with its emphasis on the unconscious repressed leading to a manifest, symptomatic transference illness (Freud, 1914, 1917) and although my respondents' clinical material did not support the idea of the consistent appearance of such a symptomatic phenomenon, their thinking was influenced by a version of the classical description of the transference neurosis that one respondent felicitously called the "florid transference neurosis of the hysteric." Most agreed that this constellation appears at times today, though some emphasized its rarity more than others. Considered the essence of the classical transference neurosis, this constellation functioned for many as a base line (see Dr. B, below). Implicitly or explicitly, such a transference neurosis was thought to be intense, erotic, and conscious in addition to involving symptom formation.

If their analytic skill and proficiency rarely seemed to them to hang in the balance, the degree to which the absence of this classical transference neurosis was associated with self-doubt or the need for justification was still notable. Some respondents described their material as necessitating a broader and by implication less pure definition (see chap. 5). One pointed to a change in technique as leading to a less delineated transference neurosis and questioned himself (see chap. 3). Another described questioning his skill because he saw the classical transference neurosis so rarely (Dr. R, below).

Because the historical constellation exerts such influence, it seemed useful to take a detour into the historical development of the concept before turning to my respondents' contemporary clinical accounts and the issues raised by them. The first and longest section of this chapter will accordingly concentrate on the evolution of the concept in Freud's writings; the next will describe the effect of the Alexander controversy on the subsequent meaning of the concept, then survey a few more developments in the literature, and finally turn to interview material to illustrate some of the problems during analytic training, to which the accumulating connotations of the concept lend themselves.

The Transference Neurosis in Freud's Writings

The language in which Freud originally expressed the concept of the transference neurosis, particularly in the period from 1905 to 1917, includes an idea of the analyst as aggressively pursuing the analytic cure by waging a solitary battle against the patient's transference neurosis. The disease in this period was a love-sickness, a conflict between the specific libidinal wish toward a specific object and those forces that oppose its emergence into consciousness. Freud conceived of the analyst both as an object representation within the patient's transference disease and as a material entity without it, doing battle with it. This disease of indirect, symptomatic libidinal satisfaction existed in the place that would come to be occupied by the death instinct in Freud's second drive theory.[1] The representation of the death drive in Freud's revised drive theory of 1920 and the larger role accorded to sadism as its external manifestation were accompanied by a change in his vision of the analyst's role in the analytic cure. Freud began to write of the analyst battling an entity defined as the patient's disease not alone but with the patient against the resistance in the patient's internal battle between stasis and change. That is, the strict and somewhat contradictory division between the analyst as within the transference disease and as without it doing battle for the sake of cure (which is implicitly a distinction between the analyst as imbricated in the patient's fantasy world and the analyst as materially real) became more blurred and problematic. The field in which cure was observed became larger and cure itself less a black and white matter. The term disappeared from Freud's writings after 1926. It has not been generally recognized how the term is historically connected

- to a vision of technique in which the analyst without the patient as ally battles a disease enemy,
- to a vision of disease as a circumscribed libidinal conflict,
- to a vision of the process of cure split between the (nonspecified object representation of the) analyst intricately involved in the development of a transference disease within an intermediate space called transference and the (nonspecified therapeutic) analyst outside that space battling the disease that has developed, and

1. Freud had already spoken of sadism as a form of libido (1905a) and was fully aware of the negative reaction to libidinal frustration.

- to a vision of conflict that excludes a sustained theoretical representation of aggression.

Moreover, the subsequent history of the concept is significantly related to that lack of recognition.

The death drive is neither theoretically nor conceptually identical with aggression. *Aggression*, as I have just used it, is a current psychoanalytic term that I apply to the action of Freud's figurative analyst battling disease. I also use it to designate that which is clinically applicable in the concept of the death drive. To the extent that I use *death drive* and *aggression* interchangeably, that usage is a shorthand designation to avoid cumbersome explanations and follows the usage of Arlow and Brenner (1964, p. 45).

From the "Dora Postscript" (1905b) to the *Introductory Lectures* (1917)

The concept that Freud would later call "transference neurosis," already embedded in his first extensive clinical discussion of transference (1905b), was immediately associated with a theory of cure.

> During psychoanalytic treatment the formation of new symptoms is invariably stopped. But the productive powers of the neurosis are by no means extinguished; they are occupied in the creation of a special class of mental structures, for the most part unconscious, to which the name "Transferences" may be given. . . . Transference is an inevitable necessity. . . . this latest creation of the disease must be combated like all the earlier ones . . . since use is made of it in setting up all the obstacles that make the material inaccessible to treatment, and since it is only after the transference has been resolved that a patient arrives at a sense of conviction of the validity of the connections which have been constructed during the analysis. . . . It is true that . . . hysteria may be said to be cured not by the method but by the physician, and that there is usually a sort of blind dependence and a permanent bond between a patient and the physician who has removed his symptoms by hypnotic suggestion; but the scientific explanation of all these facts is to be found in the existences of "transferences" such as are regularly directed by patients onto their physicians. Psycho-analytic treatment does not create transferences, it merely brings them to light, like so many other hidden psychical factors. The only difference is this—that spontaneously a patient will only call up affectionate . . . transferences to help towards his recovery; if they cannot be called up . . . [he] breaks away from [the doctor] . . . without having been influenced. . . . In psycho-analysis, on the other hand, since the play of motives is different, all the patient's tendencies, including hostile ones, are aroused; they are

> then turned to account for the purposes of the analysis by being made conscious and in this way the transference is constantly being destroyed. (Freud, 1905b, *S. E.*, pp. 116–117)

As this passage from the "Dora Postscript" clearly describes, new symptom formation ceases. Instead, a "new class of mental structures," transferences, results in "this latest creation of the disease," that is, the transference neurosis. This new creation constitutes both the greatest obstacle to the treatment and, when resolved, the source of the patient's conviction about the unconscious motives of his illness. It must now be "combated" (*bekämpfen* [1905b, *G. W.*, 5:280]) by being made conscious. In this way it is destroyed and the patient freed from the influence of the physician.[2]

Freud's emphasis is on the metamorphosis of the *neurosis*. He is also at pains to insist that "this latest creation" is not, in fact, a creation of the treatment but a product of the original illness. It belongs a priori to the patient.

Discovery of this "new class of mental structures" enables Freud to give a "scientific" explanation for cures by sanitarium and by hypnosis. Affectionate feelings by the patient allow the physician to exercise his influence and give force to his suggestions. Psychoanalysis, unlike cures by suggestion, utilizes the influence of suggestion to unearth the hidden roots of this influence. Finally, the language implies that this cure is violent: the roots of influence are to be "combated" and "annihilated."

The first use of the term *transference neurosis* occurs nine years later in a new context, that of the compulsion to repeat:

> We render the compulsion harmless . . . by giving it the right to assert itself in a definite field. We admit it into the transference as a playground in which it is allowed to expand in almost complete freedom and in which it is expected to display to us everything in the way of pathogenic instincts that is hidden in the patient's mind. Provided only that the patient shows compliance enough to respect the necessary conditions of the analysis, we regularly succeed in giving all the symptoms of the illness a new transference meaning and in replacing his ordinary neurosis by a "transference-neurosis" of which he can be cured by the therapeutic work. The transference thus creates an intermediate region between illness and real life through which the transition from the one to the other is made. The new condition has taken over all the features of the illness; but it represents an artificial illness which is at every point accessible to our intervention. (1914, *S. E.*, p. 154)

2. Freud's word *vernichtet* (1905b, *G. W.*, 5:281) actually is stronger than the translated "destroyed"; it is closer to "annihilated."

Without the concept of transference, the description of cure would resemble one for pustular infection—something that draws impure products of infection to one central, superficial, and therefore accessible location in order to permit draining or lancing. Transference, however, introduces several new elements. One is *transformation* not only of symptom but of meaning. Another is the concept of *intermediate space* in which the transformed products exist and expand; this space is the realm of the transference neurosis. A third is the element of *accessibility*; the transformations that play themselves out in this intermediate space become accessible to some action from outside the space in a way they were not before.

Freud uses language in a new way because he is constructing new concepts, and it is perhaps inevitable that apparent contradictions result. Nevertheless, if one concentrates on the language in which these ideas are expressed, it becomes evident that the interrelation of these three elements is paradoxical. The transference is first seen as a space—a playground (*Tummelplatz* [1914, *G. W.*, 10:134])—inside of which something else—the compulsion to repeat—may expand. Here, from the point of view of the imagery, transference appears as an enclosure for the repetition compulsion. Later on, however, it is the transference itself that "creates an intermediate region" (*Die Übertragung schafft so ein Zwischenreich* [1914, *G. W.*, 10:135]).

But if the space is the transference itself, and if the transference comes from the patient, how is it that the space has guardians who are not the patient? "We render the compulsion harmless," writes Freud, "by giving it a definite field. We admit it to the transference."[3] But the identity of this "we" who controls entry into the transference space is not clear. Freud began his paper not with a collegial "we" but with a magisterial "It seems to me not unnecessary to keep on reminding students . . ." In quick succession he referred to "the analyst," "he," "the doctor," "the patient." "We" enters only in a sentence in which hypnotic technique gives a more inclusive "us" cause to be grateful because it has given "us the courage ourselves to create more complicated situations in the analytic situation and to keep them clear before us (1914, *S. E.*, p. 148).

"We" may have to do with a summoning of reinforcements at a time when courage is called for and would seem to designate contemporary analysts who had freed themselves from the simplicity of hypnosis where "the patient put himself back into an earlier situation, which he never seemed to confuse with the present one" (p. 148). These analysts prepare to confront the opposite: something dangerous, since it needs courage, something complex, and something in which past and present are confused. Psychoanalysis has already moved, at this point in the history of technique, from an intellectual reconstruction of the past to the in vivo experience of the

3. *Wir machen ihn unschädlich* (1914, *G. W.*, 10:134).

transference, and the experience of transference for analyst and patient is different from the previous intellectual reconstruction. No wonder that figuratively, at least, "we" is needed for reinforcement before a dangerous enterprise; that "we" must give permission for the transference to enter the field; that its expansion is envisaged as taking place in a space both confining and innocent ("the playground").

But not only is the analyst seen as controlling entry into the transference space. If successful, he gains mastery by admitting into the transference. "We . . . succeed in giving all the symptoms of this illness a new transference meaning and in replacing his ordinary neurosis with a 'transference neurosis.' "[4] Through transference and by the physician's agency, the disease is channeled and transformed into a *transference* illness.

A useful distinction between transference and transference neurosis emerges from this passage, a distinction of *function.* Transference is an agent of transformation; transference neurosis is a product of the psychoanalytic treatment and includes the work of transference as transforming agent. In a personal communication, D. M. Kaplan has compared this relation to that between abstinence and neutrality where abstinence is a means and neutrality is an end. I have used the distinction in arriving at a contemporary concept of transference neurosis.

To return to Freud, in the interest of cure, the transference neurosis is created in order to be annihilated. In other words, what is always at issue, just below the surface, is a mortal combat: doctor versus disease. *The transference neurosis is not only an artificial illness; it is the first sign of the mastery of the physician over the disease.*

To be sure, there is a second register reverberating less distinctly along with this depiction of mortal combat. In this second register, closer to theory, the playground is within the patient and the battle is one between the systems conscious-preconscious and unconscious over the access to consciousness of unconscious wishes. In chapter IV of *The Interpretation of Dreams* Freud had described this battle in terms of political power, censorship, and disguise (1900, pp. 141–143). But this second register remains a background to the dramatic immediacy of Freud's writing of the analyst's struggle with disease.

In a famous passage in the *Introductory Lectures* (1917), however, the analyst's aggressive pursuit of cure is deemphasized by a language that stresses the insidious progress of disease. In the process of cure, disease products become "concentrated" and "rise" to the surface: "the whole of his illness's new production is concentrated upon a single point—his rela-

4. *Gelingt es uns regelmässig, allen Symptomen der Krankheit eine neue Übertragunsbedeutung zu geben, seine gemeine Neurose durch eine übertragungsneurose zu ersetzen* (1914, *G. W.*, 10:134–135).

tion to the doctor" (Freud, 1917, *S. E.*, p. 444). The organic process of the illness is further accentuated by an analogy: the growth of the transference illness may be compared in its concentration on the person of the analyst to the growth patterns of a tree in its cambium layer. In the face of this inexorable organic activity, the analyst becomes once again an apparently disinterested scientific observer: "We have followed this new edition of the old disorder from the start, we have observed its origin and growth," but the analyst is not only a disinterested observer. The disease, in its new growth, makes the analyst its core. "We are especially well able to find our way about in it since, as its object, we are situated at its very centre" (1917, *S. E.*, p. 444).

Thus the analyst has two existences. He is (literally) integrated into the disease process so that he exists within the disease. At the same time, he exists outside the illness from which vantage point he can dissect his internal presence. Stressing the immediacy of the analyst's engagement in the process of cure, Freud does not draw the distinction between the analyst's presence within the patient and his representation within the patient in the same way that he earlier situated the playground outside the patient. Instead, he elaborates the transference neurosis as an intermediate structure in which the object representation of the analyst can be seen as inside an intermediate psychic organization, the illness, rather than entirely outside it.[5]

The growth of the transference disease thus constitutes a mastery from the inside: "we are situated at its . . . centre" and can find our way in it because "we have observed its origin." Indeed, the transference neurosis develops, writes Freud, "when the treatment has obtained mastery over the patient" (1917, *S. E.*, p. 444).[6]

In the next lecture the transference neurosis is described in language that expresses even more clearly the idea of its involvement in a war, though to be sure, it is one fought over love and with weapons of love. The context is the already familiar one of the difference between analysis and hypnosis. Unlike hypnosis, which utilizes suggestion indiscriminately, analysis, Freud tells us, gets suggestion in the form of transference "into our hands" (1917, *S. E.* p. 451).[7] Then the transference "is dissected in all the shapes in which it appears" (1917, *S. E.*, p. 453). The aggressive action of the analyst in the process of cure cannot be denied: not only is transference "dissected" but "we must make ourselves masters of the symptoms."

5. It is not strictly the therapeutic analyst who remains outside doing battle with a transference illness. Even at a level of discourse at which the question of representation is accounted for, this indeterminately situated object representation of the analyst participates in an internal battle by changing the internal economic balance and thus influencing the intersystemic struggle.

6. *wenn die Kur sich erst des Kranken bemächtigt hat* (1917, *G. W.*, 11:462).

7. *wir bekommen sie in die Hand* (1917, *G. W.*, 11:470).

"We . . . compel [the patient] to come to a fresh decision." "The transference becomes the battlefield." Symptoms are "divested of libido." "Libido is forced from the symptoms." "The struggle is waged." "Libido is liberated from [this new transference object]" (1917, *S. E.*, pp. 454–455).

The transference neurosis occurs at the moment when the physician/warrior—through the transfer of libidinal wishes—has gained mastery over the forces of disease, at the moment when he or the disease process that he channels defines the arena for battle. In Freud's language, the analyst's therapeutic action is aggressive, makes use of libidinal attachment, and ends in the annihilation of that libidinal investment for the paradoxical purpose of freeing it.

It is hard to overstate the centrality of the transference neurosis in the conceptualization of psychoanalytic cure at this time. If transference is the transforming force, transference neurosis is the product of the transformation that makes the disease accessible. Together force and product constitute an intermediate locus or stage. From the point of view of cure, this stage permits the transformation of mysterious symptoms into decipherable ones because their origins are known. The analyst is the target of the impulses that are expressed as symptoms and has observed their genesis. Transference neurosis is thus a translation of a private code into a common language in which the analysis governs the rules of morphology. At the same time, this stage of transformation separates psychoanalysis from mental and physical cathartic cures. Cure is no longer a question of drawing infection to the surface to be lanced or of abreacting affects associated with newly remembered traumatic events. Cure involves the interposition of a stage in which transformation of the disease occurs. This stage also provides a temporal transition. Past struggles take present transference forms. These may involve direct or indirect editions and repetitions, but it is not always possible to infer the past from the form of the present:

> Suppose we succeeded in bringing a case to a favourable conclusion by setting up and then resolving a strong father-transference to the doctor. It would not be correct to conclude that the patient had suffered previously from a similar unconscious attachment of his libido to his father. His father-transference was merely a battlefield on which we gained control of his libido; the patient's libido was directed to it from other positions. A battlefield need not necessarily coincide with one of the enemy's key fortresses. . . . Not until after the transference has once more been resolved can we reconstruct in our thoughts the distribution of libido which had prevailed during the illness. (Freud, 1917, *S. E.*, pp. 455–456)

This stage then separates the realm of only remembering from that of experiencing and unites the two so that what is remembered is remembered and experienced, or experienced and reconstructed.

The stage of the transference neurosis also constitutes an intermediate step in the progress of the libido, bridging its devious satisfaction in symptom formations and its future and healthier availability for enjoyment in accordance with the reality principle. At the same time, it excludes from psychoanalytic therapy those narcissistic conditions in which the libido has not maintained sufficient development to cathect an object representation with continuity. Finally and most crucially, this intermediate stage separates psychoanalysis as therapy from suggestion and hypnosis by providing the means whereby the capacity for suggestibility is transformed into illness. It is suggestion that is curative in hypnosis. Suggestibility forms one aspect of transference, and transference by giving a new form to the neurotic illness becomes the disease that psychoanalytic therapy "annihilates."

In Freud's writings during this period, then, the transference neurosis appears as a pivotal and exciting discovery. By annihilating the transference neurosis, the psychoanalyst outside the disease frees the patient's libido: if the transference neurosis is the sign of the analyst's mastery over disease, the annihilation of the transference neurosis is the sign of the patient's unconditional liberation from disease. The analyst who annihilates disease does so by inserting himself in its process and thereby effecting a transformation of its terms. He then battles this enemy, which includes him, and in mastering it becomes both conquering hero and liberator.

Beyond the Pleasure Principle

Freud's next discussion of the transference neurosis (1920a) bears the traces of a larger evolution that will ultimately lead to the development of the structural theory (1923) and the revision of the theory of anxiety (1926a). Emphasizing the factor of repetition, he ascribes what is "invariably" repeated to "some portion of infantile sexual life—of the Oedipus complex . . . and its derivatives" (1920a, p. 18). With a reemphasis on repetition comes a parallel and familiar emphasis on containment: the physician must "endeavour . . . to force as much as possible into the channel of memory and to allow as little as possible to emerge as repetition" (p. 19).

Yet the analyst now has a new obligation: besides enabling the patient to remember "some portion of his forgotten life" the analyst "must see to it . . . that the patient retains some degree of aloofness . . . to recognize that what appears to be reality is in fact only a reflection of a forgotten past" (p. 19). In the 1914 passage the patient needed only, in contrast, to show "compliance enough to respect the necessary conditions of the analysis" (p. 154).[8]

8. Earlier passages in Freud seem to speak to the need for the patient's alliance. However, these do not occur in the context of the transference neurosis. Moreover, their general place in Freud's notion of technique is unclear. See Reed (1988).

This addition to the technical handling of the transference neurosis signals a change in perspective. By requiring that the analyst help the patient also observe, Freud reorients the relationship between them and reorients the field of observation in which each has a place. The two registers previously recognized, the external battle between analyst and disease and the internal disease in which the analyst is entwined, are differently integrated and presented. The analyst is no longer depicted as confronting and combating the patient's illness alone. Instead, he admits the patient as his ally in combat and regards the battle as taking place within the patient.

Freud continues the passage on the transference neurosis in *Beyond the Pleasure Principle* by describing the patient's conflict as taking place between a coherent and partly unconscious ego, which resists, and the unconscious repressed from which emanates the compulsion to repeat. This material causes the ego unpleasure, and the analyst works toward the patient's "toleration of that unpleasure." Such a process accords with the pleasure principle so long as the system-ego's unpleasure simultaneously represents pleasure for the system unconscious. But what, Freud asks in a moving passage, of childhood narcissistic injuries? They, too, are repeated by the patient. Not only is the childhood wish for knowledge reexperienced, but also the failure to know. Such a failure and its remembering are painful. How can reexperiences of this nature be ascribed solely to the pleasure principle?

This questioning of the transference neurosis is significant. Until this point in 1920 Freud introduced transference neurosis to demonstrate a clinical fact, describe the process of cure, distinguish psychoanalysis from suggestion, and illustrate the analyst's successful combat with disease. He perceived it as an answer to questions. Now the phenomenon of the transference neurosis itself raises a question.

Accompanying this change in the status of the transference neurosis is a temporary and revealing recrystallization of elements in Freud's ongoing evolution. This rearrangement of elements may be approached from the points of view of theory, of imagery, and of degree of conviction. From the point of view of theory, this shift is best observed in the new role accorded sadism:

> Is it not plausible to suppose that this sadism is in fact a death instinct which, under the influence of the narcissistic libido, has been forced away from the ego and has consequently only emerged in relation to the object? It now enters the service of the sexual function. During the oral stage of organization of the libido, the act of obtaining erotic mastery over an object coincides with that object's destruction; later, the sadistic instinct separates off, and finally, at the stage of genital

> primacy, it takes on, for the purposes of reproduction, the function of overpowering the sexual object. (1920a, p. 54)

What Freud describes is an interplay of libido and aggression within the individual. It repeats in a different arena the battle of analyst versus disease. Now represented within theory, combat need no longer be represented in the figurative language of warlike cure.

Moreover, in these new terms, the ultimate liberation from the dominance of suggestion, which constituted the analytic cure of 1917, is impossible. The danger of dominance by suggestion is replaced by the danger of dominance by sadism and its predecessor, primary masochism. In an important and frequently unrecognized sense, the death instinct itself has become the disease, so that now the ultimate liberation of cure would be the complete victory of the libidinal forces over what for Freud is the psychic representative of a biological given. Unless the analyst presumes to play God, such a victory is beyond his control. It follows that visions of therapeutic cure will of necessity be tempered.

Second, from a descriptive point of view, the theoretical change affects Freud's organic imagery. In writing of the possible evolution of the system conscious, Freud, utilizing his knowledge of embryology, describes a crust forming on the surface of a "little fragment of living substance" which

> is suspended in the middle of an external world charged with the most powerful energies, and . . . would be killed by the stimulation emanating from these if it were not provided with a protective shield against stimuli. It acquires the shield in this way: its outermost surface ceases to have the structure proper to living matter, becomes to some degree inorganic and thenceforward functions as a special envelope or membrane resistant to stimuli. . . . By its death, the outer layer has saved all the deeper ones from a similar fate. (1920a, p. 27)

Although this shield was further clarified in 1924, from the point of view of imagery it also recalls the comparison of the transference neurosis to the cambium layer of the tree where growth is concentrated on a single point. In both cases an inert crust encircles living matter. But the inert crust around the cambium layer was important only because it surrounded the cambium layer/neurosis and thus represented a capture and confinement, an eagerly awaited step toward the final dispatch of the disease. Now, more subtly and complexly, the protective shield is a compromise in which both aggression and libido combine. Moreover, in its protective function it represents a triumph of libido (or eros in the second drive theory) over aggression (or the death drive), which already contains a history of conflict.

The organic unit has also changed. Instead of a presumably substantial tree, we are presented with "a little fragment of living substance" buffeted from without. These new dimensions are hardly a setting for analytic heroism. Rather, libidinal investment and existence themselves are heroic.

Thus, the revision of the theory of drives has a profound effect on what is perceived, how it is organized, and the position of the analyst in regard to what is perceived—the analyst's technical role. In locating aggression, albeit in the form of primary masochism, as part of the original conflict with the libido, Freud removes the analyst from imagining himself as directly engaged in a war with disease.

A third manifestion of this rearrangement of elements is the presence in *Beyond the Pleasure Principle* of a discussion of conviction.

> There is no reason . . . why the emotional factor of conviction should enter into this question at all. It is surely possible to throw oneself into a line of thought and to follow it wherever it leads out of simple scientific curiosity. . . . But the degree of uncertainty is not assignable. . . . I do not think a large part is played by what is called "intuition" in work of this kind. . . . Intuition . . . seems to me to be the product of a kind of intellectual impartiality. Unfortunately, however, people are seldom impartial where ultimate things, the great problems of science and life, are concerned. Each of us is governed in such cases by deep-rooted internal prejudices, into whose hands our speculation unwittingly plays. Since we have such good grounds for being distrustful, our attitude towards the results of our own deliberations cannot well be other than one of cool benevolence. I hasten to add, however, that self-criticism such as this is far from binding one to any special tolerance towards dissentient opinions. It is perfectly legitimate to reject remorselessly theories which are contradicted by the very first steps in the analysis of observed facts, while yet being aware at the same time that the validity of one's own theory is only a provisional one. (1920a, pp. 59–60)

This discussion of emotional conviction partially replaces the conviction or what I have called in another context certainty (Reed, 1985) that characterized the earlier discussions of transference neurosis. Of course, Freud is here referring to a far-reaching theoretical hypothesis rather than to something clinically observable as he may have been doing in the earlier writings on the transference neurosis. The tone of these earlier passages, however, is not easily ascribed to the lesser degree of abstraction only. Instead, there is an intense emotional involvement in imparting and pronouncing the (discovered) truth: "the formation of new symptoms invariably stops." "Transference is an inevitable necessity" (1905b). "We render the compulsion harmless" (1914). "We, by summoning up every available mental force [in the patient], compel him to come to a fresh decision" (1917). In contrast, the passage about conviction takes into account the unconscious meaning of theory to the theorizer. It alludes to the unconscious reasons at work in any fervent attachment to a hypothesis. With the theoretical representation of aggression, Freud has given the analyst the option of partially disengaging himself from combat with disease to better observe the combat within each individual.

The Transference Neurosis after 1920

This evolution is neither sudden nor complete, for the earlier heroic tone reappears once more in connection with a mention of transference neurosis. Freud's last reference to the term, six years after *Beyond the Pleasure Principle*, recalls in tone the earlier writings on the transference neurosis as an external battle, though it also bears traces of the evolution discernible in *Beyond the Pleasure Principle*. In the context of a discussion of cure, he writes:

> As you see, the requirements of analytic technique reach their maximum at this point. Here the gravest mistakes can be made or the greatest successes be registered. It would be folly to attempt to evade the difficulties by suppressing or neglecting the transference; whatever else had been done in the treatment, it would not deserve the name of an analysis. To send the patient away as soon as the inconveniences of his transference-neurosis make their appearance would be no more sensible, and would moreover be cowardly. It would be as though one had conjured up spirits and run away from them as soon as they appeared. Sometimes, it is true, nothing else is possible. There are cases in which one cannot master the unleashed transference and the analysis has to be broken off; but one must at least have struggled with the evil spirits to the best of one's strength. (1926b, p. 227)

The transference neurosis is the phase of "gravest mistakes" and "greatest successes." In dealing with it the analyst needs the greatest technical skill, for he contends with a wild and unruly force that, once "unleashed" threatens rupture. The analyst is a conjurer who has summoned up "evil spirits" and must struggle with them "to the best of [his] strength." What is more, only this struggle "deserves the name of analysis."

But in the very next sentence this struggle with evil spirits becomes one involving countertransference temptation: "To yield to the demands of the transference, to fulfill the patient's wishes for affectionate and sensual satisfaction, is not only justly forbidden by moral considerations but is also completely ineffective as a technical method for attaining the purpose of the analysis. A neurotic cannot be cured by being enabled to reproduce uncorrected an unconscious stereotype plate that is ready to hand in him"

(p. 227). The analyst is no longer so clearly divided between the materially real warrior outside the patient's transference disease and the illusory figure at the core of the illness. This struggle with evil spirits is also, by implication, within the analyst himself.

The preceding paragraph depicts a third struggle within the patient that is also now seen in more relative terms: "Analytic love is not manifested in every case as clearly and blatantly as I have tried to depict it. Why not? We can soon see. In proportion as the purely sensual and the hostile sides of his love try to show themselves, the patient's opposition to them is aroused. He struggles against them and tries to repress them before our very eyes. . . . The patient is repeating in the form of falling in love with the analyst mental experiences which he has already been through once before. . . . he is also repeating before our eyes his old defensive actions" (p. 226). This portion of the passage includes in the analyst's observational field those forces that oppose change; thus it continues the reorientation of 1920. It locates the struggle within the patient and speaks of the *relative* degree to which the patient's libidinal wishes toward the analyst and defenses against them are present in the manifest content of the transference.

This rich passage, then, ascribes three separate component struggles to the transference neurosis: that between the conjurer and the evil spirits—that is, between the heroic analyst and the patient's disease; that, by implication, within the analyst between gratifying the patient and continuing to analyze him; and that within the patient between his transference love and the defensive maneuvers that seek to maintain his ignorance. These three aspects of struggle are probably condensed in the earlier dramatic passages in which the analyst battles disease, but the last two especially hint at a greater similarity between analyst and patient in their respective and in some way similar struggles even while the first apparently returns to Freud's earlier version.

Since in that earlier passage in 1926 especially, the heroic connotations of the transference neurosis reappear, it is important to stress that the evolution away from the vision of the heroic analyst battling disease seems to reveal itself most tellingly by silence: Freud never again uses the term *transference neurosis*. Some have even questioned whether he meant by his silence to discard the concept (see Bergmann, 1976). I think it doubtful. In *Beyond the Pleasure Principle* he still describes the conflict in the transference neuroses as between "the ego and the libidinal cathexis of objects" (1920a, p. 42), and later references to cure assume his earlier discussions, in which the transference neurosis is central. In the *New Introductory Lectures*, for instance, referring his audience to his 1917 lecture on psychoanalytic therapy, he continues to endorse his earlier description of cure: "I cannot formulate it in any other manner today" (1933, p. 151). In 1937 once again he writes that the matter of how a psychoanalytic cure comes about "has been sufficiently elucidated" (p. 221). The tepid tone of both these endorsements, however, so contrasts with his earlier excitement that it is not surprising to discover in the 1933 paper that he has modified his earlier attitude, declaring himself no longer "a therapeutic enthusiast." Inevitably, personal reasons for this change in tone must be considered—disillusionment, loss, old age, cancer—but they are both beyond the purview of this exposition and, to my mind, insufficient.

For, when the heroic attitude toward cure returns in a burst in the *Outline* (1940), the term *transference neurosis* does not. Freud's description there of the course of the transference includes many of the familiar components of a description of the transference neurosis—the language of battle, the "undreamt of importance" of the transference, the taking of the analyst as object from childhood, the connection between suggestion and positive transference, the resistance aspect of the transference, and the tempestuousness of the negative transference. The patient then

> behaves like a child who has no power of judgment of his own but blindly believes anyone whom he loves and no one who is a stranger to him. The danger of these states of transference evidently lies in the patient's misunderstanding their nature and taking them for fresh real experiences instead of reflections of the past. . . . It is the analyst's task constantly to tear the patient out of his menacing illusion and to show him again and again that what he takes to be new real life is a reflection of the past. . . . Careful handling of the transference on these lines is as a rule richly rewarded. If we succeed, as we usually can, in enlightening the patient on the nature of the phenomena of transference, we shall have struck a powerful weapon out of the hand of his resistance and shall have converted dangers into gains. For a patient never forgets again what he has experienced in the form of transference; it carries a greater force of conviction than anything he can acquire in other ways. (1940, pp. 176–177)

While this description of transference developments is of a regressive, unpredictable, intense, and irrational transference, what Freud might formerly have described as a transference neurosis, he does not call it a transference neurosis. Nor does he describe the battle as one between analyst and disease.

These two facts have, to my mind, a causal relation to each other. It is not the concept of the transference neurosis which Freud discards, but its connotation as an independent disease the analyst must engage in battle by himself and defeat. As the death instinct takes over the function of what once was the dragon of neurotic libidinal conflict, there is no longer a place for the transference neurosis as a defeatable and thus curable entity independent of the patient. Thus the neat division of the analyst into a portion at the center of the transference disease and a therapeutic hero outside, doing battle, no longer is possible. Although Freud maintains the idea of analytic objectivity, the opposition transference disease-"fantasy" and reality-"therapy" no longer holds. On a theoretical level the death instinct is a great equalizer. On another level, one may speculate that various regressive phenomena he encountered—among his disciples, Jung and Ferenczi's sexual involvement with patients; in his own countertransference struggles; and in his clinical work, perhaps including projective processes—probably were its clinical equivalent. It is Freud's interest in a widening panorama of pathology that led to the wider focus in which symptomatic libidinal conflict no longer is the only pathological entity, but he does not attempt correspondingly to broaden the concept of the transference neurosis.

If Freud himself does not attempt to broaden the concept of the transference neurosis to bring it in line with his widening field of focus, he nevertheless continues to conceive of psychoanalytic therapy as in part a struggle, this time between the analyst and the patient's resistances; however, he locates the conflict more fully within the patient. He writes, for instance, of the need for an alliance with the patient: "if we succeed . . . in enlightening the patient on the nature of the meaning of the transference . . ." The clinical concept of an intense regressive transference in which the past is repeated remains, but Freud no longer refers to this phenomenon as a transference neurosis because he no longer thinks of it in terms of a circumscribed disease that the analyst battles alone. The analyst now contends with a patient and his character.

One year before he wrote the *Outline*, in "Analysis Terminable and Interminable," Freud repeated that the process of psychoanalytic cure had been sufficiently clarified and redirected attention toward obstacles to cure (1937, p. 221). In this larger field, the transference neurosis as artificial disease is no longer that which opposes cure. Obstacles to cure are not conceived of as disease entities; they involve a new kind of crust, the rigidity of the ego's alterations by its characteristic defenses. Mobilized originally against drive derivatives and now against the revivification of these drive derivatives by the psychoanalytic process, these defenses react to recovery as to a danger and may interfere with the patient's ability to adhere to the analytic pact: "Analysis can only draw upon definite and limited amounts of energy which have to be measured against the hostile forces. And it seems as if victory is in fact as a rule on the side of the big battalions" (1937, p. 240).

Disease in its earlier meaning of libidinal conflict is not an issue in this battle because of the destructive power assigned to the death drive. More precisely, the death drive replaces a disease based on libidinal conflict in that it opposes life. Libido, or eros as it has become, does not have the same unrestricted power it was formerly accorded. The power of the analyst to attract libidinal impulses to himself is also restricted: "The patients cannot themselves bring all their conflicts into the transference; nor is the analyst able to call out all their possible instinctual conflicts from the transference situation" (1937, p. 233). By implication, Freud sees the death drive as a formidable opposition to cure through the transference neurosis rather than, in the form of aggression, as a potential part of a differently constituted transference neurosis. Although the conception of psychoanalytic cure in its narrowest sense has not radically changed, the radicality of cure per se has been tempered by greater acceptance of the limitation of the human condition.

By conceptualizing the transference neurosis in the first place, Freud defined psychoanalysis as a radical therapy of deep change. By depicting the transference neurosis as a result of the transforming work of transference and as a midstation that will need to be dismantled, not as an end of the cure, he identified psychoanalysis as a therapy requiring a process of symbolic transformation in which the analyst and the patient together verbalize their understanding of that internal symbolic transformation in order to effect change. The conceptualization of the transference neurosis thus placed psychoanalysis very far from both personal suggestion on the one hand and physical cures on the other.

In general, the concept of the transference neurosis as Freud elaborated it between 1905 and 1917 fulfilled several simultaneous functions. It defined psychoanalysis as the cure of a libidinal conflict in which transformation of that conflict occurs; it distinguished psychoanalysis from suggestion; it encouraged the reexperiencing and understanding of unconscious childhood attitudes and wishes; and it gave a predictable course to the treatment. Because it accomplished so many functions, it readily lent itself and continues to lend itself to a reification that may excite the fantasy, among others, that the possessor of this tool has control of powerful knowledge that enables him to rescue the patient held captive by disease.

But this possible overestimation is certainly not inherent in Freud's original concept. It may adhere to the concept because of the countertransference danger inherent in the transference relationship itself. Freud implied countertransference dangers in relation to the transference neurosis in *The Question of Lay Analysis* (1926b). Later, he noted the unconscious meaning of theory as a factor in conviction. At about the same time, his own attitude, as it emerged in passages about the transference neurosis, showed some signs of modification, tempering descriptions of warlike aggression in the service of libidinal cure, representing aggression more explicitly, and reorienting the focus and field of observation.

The result of this change of perspective is an eventual modification in the conceptualization of cure. The patient becomes the ally, and resistance in the sense of the conservative forces, not disease in the sense of libidinal conflict, becomes the enemy. It is thus difficult to speak of a transference neurosis in the circumscribed way Freud originally meant it. In this broader perspective, cure must now be seen as a reorganization of structures, and relative resolution of conflict within the patient replaces radical liberation of the patient from disease.

Some Connotations of the Transference Neurosis after Freud

Despite the gradual change in Freud's concept of the transference neurosis, in the 1950s the figure of the heroic analyst battling disease reemerged in a new and surprising form. A number of analysts, concerned about cases that seemed to be stalemated, began to advocate transference manipulations (see Weinshel, 1971). Inevitably, their attention was drawn to the transference neurosis. For instance, to support his more active technique, Sacha Nacht in France attacked the transference neurosis: "It is the excessive development of the transference neurosis which must be held principally responsible for [the treatment's] interminable character" (1957, p. 196). In America, Franz Alexander was the most prominent of the analysts reassessing the transference neurosis. In 1954, he contended that transference might lead to a malignant wound rather than an artificial illness: "The medicine of artificial regression in the transference can be given in overdoses. Like radiation therapy, it is a powerful new weapon, but can become the source of new illness" (p. 733).

The Alexander Controversy

Nacht, Alexander, and others who followed them were struggling in good faith with perplexing clinical problems. Analyses frequently became stalemated. The passive silence of many analysts of that epoch, itself reflecting a technique tied to the topographic theory as well as to the related belief that the transference neurosis grows spontaneously and organically, fostered some of these stalemates. In response to the problem, Alexander (1948) focused on patients' dependence: "The analyst is the natural target for these regressive emotions. The core of these reactions is a dependent attitude" (p. 281). He thus argued that the analytic frame itself encouraged too much regression. Like the silent analysts who waited for the transference neurosis to take root, he saw the transference neurosis as something that developed on its own: "Assuming a tolerant attitude and avoiding any evaluation of the patient's material suffices after a time to encourage the development of a transference neurosis. It requires no particular activity on the part of the analyst; the prevailing neurotic tendencies within the patient take their free course and express themselves uninhibitedly"

(Alexander, 1948, pp. 281–282). He began to advocate varying the frequency of sessions to prevent too much dependence:

> Experience has shown that the transference neurosis develops spontaneously as the result of continued contact with the therapist. The outlook for a prolonged treatment favors the patient's procrastination and disinclination to face the problems from which he escaped into neurosis. The transference neurosis soon loses many of the unpleasant features of the original neurosis because it is seen to be a necessary part of the treatment and the conflicts provoked by the regressive tendencies are reduced by the analyst's attitude. This allows the patient to be neurotic during treatment without too much conflict. It must be remembered that the transference neurosis develops naturally and that effort is required on the part of the therapist to counteract it. Reducing the frequency of interviews is one of the simplest means of preventing the transference from becoming too powerful an outlet for the patient's neurosis; if the dependent tendencies are frustrated, they are thrown into relief and the patient is compelled to resist them consciously. (1948, pp. 283–284)

Alexander continued to call his treatment psychoanalysis despite its authoritarian stance and radical manipulations of the transference. A sharp reaction from those who believed these departures were attacking the very principles upon which psychoanalysis was based was inevitable.

With the benefit of hindsight, it is possible to understand that his concern was valid even if his assessment of the problem was misdirected. Part of the problem was his belief that a transference neurosis emerged on its own. The passive technique that followed from it led indeed to stalemates. It also led to a misunderstanding about the clinical appearance of the transference neurosis. The frustrated attitude toward the analyst that may be the patient's response to the analyst's passivity and silence is seen as the transference neurosis itself rather than as a possible iatrogenic product of that passivity. Successful treatment requires activity from the analyst: the analysis of resistances and of defense transferences and of the unconscious fantasies of which the resistances are a part. Yet this necessary activity was discouraged by the ethos of silence that prevailed in the 1940s and 1950s.

Like Freud, Alexander believed that what he identified as the transference could create a new illness. Unlike Freud, he did not welcome the new illness as something to be analyzed but regarded it as something that had to be "handled." The analyst once again battled a transference disease not to cure the illness of which it represented a transformation but to *prevent the transference neurosis from coming into being*. In this strange permutation of the battle of doctor versus disease, it was the physician who controlled the course of the disease, decided what was right for the patient, and by manipulating the transference, re-placed himself in the position of the hypnotist.

And if the transference neurosis was a dangerous affliction, then psychoanalysis itself, with its intensity, frequency, and encouragement of regression, had to be questioned. Indeed, for Alexander, those who continued to insist on psychoanalysis as a form of treatment separate from psychotherapy did so to enhance their status vis-à-vis psychiatrists. Alexander believed that since psychiatry had become dynamic and psychoanalytically oriented, there was no more need for a psychoanalytic subspecialty. "All psychiatrists become more and more similar, even though one may practice pure psychoanalysis, and the other psychoanalytically oriented psychotherapy." To restrict the number of sessions per week in order to control the infliction of a transference wound was to accept the inevitable absorption of psychoanalysis into medicine (1954, p. 725).

Finally, in 1954, the American Psychoanalytic Association convened a panel devoted to defining the difference between psychoanalysis and psychotherapy. It included Alexander himself, Freida Fromm-Reichman, Leo Rangell, and Merton Gill. Both Rangell and Gill made explicit what Alexander had already implied. Rangell defined psychoanalysis as "a method of therapy whereby conditions are brought about favorable to the development of a transference neurosis, in which the past is restored to the present, in order that, through a systematic interpretative attack on the resistances which oppose it, there occurs a resolution of that neurosis (transference and infantile) to the end of bringing about structural changes in the mental apparatus of the patient to make the latter capable of optimum adaptation to life" (1954, p. 740). Gill defined it as "that technique which, when employed by a neutral analyst, results in the development of a regressive transference neurosis and the ultimate resolution of this neurosis by techniques of interpretations alone" (1954, p. 775).

These definitions, enunciated in an official setting, restored to the concept of the transference neurosis its scientific and clinical meaning. They also revived one of its oldest functions: that of distinguishing psychoanalysis from cures based on suggestion. But *Alexander's polemic shaped their conceptualization*. Reacting to what they regarded as a particularly wrongheaded view of psychoanalysis, they inverted Alexander's terms: if Alexander saw the transference neurosis as destructive and the motives of those who upheld it as self-serving, it was precisely because he did not practice psychoanalysis. By maintaining the equation between psychoanalysis and transference neurosis while removing the negative political sign Alexander had placed on it, they nevertheless gave the transference neurosis a possible ideological function. As a result, the transference neurosis became the common term in a series of diverse cures: Freud envisioned the transference neurosis as curing his patients of suggestion and disease; Alexander sought to enforce a preventive cure on his patients by protecting them from the transference neurosis; Rangell and Gill attempted to rescue the transference neurosis from Alexander's characterization of it as political and nontherapeutic by resuscitating psychoanalysis as a valid, scientific, and therapeutic discipline.

The pathway to politicization was well established by this last linking of transference neurosis with cure. If psychoanalysis was, in fact, a therapy it had to answer the accusation that its only function was to give status to its practitioners by insisting that it had an exclusive means of cure. The transference neurosis became that answer. And if, of course, an analyst believed that in order for him to do psychoanalysis his patient must "have" a transference neurosis, then a transference neurosis would no longer constitute a step toward the liberation of the patient from suggestion as Freud conceived it, but would become the occasion for suggestion. The more it was pressed to function politically as a buffer demarcating psychoanalysis from psychotherapy, the less the transference neurosis could continue to separate psychoanalysis from suggestion.

The Written Literature after Alexander

The process of *scientific* discourse led fairly quickly to a correction of the polemical overreaction to Alexander. Greenacre (1959) was the first to introduce modifications in the equation of transference neurosis with psychoanalysis, pointing out that not every important conflict we analyze appears in the transference. Kepecs (1966), in a useful review of the literature, elucidated two contradictory concepts in Freud, the concept of the artificial illness related to cure, which was adaptive, and the concept related to the repetition compulsion, which saw transference as a resistance. These, he noted, have been conflated and confused by analysts since the thirties who have tended to adopt the second concept and to condense transference and transference neurosis. He suggested that the transference neurosis apply to the activation of the acute, original terms of the infantile conflict, not to its characterological result.

The modern concept of the transference neurosis evolved in two directions, reflecting Kepecs's categories. In one, it was restricted quite narrowly to the development of a new symptom representing the infantile conflict within the transference (Harley, 1971; Gann, 1984) with no expectation that this phenomenon was to be expected in every analysis, particularly not in character neuroses. In the other, it was broadened for the first time explicitly to include character analysis (Loewald, 1971; Blum, 1971).

Loewald remarked that the contemporary focus on "ego analysis carries with it the danger of concentrating too heavily on autonomous ego functioning and losing sight of the instinctual-affective, experiential roots and determinants of ego development, thus neglecting the infantile neurosis and its object-related instinctual nature" (1971, p. 60). Returning to Freud's (1914) definition but replacing symptom with "the wider areas of character and ego pathology," Loewald defined the transference neurosis operationally as "the retransformation of the psychic illness which originated in pathogenic interactions with important persons in the child's environment, into an interactional process with a new person, the analyst, in which the pathological infantile interactions and their intrapsychic consequences may become transparent and accessible to change by virtue of the analyst's objectivity and of the emergence of novel interaction-possibilities" (p. 61). Blum "would retain the designation of transference neurosis bearing in mind a modern concept of neurosis which takes into account structure and character . . . [and] includes not only symptoms, but all transference-neurosis phenomena in a concentrated revival and continuous unfolding. The analyst remains the central transference object. . . . I would underscore the concentration and continuity of conflictual transferences" (1971, p. 44). This definition, in its emphasis on what Greenacre called the "constant panoramic procession of transference pictures," is much broader than the transference neurosis as first described by Freud, as is Loewald's. Significantly, Blum's definition is broad enough to retain the designation of the transference neurosis as "a development unique to analysis" (p. 44).

Bird (1972) wrote an influential paper that reiterated Loewald's concern that the disregard of the transference neurosis was synonymous with the neglect of an instinctual crux and mentioned the analyst's reciprocal transference involvement. He objected to the tendency he discerned in contemporary analysts to abandon transference neurosis for more pallid, more easily dealt with transference reactions. "We forget sometimes," he wrote, "that a neurosis is based upon conflict and that what is specific about a transference neurosis is the active involvement of the analyst in the central crunch of the conflict. . . . If a transference neurosis is to develop and be analyzed, the analyst cannot pull away, cannot merely sit back, observe, interpret and 'practise . . . explanatory arts'" (1972, p. 279). In a transference neurosis the patient not only displaces "certain cathexes from early memories of his father onto me as if in the present," which is how he understood transference. Rather the patient "replaces *in his neurosis* mental representations of a past person, say his father, with mental representations of me" (p. 281). That is, Bird described the experiential dimension of what is meant by the transference neurosis as a new organization (see chap. 5). Both Loewald and Bird seemed to be reacting to an intellectualizing tendency in many analysts who adopted the predominant ego psychological framework of the time.

In 1982, however, Brenner argued just as forcefully against the concept. With his tendency to reduce the number of concepts and the terms referring to them in order to minimize the number of theoretically inferred, non–clinically observable terms, he found the compound *transference neurosis* redundant. Since both *transference* and *neurosis* designate compromise formations, he recommended *analyzable transference* as a more accurate substitute. Brenner's argument is certainly with the term, but not necessarily with the clinical phenomenon it attempts to designate. His heavy emphasis on praxis begs the question of whether every analyzable transference is a transference neurosis or whether it matters. An analyst ignorant of the concept might stop with the analysis of the defensive function of the character trait of stubbornness, for instance, and miss the acute infantile oedipal origins (see Kepecs, 1966). Although Brenner would no doubt respond that the analysis of the character trait would then be incomplete, one might legitimately counter with the question of how the analyst would know. Concepts influence clinical expectations and thus technique.

At a 1988 panel of the American Psychoanalytic Association on this issue (Shaw, 1991), the participants flatly disagreed on the utility of the concept, with Abend and Cooper finding it of no value and Renik, Tyson, and Shaw arguing variously for retention of the concept. Significantly the proponents did not agree on a definition. Tyson considered the concept, following Loewald (1971), as operational, treated the word *neurosis* in the term not as a description of content but as a sign needed to distinguish one particular form of transference from others, and understood the particular form of transference designated as expressing an overlapping and intertwining of a relatively small number of pathogenic relationships from the past with increasing continuity and persistence. Renik, in contrast, while acknowledging a built-in circularity in the argument based on the requirement that the patient be neurotic, nevertheless offered an explicit manifest definition that described a series of transferences ending in the analyst's involvement in structured oedipal conflict as the ambivalently loved rival who impedes the realization of the patient's deepest wishes (see Renik, 1990). Shaw disputed Cooper's contention that the transference neurosis does not occur in character analysis by describing common clinical material in which an infantile neurosis presented itself as a current depression. She questioned Renik's definition by pointing out that the recurrence of the infantile neurosis may take a preopedipal form because it incorporates regression as a defense against oedipal conflict.

This panel so testified to the wide variations in current conceptions of the transference neurosis and also in opinions about its utility that one might easily conclude that the transference neurosis no longer represents the sine qua non of analysis. More or less contemporaneously, however, Kern (1987) stressed its lasting clinical relevance, and Rosenblatt (1987) pointed out that if we discard the transference neurosis, certain phenomena in an analysis will exist in search of a referent. Moreover, with more recent attempts to define the quintessentially psychoanalytic through a specification of the psychoanalytic process, the concept of the transference neurosis has reemerged as a central criterion. An issue of the *Psychoanalytic Quarterly* (1990) entirely devoted to deliberations on the nature of the psychoanalytic process underscores this fact.

The transference neurosis was implicit in Compton's list of criteria, at least in my reading of them (cited by Boesky, 1990, and Weinshel, 1990). Other authors used the concept explicitly. Dewald (1990) examined the psychoanalytic process by asking participants to characterize verbatim material from sessions in early, middle (early, middle, and late), and termination phases. "Criteria for identifying the early middle and middle sessions involved changes in the process toward deepening of the transference neurosis" (p. 710). Attempting to distinguish psychoanalysis from psychoanalytic psychotherapy, Weinshel (1990) cited Willick's (1989) criterion, "the mobilization of an intense transference relationship": "I assume that what Willick describes as intense transference relationships others (including myself) would designate as *part* of the 'transference neurosis.' I submit that the terminology is not as critical as the concept itself: that is, the concept of a somewhat indeterminate stage in the course of a productive analysis at which the major transferences (some, but not necessarily all of which are related to the oedipal stage) come together around the person of the analyst."

Weinshel was concerned to clarify the misconceptions of the transference neurosis in the psychoanalytic process.

> The transference neurosis [is not] . . . a simple replication of the infantile neurosis [but, according to Freud], . . . a repetition in a different setting, . . . with a new object (the analyst) of certain psychic conflicts (predominantly oedipal). Furthermore, the transference neurosis does not just happen, and it does not emerge suddenly or magically as a full-blown entity. It is invariably the product of a good deal of prolonged analytic labor (working through), with many transferences and resistances associated with them. . . . The transference neurosis neither guarantees the success of a treatment . . . nor destroys it . . . [but] will [likely] result in a more effective "re-solution" of crucial intra-psychic conflicts. (pp. 641–642)

It is surely no accident that in making the transference neurosis a central criterion of the psychoanalytic process Weinshel refuted persistent connotations that either arose in consequence of the Alexander controversy or were perpetuated by it.

Countertransference Dangers

Despite the difficulties inherent in integrating the concept with the structural hypothesis, contemporary analysts obviously value the transference neurosis as an organizer of the clinician's perception, as Tyson and Shaw implied at the 1988 panel. It may have gradually acquired this relatively unrecognized significance in addition to its meaning as an artificial illness. It is useful to think that a current resistance might be reproducing a central childhood conflict, or to think in terms of an organized transference configuration to be analyzed, especially when rapid shifts are subsumed in that organization. Thus the diminution of the disease meaning of the concept may have led to the concept becoming less recognizedly defined, not less significant. In this sense, the broad definition has its roots in the inductive observation of what concepts help the clinician think analytically.

Some clinical material of mine will help illustrate this point. A woman patient with bisexual conflicts shifted between mother and father transferences. These shifts corresponded to shifts in opposite masculine-sadistic and feminine-masochistic behavior (as the patient herself understood it) toward me. That is, the father transference elicited the patient's "feminine" and masochistic behavior while the mother transference brought out her "masculine" and sadistic behavior. The panorama of transference and behavior together with other factors suggested the reenactment of a sadomasochistic primal scene fantasy-memory complex. It was helpful in synthesizing understanding of the analytic events to bear in mind the larger panorama of the shifts in transference objects and to coordinate them with the behavior toward me that appeared simultaneously rather than think only of the more fragmentary individual transference manifestations.

It is, however, hard to separate the concept from the superego conflicts it so easily evokes. The idea about the uniqueness of the transference neurosis to psychoanalysis (see Blum, 1971) always threatens to invest useful clinical observation with connotations about a right way and a wrong way to conduct an analysis. For example, Greenson (1967) identified the transference neurosis by "the patient's preoccupation with the person of the analyst and the analytic processes and procedures. . . . Not only do the patient's symptoms and instinctual demands revolve around the analyst, but all the old neurotic conflicts are remobilized and focus on the analytic situation" (p. 184). He placed responsibility for the development of a transference neurosis squarely on the shoulders of the analyst: "if these early transference reactions are properly handled . . . if the analytic atmosphere is that of compassion and acceptance and if the analyst consistently reaches for insight and interprets the patient's resistances, a transference neurosis will develop" (pp. 184, 189). Although Stone (1967) immediately took issue with Greenson's emphasis on the overarching importance of the analyst in the patient's life, suggesting that such an occurrence rarely took place, Greenson's description mirrored conventional wisdom and was therefore generally acceptable and accepted. It is a very small step from Greenson's formulation to the assertion that if such a transference neurosis does not develop, the analyst is not an analyst at all.

Further, there is a danger that manifest requirements for a transference neurosis such as the patient's conscious involvement with the analyst and cessation of symptoms not connected to the analyst may prevent the analyst from identifying a crucial piece of transference because it does not fit the manifest definition. One patient conformed rigidly to the external demands of the treatment for several years, filling hour after hour with accounts of work problems that had elicited unpleasant affects in her. If I inquired into the significance of the accumulated detail, she would make a connection between the events she was describing and events from her childhood, a genetic connection useful to her self-understanding, but she would not explore the fact of the accumulation. She reported no thoughts or feelings toward me except annoyance at having to come daily "in order to have a happy life" and at my attempts to explore the function of her fact-filled associations.

As a child this young woman had dutifully eaten a particular cereal daily because the box promised that if one did so one would be able to fly. Her inability to fly despite following instructions represented to her one more in a long line of disappointments, disillusionments, and broken promises from the adult world. She was more than ready to add analysis to her disappointments.

Gradually, work on some of the formal elements in these resistance phenomena, especially on the "Well . . ." with which she began each session, uncovered the guilt associated with a second reenactment: dreaded visits to the pediatrician who poked her stomach, announced that she was constipated, and prescribed an enema. Among the multiple transference meanings eventually established for this manifest behavior was the childhood fantasy/wish to be close to her father by being his phallus (and flying); the wish to have a phallus, an identification with a phallic narcissistic, powerful mother; the wish to defy the analyst/mother and retain a feces/baby; the wish to defy the analyst/mother's masturbation prohibition; the wish to shut out the analyst/mother from knowing about (fantasied) creative endeavors with the father; the wish to prevent the analyst/mother from having babies (functioning as an analyst); and hostile and sadistic wishes toward her younger brothers. This work was never marked, however, by a sustained, *conscious* involvement with the analyst. Instead it was dominated by the defiant enacted death wish represented by not acknowledging the analyst's importance to her. At a certain point, it was necessary to point out this wish as it was enacted in the sessions. Anal conflicts had so organized the patient's character that all subsequent conflicts were organized around them.

In working with such a patient, the belief that the development of the transference neurosis, understood as a conscious involvement with the person of the analyst, is the mark of one's analytic ability is not productive. Indeed, the sense that one is working under the gun and that the patient "must have" a transference neurosis to get better is probably a countertransference reflection of the patient's central conflict with the analyst experiencing the severe superego condemnation for hostile wishes that the patient is warding off. Insisting on the patient defending against manifest transference becomes a sure way of colluding with the patient to avoid analysis of transference wishes being enacted and their ensuing guilt. The patient experiences the insistence as a judgment on his qualifications as a patient. The analytic sessions become his suffering atonement for his hostile wishes. Since he is suffering, he is being punished and need not experience his guilt.

Although descriptions of manifest configurations can be useful guides, defining the transference neurosis according to manifest criteria always risks evoking analysts' submission to rules when they need to respond to the patient's material appropriately and flexibly without feeling obliged to live up to a requirement to prove their ability. A definition of the transference neurosis that stressed the development of the patient's *conscious* and sustained libidinal preoccupation with the analyst would have excluded my last example and could have led to a countertransferentially motivated enactment of an anal struggle gratifying the masochistic wishes of the patient (see Dr. Q's case, chap. 5). Other definitions could evoke other reactions.

Perhaps those most vulnerable to feeling the pressure for the patient to "have" a transference neurosis are candidates who face the necessity of demonstrating that they have conducted a "true analysis." One analyst who heard me present the material on the Alexander controversy had been a candidate at the Chicago Institute right after the 1954 panel in which both Rangell and Gill linked the transference neurosis to the definition of analysis. He recalled the worry he and his fellow candidates had about whether their patients had developed transference neuroses. At the same time, he remembered that candidates' anxiety was compounded because no one was sure what a transference neurosis was or how to identify it.

Candidates are, of course, generally anxious and unsure of themselves, and the difficult task of discovering their own unconscious conflicts in training analyses while learning a complex theory and its technical application can be both daunting and disruptive. On the one hand, in these circumstances, certain concepts can become a lightning rod for deeper and more personal conflicts. A candidate's transference neurosis can be played out in a disagreement with a supervisor over the concept of the transference neurosis. On the other hand, candidates can also reflect the effects of connotations arising from political polemics more clearly. My interviews contained two accounts in which the analysts' difficulties as candidates seemed to be connected with supervisors' concepts of transference neurosis.

Dr. I developed the impression that the transference neurosis was "a religious issue for the Inquisition. The good ones believe in it; the bad ones don't." She continued:

> I had felt free in my own transference to develop every pathological thing, to go from being a child kicking at my crib to a grown-up person and back again to being a child in full freedom. But the supervisor of my first case had a fixed idea of what a patient should do.
>
> I had had a lot of experience with borderline patients. I could tell that the patient whose analysis I was presenting was not borderline; she was very obsessional and had some wild imagery. My supervisor fixed on the idea that since the patient was constantly dreaming of eyes looking at her, she had to be borderline. My supervisor decided that since the patient was borderline, she would not develop a transference. She demanded that I have the patient sit up.
>
> I said "No. This woman is in analysis, wants to continue analysis, why should I interfere?" "Well, she won't have a transference." It was all uphill. It was an overwhelming task. I could not live with myself if I lied to my supervisor, and I could not live with myself if I mistreated the patient. So I felt like a pretzel. Really, like a pretzel. I did what I could to allow the transference to develop, but the supervisor would interfere.

Dr. M described a similarly uncomfortable situation with the supervisor of her first case:

> I had a case I realized I would never have treated the way he did. For me, this experience defined who I was in reference to psychoanalysis, and how I would conduct a psychoanalysis in the future. I think the transference neurosis that developed was iatrogenic. She was made almost psychotic. The propensity was in her, of course, but the "therapeutic environment" brought it about.
>
> The technique that my first supervisor favored was going after hostility and aggression but in such a way that the patient was never accompanied in the pain of discovery. It made the patient guilty and furious, uncovering hostility in such an untimely way. Today I wait until after the analysis has been going for years and the basis in trust and the transference are so firm that the patient and I can talk about anything without the relationship being shaken by it. So I do not obtain these waves of aggression and despair and depression.
>
> This analysis was very successful. But it was fourteen years of pain and hard work for both of us. I was desperate because, more often than

not, I wasn't doing what I thought I should be doing. I couldn't stand her suffering. She really had to recollect traumas from her childhood and she needed to feel comfortable to do so, but following the demand of my first supervisor, I interpreted her intense hostility, with no support from where the hostility came from. This was very much against anything I had gone through in my own analysis. When I had trouble doing this, my supervisor told me that I had terrible problems with aggression. There was no way I could come out clean. This technique was terrible. So more often than not, I was desperate because I wasn't doing what I thought I should be doing.

Fortunately, after two years, my supervisor thought I was doing a superb job and didn't want to continue. I did quite well for another two years and then, because the situation was so difficult, I went to ——— and asked him to supervise me. He did so for several years, and the analysis continued on after that supervision. With this supervisor the technique was different and I no longer saw the same reactions.[9]

Dr. A spoke from a supervisor's viewpoint:

I find, for instance, that our candidates have learned about transference and transference neurosis so thoroughly and so well before they ever become candidates, you have to spend a lot of time helping them to undo that, to look at something else, not to scotomotize in a particular way that they've been trained to since they got into psychiatry. I think that's a nice problem to have. I mean, I begin with students who really are fascinated by transference, pay attention to it, and fascinated by the problem of the difference between sporadic transference reactions and something or other that seems to go beyond that which we call a transference neurosis. But they're so fascinated often that they can't look at anything else. Or they're afraid to look at anything else. And also many of them, of course, have the shadow of imagined teachers or imagined scorers who someday will look at what they're saying to see whether they could become members of the American. So they must be sure to say enough about the transference neurosis.

So I spend some time with many students helping them to "forget about" the transference neurosis, and look at other matters. Or to put it more precisely, to allow a more spontaneous interest in the transference neurosis, and to allow the transference neurosis to develop more spontaneously, without dragging it in by the heels.

A student recently presented a first case to me in which the patient was speaking about the memory of a tonsillectomy at age five. And she was terrified of this procedure. She spent a fair amount of the first

9. This case in continued in chap. 7.

hour of analysis talking about that terrifying procedure. And this student of course immediately recognized it must have something to do with beginning analysis—the memory of it, this amount of attention to it in the first hour—it must connect in some way. And he rushed in—after I think a minute—a remark about whether she was frightened, or that was she not indeed frightened about beginning analysis. He made it in that "What about me?" style of intervention: "Aren't you really talking about me?" And so I suggested that probably she was really talking about both things, but that she wished so much to talk about this early operation, that it looked as though the response to his intervention was that she felt misunderstood. She took it, I think, that he was saying, "Look, I'm not interested in your memories of your operation; I'm interested in what's going on here." Well, with a little better timing, and in a slightly different style, it seemed to me, she might have looked at both and been interested in both—to have seen that there was something probably that was stirring up this memory at the moment, but it was an important memory in its own right. So by saying I have to sometimes help the student not to focus on transference and/or the transference neurosis, I mean not to leap upon it, not to break it open in the first few minutes.

The interesting thing about that particular example was that she seemed to be trying to describe how difficult it had been for her to tell anybody how frightened she was about that operative procedure. And in telling about it, she gave many possible opportunities to discuss with her, in terms of that operation, the ways in which she avoided talking about it and the reasons she avoided talking about it, and to let it unfold in terms of the distant experience first, before dragging it into the analytic situation.

This is a very good student. And it was quite unusual for this student to say things like, "Are you really talking about . . . ?" If a patient is speaking about one thing, I'm sure this is not the kind of student who would say, "What you're really talking about is so-and-so." Except he had this notion of transference, and transference is the realist thing. So that "what you're really talking about" seemed to him an appropriate remark. He has no trouble with the idea that people are doing about ten things at once.

This was not a special problem of his in respect to the material, but in respect to his proving to me and to the school and to the American that he knows what really counts. And I think it just led him, in his own anxiety, into this kind of overstatement which was quite disruptive to the patient—only temporarily; but, you know, if he kept up that way, I think it could have been a major problem.

Let me come at it a different way. The Gill business strikes me often as a marvelous way of focusing upon things that people often neglect. But I don't think it's a marvelous way of proceeding with analysis. I mean, I think it's a marvelous intellectual scheme for helping a student to think about these matters, if the student is capable then of allowing that to fall back into the free conscious—or, as I like to say, you can learn it so you can forget it. But Gill doesn't talk about the problem of forgetting it, nor does he demonstrate the problem of forgetting it and coming upon it more spontaneously.

The transference neurosis can also become a focus for the inevitable reappraisal of concepts and technique occurring in tandem with a de-idealization of teachers, supervisors, and other transference figures that is part of the growth of the young graduate analyst (Fogel and Glick, 1991). Dr. R affords us a glimpse of this process in describing the development of his attitudes about the transference neurosis:

When you first asked me about the interview, I began to think about the evolution of my own thinking about the transference neurosis. When I was a psychiatric resident, I had one patient who became very preoccupied with her feelings about me, about what my feelings would be about her, and she struggled with this preoccupation with me. Most of the other issues in her life became secondary. I thought to myself, "Aha. This is what the transference neurosis is." My supervisor said to me, "She's got a good old-fashioned transference neurosis." So I read about the transference neurosis and thought about it and talked about it and learned about it. This was a woman in once-a-week psychotherapy who had a hysterical flavor to her character. We increased the treatment to twice a week so that we could work more actively on her feelings and it wouldn't be so hard for her to sustain her feelings from one session to the next. I got the notion—which I later realized was mistaken—that this is what analysis would be like. Well, very little of that happened in my own analysis, although there were important transference feelings and manifestations. I don't know how my analyst would describe it, but in thinking about it myself, it certainly wasn't like that patient's reaction. And in subsequent analytic work, I think that that kind of reaction has been the exception rather than the rule.

At some point I was also very perplexed about it, and wondered was this some failing in me? Some failing in my analytic work? It didn't appear in my own analysis, did that mean I had a limitation? I talked about it with older colleagues and supervisors and so on, and talked about it with contemporaries. I was liberated, I think, maybe mistakenly so, but I was liberated when I read Loewald's paper on the transference neurosis, where he pointed out that with the shift from symptom neurosis to character neurosis, you don't see the kind of

> transference neurosis in the sense that Freud described it. You see it fractionated throughout the entire analytic experience. And I thought to myself, Okay, well, maybe I'm not missing something. Maybe it's just not what it used to be, or maybe this isn't quite what Freud meant, it's a mistaken assumption. Because there are so many assumptions that one has about the work before one gets into it. Then my notion of transference began to change, to become more subtle and complicated. In fact, my whole thinking about transference is now quite different.

In contract to Dr. R's worry, Dr. B described the reassurance afforded him by having had a case, early in his career, that conformed to the historical criteria of a transference neurosis.

> I was blessed with the rare good fortune that my first completed case after graduation was a young man who came for analysis as a freshman in college, stayed his four years, and then properly moved on. I've never had another case quite like it. If a textbook were to be written about transference neurosis, this was a classic case. He came for his original consultation, sat in a chair opposite me, asked if it was all right if he smoked, and then told me that his grandfather died of lung cancer, and then told me about a dream in which he was responsible for something bad happening to his father. And looked to make sure that I didn't mind, that it didn't bother me that he was smoking in my office. Over the four years, the analytic work, retrospectively, was the center of his life. It was a negative center. We talked a great deal about his sexual problems, his social problems, the genetics. But there was a heat going on.
>
> He had major problems with identifying with his parents. I realized that he noticed that I had an Israeli painting. This was a man who had great anguish over his Jewish identity, because it's hypocritical not to buy German goods as his parents would not when you don't believe in God anyway. All I'm saying is that in the background was my being Jewish. He was constantly testing the taming of his impulses and his identity against me. And we did get to talk about it. That's the point that I think is exceptional and essential to the analytic process. Toward the end, when it came time to terminate, he really gave me a hard time—he started destructive acting out. I thought "My God. I'm destroying him rather than helping him! This is not supposed to happen!" Then I realized my feeling of failure was the gist of what was going on; it had to do with him and me. And I interpreted it on that level.
>
> In his senior year, he was giving a talk before his class. He fainted, bumped his head against the desk, was hospitalized, and insisted on telling everyone that his analyst, who was undoubtedly charging him

for his sessions while he was in the hospital, would think this was all psychological; and he did not waste time letting them all know my name; and he had the neurologists in quite a snit till they finally decided to discharge him because they couldn't find anything neurologic. When he did come in, I didn't have to make a transference interpretation to him. He made it. We were getting ready to close.

Well, to the extent that the classic transference neurosis—I don't mean it in a negative way, I mean in its ripest form—has to do with summoning up a lot of free-floating urges, needs, inhibitions, symptoms, drives, hooking on to a center point of another person, and then allowing them all to become exposed and organized in relation to the other person, and sorting them out in terms of their origins, his was the most classic transference neurosis I have ever seen.

That's classic transference neurosis, in its nicest form. And it's useful to me because having been through it with one person, I had a sense of a baseline, a model in which I could see variations, so I didn't get so scared. If I had never had that experience, I would have had doubts that such things could ever happen.

While none of these examples need diminish the inherent clinical value of a properly understood and used concept of transference neurosis, they indicate the nature of the conflicts and conceivably resulting technical errors to which the concept, by its history, position, definitions, and connotations, may lend itself. Indeed, they emphasize a paradox especially relevant to the transference neurosis. If our clinical theory prepares us to begin each analysis anticipating a transference neurosis, we need to create an atmosphere in which the patient's material evolves with all possible freedom, subject only to those internal constraints that we must also help him or her analyze. To create such an atmosphere, we need the freedom to feel that the treatment need not live up to a theory of cure. That is, a successful analysis may indeed depend on the resolution of a transference neurosis, but it also depends on our willing suspension of disbelief that that is so.

The struggle for this freedom characterizes my respondents' accounts. Whether an analyst talked primarily of inner freedom from conflict for responsive understanding or of technical freedom from repressive rules, the struggle for freedom to practice analysis proved ubiquitous. Significantly, none of my respondents ended believing that the transference neurosis in its narrow definition is the only path to psychoanalytic cure or that its manifest presence is a measure of their clinical skill. The need of individual analysts to work themselves free from what they perceive to be repressive rules and rediscover the transference neurosis for themselves may, in fact, explain much of the current instability of the concept.

CHAPTER THREE

Working Free: Two Evolutions

If an individual analyst's concept of the transference neurosis is partly a product of transferences to teachers, supervisors, Freud, and one's own analyst, it follows that an evolution away from blind acceptance of received opinion toward an independent judgment on the concept and its clinical utility constitutes, in part, the working through of conflicts bound up with those transferences. Indeed, when an analyst makes the concept his or her own and integrates it into a personal way of practicing analysis, the concept acquires the stamp of a personal working-through process. Two interviews not only illustrate the relation of individual definitions to the process of personal evolution but also suggest the role of internal conflict in the attitude adopted.

Dr. A

Dr. A, in an account colored by conflicts with authority, described an odyssey away from an overzealous reliance on the transference neurosis toward the clinical freedom to explore more subtly.

> We've become so politicized. If someone asks you, under formal circumstances, what you mean by a transference neurosis, what you respond often depends on the local political situation. I first became aware of the transference neurosis posing this problem for me when the definition of analysis, in America at least, became popular as the optimal or fullest possible development of a transference neurosis, and its subsequent resolution. One could have struggled along without too much trouble, even with that definition, but the use of it soon became a way of distinguishing between true believers and nonbelievers, between those who were good analysts and those

who weren't good analysts. The wish to have a definition that would distinguish between true believers and infidels shapes the definition, which in fact then becomes taken so seriously in this odd way that one thinks one has the instrument, then, for distinguishing the good from the bad. So I've had a lot of trouble with this for many, many years.

Yet, if I'm dealing with a student who's just beginning, I would also put a bizarre emphasis on transference and transference neurosis. You know, it's like: the English watercolorists begin by painting in sepia. Now, nobody thinks you should paint in sepia for the rest of your life, or that that's the whole medium. But it isn't a bad way of beginning, to make sure that at least you pay careful attention to some particular crystallization.

The problem is not so much even that we've overdefined or too narrowly defined what analysis is. We could do that if we would then forget it, allow it to appear, and allow your own preconscious interest to focus on it from time to time, as it will. If you really believe in transference, and you really believe it's important, and you really fully intend to analyze it, then you can say, don't hammer it.

The more codification that occurs, the more it demands of us that we should study and learn it, and then learn how to "forget it"—to function with that at the edge of awareness rather than at the center of awareness, which I think is a special problem with any concept, but a very special problem with a concept that becomes holy, as the concept of transference neurosis has.

I would not necessarily restrict the notion of transference neurosis to those circumstances in which a patient is centrally preoccupied in the manifest content with the analyst. I would spread it beyond that. There's a gray area, a shadowy area. Sporadic transference reactions at some point with some patients begin to be more intense, more continuous, and remain in the same configurations for longer and longer periods of time. At what point one calls that a transference neurosis, I can't say. Although I can't define it, I think there comes a point where I get the sense that something has changed. It's not simply a matter of intensity; it's some mix of intensity and continuity. Some mix of preoccupation on the part of the patient and unfolding of whatever is being unfolded in respect to the analyst, sometimes consciously, very often not consciously, but preconsciously.

I suppose that the problem is something like: water gets a little warmer and a little warmer and a little warmer, and then it's not just a quantitative change when it becomes steam; there's a qualitative change. I don't know how to describe what that means in the analytic situation. There is some crystallization, some integrative process when the intensity of the transference becomes sufficient and when it becomes central enough such that a new configuration appears; and one has the sense that it has, as I said, not only a greater intensity but a greater continuity.

It can be pretty much relied upon. At that point, if one watches what the transference reactions are, one will get rather consistently a notion of what is most important for the patient in that moment. Or going at it the other way, if one gets some sense of what's most important for the patient, it will almost invariably also be appearing in the transference.

There must be some kind of integrative process; there's a regression, but it's not only a regression: something new is built. Something is shaped. I would say that the transference neurosis is pushed both by the emerging urges and by defenses against them and whatever is brought to bear on that; but it is also pushed by some preconscious ego interests in the patient, some intention to bring something forth, to examine, to explore, to look into.

To think of the transference neurosis as only the product of conflict leaves out that it's a product of analytic work, of the patient's strengthened intentions to bring forth, re-create, examine something. Otherwise, we have a runway transference in which the intention to look at it, to use it, is minimal; and the intention to simply reexperience it in one way or another is maximal.

I look on it as a double crystallization: a crystallization of something in the patient that evokes the analyst's analytic attention, but also attention for very personal reasons, and inclines the analyst toward focusing increasingly upon that which is extremely important in both the patient and the analyst. We hardly have a language for trying to talk about it. We describe the transference neurosis as though it were occurring only in the patient. We need a unitary theory and language which describes an evolution in the patient, an evolution in the analyst, and how the two are connecting and integrating, and how the analyst's interpretive activity is helping both the patient and the analyst to master what is being stirred up.

Not only with my own work, but with all the supervision that I've done, and all the discussion of other colleagues' cases, you know there's a transference neurosis when there's something like a countertransference neurosis occurring. I would say it's not to the same extent, and one hopes there's more distance from it, more insight into it, and so forth; but there's some parallel phenomenon, which I think helps the analyst to maintain that fanatical attention to the phenomenon. I mean, we're most interested in things that are important to us. The trick is to be sure that it's important to the patient as well as to the analyst.

When things go best, and also that's when things are most advanced and hindered, there's no getting around it, one is working with the interface of one's inner world and the so-called outer world, and one is helped by the intensity of the inner impulses, and one is hindered by them. Otherwise, I think we work in a rather mechanical, tepid kind of climate—which is not without use, and I don't mean to imply that one needs always to be working where it's fiery hot—but I think the best moments are generally moments that could be disaster; that the analyst could get lost in his countertransference phenomenon, but transcends it in his own way, and does something that is mutually instructive and mutually beneficial.

One of our other troubles in discussing the transference neurosis is related to another political myth. Both for purposes of simplicity and also for purposes of I guess I could say duplicity, we talk sometimes as though our own countertransference reactions are less intense than they are, less problematic than they are; as though there are two classes of analysts, those who have really transcended their conflicts, and others who have not and it's just because they're not good analysts, they haven't been sufficiently analyzed, they should be back on the couch.

For me the truth is when one works where the transference neurosis is most intense, one works where there is an intense countertransference. For good and for bad. And that's the fascination of the work, and the difficulty of the work. And we do things in that climate that are readily observable as both helpful and intrusive. I think one needs a concept something like this: in the throes of the transference neurosis, the analyst will be in the throes of something related to, synonymous with, certainly not identical to, what could be called a countertransference neurosis; and that the analyst at these times is trying always both to advance and to retard the analysis.

I don't think that that is only a certain strange kind of analyst or only an analyst in trouble. I think that's a universal. And I think we will simply need a lot more practice in looking at those things and arriving at something that is more honest. You know, it seems to me, for instance, here we speak not only of how the analyst reacts to the so-called transference neurosis. What you perceive as the transference neurosis, it seems to me, is already partly a matter of what you are searching for that might be important to you, and important to this particular patient. So it isn't just that the transference neurosis unfolds spontaneously, and then the analyst reacts to it. The analyst is with the patient shaping a particular transference neurosis that serves the purposes of both parties.

So optimal technical intervention means to me that those interventions should be appropriate not only to the patient but appropriate to the particular analyst. I could conceive of a transference neurosis unfolding with the appropriate counterreactions that would be different in a particular case, with a particular couple, patient and analyst, and perfectly appropriate and perfectly useful, although different from what it would be with ten other analysts.

What I used to experience as the transference neurosis in my early work was artifactual and based on my own tendency to overinterpret the transference, to interpret it more rapidly than I would now, more exclusively than I would now, and perhaps more important, to interpret it with the notion that this is what really counts, and that the rest of it was just paving the way for the transference interpretation.

When I did that, I believe I saw transference neuroses that were clearer, more pronounced, more dramatic, than now. I don't want to overstate things because there are other features involved. For instance, certain patients are inclined toward that kind of reaction; a hysteric classically would be such a patient. But on the average, I think it is true that the kind of persistent hanging up on the analytic situation that some patients get into, hanging up on their reactions to the analyst, where everything that is wrong would feed into the immediate relationship, also requires an analyst who thinks that's what should be done and can send thousands of signals saying to the patient, "If you're going to get my interest, don't talk about everything under the sun. Talk about the transference."

I don't mean that explicitly or even consciously I made such a suggestion, or that patients even heard me doing it. But I think we got that going more often than I would now. Now I'm happier to go with different things. Some conflicts come out with extraordinary clarity, probably the most important on the average, in the transference neurosis. But some things do not come out, need to come out by displacement and unhappiness.

Occasionally I see a patient who I think is a good analytic patient and works well, who developed nothing that I could call a transference neurosis except by the loosest definition, you know, by stretching it and stretching it and stretching it. This is not in my view necessarily a matter of healthier patients versus sicker patients. It's much more complicated than that. I don't know anything that could identify or predict specifically which patients work things out in the transference and which do not. Some patients work things out more in the immediacy of the analytic situation, and some in the external, extra-analytic situation, or even work things out in respect to memories of more distant material. With affect, I mean, with intense affect, and with what I would regard as structural changes, not just an avoidance of the relationship to the analyst.

At the extremes people who don't bring things into the transference neurosis can surely be identified as having certain complicated defenses and resistances. But I think their character style is different. Some people not only don't work their transference neuroses out all in the same particular way, with the same intensity, but they don't work anything else out that way. They have personal relationships, and they're warm, but they don't have that white heat that other people do. And I think to ask them to is to be doing something that's not analytic, turning one kind of human being into another kind of human being.

A patient who might be an example of a more tepid set of transference reactions? The material would unfold, by and large, in terms of daily events, with intense affective experience during the analytic situation as those daily events were recounted. The exploration would take place about those current affective reactions in relation to the everyday events, but they would not center consistently upon me, except in one respect. If the patient couldn't—if what we were dealing with was too intense or too conflicted to go any further, the patient then would experience something in regard to me that would need to be interpreted. It would be a resistance. And it would serve as a resistance. So, for instance, say this patient would talk, would explore very well the feeling of being pushed around, and get into new discoveries about it. Everything would go well until at a certain point I might ask the patient to say more about something, I might make an interpretation, the patient becomes silent, and I would ask what had happened there, and the patient would describe something without any recognition of it, which would essentially be a feeling of having been pushed around in my intervention in respect to the phenomenon we were talking about. And then I would ask, "Is what you are experiencing now something parallel to what you were discussing?" "Oh, yes." And then the patient would notice something about it—and return to the material of everyday life which we had been working with and had stopped; and then the material would move ahead. I think this was very consistent with this patient. Things became necessary to interpret and useful to interpret only as intrusive. The rest of the time, the tale would unfold very nicely in respect to other matters; and then would stop, and almost always, when it would stop, it would be in the context of a transference reaction that would re-create the other material that we'd been looking at. I cannot account for why this happened with this patient in this particular way, although I have a suspicion. . . .

It was a family style with this patient; that is, as I understand some of the conversation and the kinds of exchanges that went on in this patient's family, they would frequently discuss very intimate matters—they would discuss them in relationship to neighbors, friends, relatives. They had a private language, almost code words, in which they would describe and investigate these intimate matters. Of course it was defensive, partly that they couldn't face talking more directly to each other; but I think it was also an autonomous style in these people. They did get around to these matters. They did discuss them. They even had some notion of what its more immediate consequence was. They were very gifted at using the world around them for a discussion of mutual personal concerns. How does one look at that? Partly it's an avoidance, and partly it's a talent. With this patient that I'm describing, it had both qualities. But by and large, it seemed to serve as a talent; it seemed to serve the ability to look at immediate everyday events and gain from it with my help, but without embracing the analytic situation to the degree that most other patients would.

She was able to get to her core conflicts by this maneuver; and whether she could have gotten there better if we could have uncovered more resistances to allowing it to unfold in the transference, I'll never know. In theory, I'm worried about that. I would still worry about that. One always worries when it doesn't go the way your general experience and your theory ask you to believe.

I have had patients who have had profound transference neuroses and the analysis of them was, I think, useful, but no more useful than the work with this patient, in analyzing experiences that we think of as once removed. Clearly what she experienced was not once removed. She had a marvelous intensity with which she could re-create events outside the analytic situation and explore them in the analytic situation. Most of us, I would include myself, my experience on the couch, can't unfold things that vividly and with that intensity and that conviction, without involving the other human being to a greater degree. But there are people who can. I think there are people who are capable of involving the other person, and I think there are people who are capable of it, but don't find it so exclusively necessary. This was a very imaginative patient, who could think of various events, and in thinking of them, reexperience them and relate to those things that she was reexperiencing the way one sometimes sees, or even often sees, only in a more florid transference neurosis. It is evocative, in a way, that most people don't find their everyday descriptions evocative. I thought when I first worked with this patient, that this way of working was a shield. I listened, I didn't intrude upon it, but I really thought that we were going to have to get through this. Sometimes it was a way of shielding herself. But most of the time it was not. I came to understand that this patient worked where she worked best.

The only proviso I put is—I've overstated how absolute it was, but, I mean, as a matter of degree, it was quite remarkable how often the immediate personal stimulus was unnecessary. This patient would describe what manifestly would seem to be a remarkable array of different incidents, different stimuli. She would come in and describe a tree. Almost anything. Sometimes it was personal, sometimes not. We'd get started on it and rather quickly get into the kind of affect-laden material and conflictual material that ordinarily one would expect from a patient who was describing a dream, or who was in the throes of a transference neurosis and was describing some element of that reaction. It had the richness to it. She could make something out of very little.

One of the ways in which I like to think of analytic material, and it must shape how I think of the transference neurosis, although I haven't thought of it before, I like to look and see whether I myself, as I'm paying attention to the patient—from time to time, not all the time—I like to see if I'm paying attention to what the patient is talking about, how the patient is talking about it, and to whom the patient is talking about it. And I find that if I get too exclusively involved in one or another of those, it's worth examining why I'm doing that, what's going sour that's making me do that.

If I move fluidly from the one to the other, I find that I can be more helpful, but I've found also I will analyze—it won't sound like I'm analyzing the transference neurosis sometimes. For instance, the patient will speak to me in a particular way, and I'll pick that up and call attention to it; the patient will then be reminded that this particular pattern of speech was characteristic of an earlier age. The material will have begun with how the patient spoke to me, but it will move into some aspect, say, of the past, which comes back later on in the transference situation, but which for the moment moves away from the transference situation.

So I find if I am doing what I set as my own ideal, the material moves all over the place. Whereas if I get fascinated by to whom the patient is telling the story and all my interventions tend to be in that direction, the material will not move around in this way and I think the analysis won't go as well.

So when I get my best "transference neuroses," it could mean the clearest and most easily traceable and the simplest, it often is when I'm not working in what I regard to be my own best way. Nevertheless, if I were working with a beginning student, I would encourage the student to focus most particularly on to whom the story is being told. In parentheses I would stress I'm not saying do this forever, I'm not saying this is all you should do, but I'm saying one can't practice this too much, especially at the start, so let's you and I focus in on that. But I try not to take that too seriously with the student or with myself.

And I think it's out of that change of my own focus that I have begun to find that there are some patients where the material is incredibly rich in respect to how they're telling the story. A little bit separate from to whom they're telling the story, or that this particular story that's being told now is—if I listen to it sharply enough—just as rich as what I would get from the transference neurosis, and in some instances more rich.

It's a problem. I don't know whether I'm analyzing anymore. It seems to go better for myself and for my patients with increasing experience; but my God! where is the transference neurosis? Why isn't it as clear as it once was? I like to think it's because I'm analyzing in a richer way, a more fluid kind of way. But we could be wrong. I mean it could be that I'm getting sloppy, that I'm not focusing the way I once did.

I think an analyst's job is to worry; to have fun, but also to worry. It's maybe a grand rationalization for avoiding what is part of the case. But since you asked for personal experience, from personal experience it is that my analyses are not as neat now as they once were. And I don't imagine they'd be as accreditable as they once were. I used to do impeccable analyses where the transference neuroses were very clear; I hammered them and sawed them and paid I think considerably less attention to the other elements.

Obviously I've come to feel that pulling everything into the transference and the transference neurosis is not the ideal way, at least for me. I think that there are some analysts who do better following one pathway, and some another pathway; and if an analyst can follow it richly enough, I see no reason why being a nut on the transference neurosis is as good as being a nut on some other element, or a nut on what I think I have come to be a nut on: fluidity, moving quickly or easily from one to the other; I think these are stylistic differences. And I don't like to call everything style. By style I mean something that has been worked out by a great deal of hard work and continuing examination. Not something that is just habitual, but has something more creative to it. I think different analysts can work better with a greater focus on the transference neurosis, or exclusive focus, a more cognitive focus; and others better in the way that I've been trying to describe.

I do my best work when I do a hell of a lot of thinking between hours, and very little thinking, you know, cognitive recognition, during the hour and move much more fluidly during the hourly sessions. And doing that, it seems to me, has changed my view of the transference neurosis, has changed my view of the analytic process.

Before, the transference neurosis was the royal road to the id, parallel to the old notion about dreams. That's where you should look.

That's where the most important things will happen. The rest of what you do, I thought, was really preparatory to that. Preparatory not just in the sense that you do that early in the analysis and analyze the transference neurosis later, but that day by day, you know you have to get away from the transference neurosis occasionally and look at something else so you can get back to it, get on with it. And my view now is different. But if the transference neurosis disappears or seems to disappear for a long enough period of time, I don't know precisely how long, I begin to wonder, am I missing something? Or is the patient involved in some kind of specific resistance?

I asked Dr. A to give an example of what he today would consider a transference neurosis.

The patient's father was anxious and controlling. The patient had an extraordinarily intense relationship to him: manifestly a rebellious relationship, a hostile relationship, but there was an extraordinarily passive imitation of everything that this father did and stood for. And most or much of the manifestly hostile reactions would be defensive against this terribly crippling passive relationship, which in turn also defended against certain aggressive impulses; but at least where the conflict lay manifestly was that he was always fighting with his father, who he was always terribly impelled to be like, follow in his footsteps. There was also the curious coincidence that this man's father was involved in his life and met with him in ways that could easily be re-created and reexperienced by the patient in the analytical situation. As the analysis unfolded, I found the ways in which the patient did re-create and reexperience those experiences remarkably rich. Much that was going on in or immediately around his hours, whether what happened on the street on the way to the analysis or what he anticipated doing after the hour, whether a tiny change in the conditions of the office, or a change in me—some way I spoke, etc.—would lead to the reactions to me that led back into that heated situation with his father. And the emerging conflicts were always most richly available in those reactions to me. When, in contrast, the patient would reexperience the conflicts from his past at a greater distance from the analytical situation and would talk of them at a remove within the analytical situation, everything would go tepid. We followed the current re-creation of the situation with his father (real and imagined) wherever it appeared, and it would usually lead clearly to the past. But when that re-creation began with some extraanalytical person, then nothing much would go on in the analytical situation, except that we would look at what was emerging in the account of the extraanalytical events. And then, in time, those configurations would come back with a much greater intensity in the analytical situation with me, and the analysis would go forward more richly. When the material had its focus elsewhere, in contrast to the patient I spoke of before, you could see the conflicts but they were much less analyzable. They were not only less intense but less convincing to him; that is, they weren't of a kind we could subject, with the same satisfactory analytical cooperation, to an analytical examination. And even when he developed insights in those areas, they were much less gripping. We really needed the richness, intensity, and conviction that came with the development and analysis of the transference neurosis to follow fruitfully the very same conflicts that came out more mildly—and for him, less convincingly—in the extraanalytical transferences. The analysis of extraanalytic events seemed to function largely as introduction or supplement to the main work of analysis of the transference in the analytical situation.

At best he learned enormous amounts from his father. And wanted that gratification. And at worst they drove each other crazy. And he wanted that gratification. Yes, that's what analysis went from. It was a continuation of his infantile relationship with his father. And he wasn't about to examine the material in the same way elsewhere.

This patient's discourses with his father were not only very elaborate very early on, but they happened to be always about the patient. In other words, the anlage, the prototype, of the analytic situation was not only this relationship to his father in general but these elaborate discussions he and father would have together—on what the boy had done, what he should do, why he had done what he'd done. They didn't discuss subjects together; the father asked him endless questions and got him thinking about himself and thinking about what he was doing; and then this process came forth in both libidinal satisfaction and a state of anxiety; but this was being re-created in the analytic situation in a very curious way. And in fact the father had a Socratic style and would ask all these loaded kinds of questions, which the boy came both to enjoy and to fear.

I found that when I asked questions, or when I encouraged him to look at something, it often had the most peculiar, untoward effects. And it took a long time to find out. It was too close to the father's "Hmm" analyzing style. The father was a self-styled psychologist. He was not actually a psychologist, but in talking to his son he used what he thought of as some mix between the Socratic approach and modern psychology. Also, I found the opposite; that is, if I made interpretations that were unrecognizable as interpretations, that looked like a casual comment or looked like a question or an association—"What you say reminds me of something"—they often worked fairly well if they were on the mark. If they were formal in their quality, if they sounded like what this man took to be an interpretation, he couldn't stand it at all. It fractured the repetition of the relationship to his father. His father didn't make formal interventions. It took the longest time before he could tolerate that. It didn't satisfy either the libidinal side or the way they worked effectively together. So it was a very peculiar detailed repetition of the early relationship to his father.

It brings in another point that I left out before. I think one of the fascinatingly rich areas of the countertransference neurosis,[1] when it does evolve, is around the analyst's analyzing style—not just his character in general, not just his appearance, but the specifics that the patient slowly recognizes as the way that this analyst analyzes and then becomes connected by the patient with specific figures from the past, and so forth.

The transference neurosis is made not only of the latent intentions of both parties to look at certain things they hold in common; but it's made out of the patient's analyzing style and out of the analyst's analyzing style, and what that stirs up in both of them, and how they react to the scrutiny of it, to the patient's reactions of it; and, for instance, whether the analyst simply holds constant, whether the analyst changes, whether the analyst holds constant in some ways and changes in others; the patient is constantly testing out in respect to the analyzing style repetitions from the past situation.

One thing that this patient—and that's what made me think of it—used to do with me persistently: he used to try to turn the analysis to examine what was going on with me. It's not an uncommon device. He was very adept at it. And it turned out after a long time that this was a repetition. His father would never talk about himself. His father would always question him, focus upon him. And he was trying to gratify this long-standing frustrated wish to have the father tell about himself, partly to avoid being the center of attention, but partly also because he wanted to find out things about his father that his father wouldn't tell him. It became a very central part of the analysis that I was constantly frustrating that wish. For the longest time, things like trying to find out what he wanted to know about—that was hopeless. You know, to caricature, if he would say, "I'm wondering if you're feeling so-and-so," and I would say something like, "Could you think more about that?" or "Do you have some more thoughts about . . . ?" he would go crazy. He could not deal with that at all.

1. Dr. A referred to countertransference instead of transference several times at this point in the interview. When I asked him whether he meant countertransference or transference, he became conscious of and acknowledged his error.

For the longest time, what we had to deal with were the very frustrating affects, how terribly frustrating it was for him to speak so freely and be questioned so much, and for me not to, and all that that reminded him of. After years, he could then tolerate a question like, "What were you curious about?" or "Was there some particular curiosity?" or "Is there anything about that that reminds you of anything?" So we were working all the time in the analytic situation at first to accommodate to his inability and also to expand his ability: to get him to a point where he could allow other things to go on in the analytic situation above and beyond what went on with his father. So I think the conflicts with the father were repeated with me, and also the formal characteristics of whatever it was they were doing together besides driving each other crazy.

So I guess what I'm really saying is that I think there are patients who do utilize the analytic situation to wonderfully repeat almost everything of importance, and it seems to me there are others who do not. And it frustrates me and I can't predict which is which, nor can I say in my experience that one analysis necessarily goes better than the other.

Dr. Z

Dr. Z, in contrast, described a self-analytic struggle with guilt for greater inner freedom, which led to greater emphasis on the transference neurosis as a therapeutic tool.

The transference neurosis is sometimes much more difficult to define than we teach, and I think it's very variable. But I do think it's an entity. What strikes me as more significant is the tremendous variability with analytic patients. There are some in whom the reflection of the past comes through so clearly in the experience with the analyst; and there are others where I feel I have to settle for being able to help the person define and discover things about themselves that they had not seen before. And that very often helps them to learn more about the past. But the fidelity of the reproduction is just not there.

I wish the differences *were* more clear. I'll just let myself go, because I haven't really been thinking about it. There are a number of patients that I've analyzed—I feel I've analyzed them, and I feel there's been some kind of analytic process going—and yet I've never felt that there was a transference neurosis in the sense that I've seen it with other patients. I've seen certain transference reactions, and I've seen something that happened to the patient which I would consider the onset of an analytic process, in that they began over a period of time to be able more and more to make sense out of what they were talking about. They could both experience it and reflect about it. And the knowledge they had of themselves deepened. But I never did get the sense that it was reflected upon me. And yet I would say from the results—I felt somewhat vaguely dissatisfied—but in a number of instances, one was a fairly classic obsessive compulsive neurosis, I never saw the transference neurosis part of it in relation to me. There were transference reactions, and we were able to establish a continuity with the past that was missing on the basis of what was learned; so that their understanding of their earlier life expanded, and that in and of itself, that new set of knowledge, gave them a different feeling about themselves in the present—but not with the intense feelings coming out in relation to me at all. And yet I would still say it was conducted as an analysis, it wasn't psychotherapy, and there was a process that was started. But I always felt on the outside, never really felt involved. I felt excluded; and it was something that I couldn't really interpret with the patient. I don't think they ever understood. It was something about their style of interaction, which was much more intellectual. I was never completely satisfied with the results, although the patients were.

I think over the years what has happened with me, I think I've learned that there are some patients I work with much better than with others; and with those that I have that experience with, it's always a mutual thing. That's where I see the transference neurosis with tremendous intensity. And it's an affectively different kind of analytic experience, both for the patient and for me. I feel more comfortable and the patients feel more comfortable with me. It may take awhile. It's a much more intense experience for both of us. With those patients I am unhappy when the analyses are over, although it's very clear when they are over. In that sense it's much more clearly a transference neurosis because I get the feeling we're both involved in something that transcends each of us. Yet at the same time, I have enough of a sense of the process that's developing to be immersed in it and yet distant enough to permit it to evolve. In those patients, the amnesia removal is much, much greater. The early experiences come out much more clearly. I have the feeling that I've done a better job.

The thing that I've noticed is that I have more patients where that's happening with now. I'll be very honest with you. What flashed through my mind was, I've had a number of analyses myself, and it wasn't until I had a personal tragedy, a younger sister died, almost sixteen years ago, long after I'd finished my own analyses. I went into a reaction of intense anxiety, more than I had ever experienced before, and I found myself troubled and trying to figure out what the hell I was going to do. I never thought of going back to analysis to try to figure it out, but I found myself working on what was evoked by the experience; and what happened with me was that I continued my previous analytic work at a much deeper level, but with a different feeling, a feeling almost of triumph, at being able to do it myself.

I think that independent work liberated me, in the sense that I had the feeling, I had the conviction, that the analyses I had worked because they provided me with a tool that I could then use on my own in a situation which was, for me, terribly traumatic. It was traumatic for a number of reasons. She had had a brain infection and—my life was a complicated one. The two of us had never really gotten on that well. She was younger and we had just, really on the basis of my efforts, established a really close relationship in the last year, where we both got to know each other much much better, and then this thing happened. A friend of hers called me, and I went to an apartment and saw her, where she was confused. . . . I knew something terrible had happened. I got her a doctor. She had an infection in the brain and they finally operated, and it was terrible, and she never fully recovered, and I saw her through the next night and it was about nine months, she kind of lingered; she was a very sturdy person. I'll give you a little story that tells you the tragic part of it. I remember bringing her a picture book; my wife and I went to visit her, and she tore the pages out and ate them. This was an unusually talented woman, not intellectual, although I'm pretty sure she was brighter than I was. But she didn't have the capacity for concentration, the drive that I have.

The anxiety was related to my various feelings as a child, which I had never fully grasped affectively. She was born when I was a little over five, and we came from a background with a tremendous amount of turmoil. Strange, I'm telling you about my life; but I think it's important because I think it fits in with—in fact, I'm convinced that whether you really enjoy your work as an analyst and whether you really do analysis depends on your having attained an openness within yourself. If you don't have that, I think it's a charade; and I think it can be a tragedy. I have lots of colleagues who really don't enjoy the work. I think if you don't, and you don't continue to develop as you grow older, it must be awful. I mean, I love it. But I have the conviction that it works, you know. I think that without that—I don't think that depends on theory.

With my sister, I remembered not only the fantasies, which were there, but things I tried to do to her. I think what accentuated the murderousness was the family setup. My mother was married when she was twenty; when I was born she was twenty-two. She was really a child, an infantile and beautiful woman. My father was a strange kind of man who I never really got to know very well. My parents got divorced not that many years later. But my father was essentially not around in the house. It was my mother and myself. So that I felt betrayed when she became pregnant.

A tragedy happened to her at that time, which I remember. Her mother died when she was pregnant with my sister. In reconstructing what went on, I think she had a psychotic depressive reaction. Because she didn't want to have my sister. I remember this. I was a little less than five. I remember she tried almost to destroy me. Vivid memories. This came from my reanalysis. My first was a training analysis, which was nothing. It was really almost worse than nothing because—and this is something else I must say. I was an excellent student, probably one of the best they thought they had trained. I swear I didn't know what analysis was during my student days, even though I analyzed four patients and really had reasonably good results. I didn't know because my analyst never analyzed me at all. I mean, what that analyst did was to reinforce some of my narcissism, which was not the best thing for me, which made for all kinds of troubles in many ways personally in my life, and made me a much more difficult person to live with, I'm sure; and I realized—this is the other thing—I did realize that I hadn't had a good analytic experience. I won't tell you the sequelae; I had trouble with my first analyst, who did something that was really terrible, that sent me back into analysis. And so maybe in a way it was helpful to me. But the second time, I had an analyst who was able to work with me on a much more emotional level. I was finished with my training, and I felt freer then.

This first analyst had picked me out as someone who was special, and I felt it was great during my training. I'm sure this first analyst didn't know how to do analysis, because he never got any of my past out. This analyst was very silent. I enjoyed just going on, but nothing happened, not in a fundamental way. The second analysis was different. It really opened me up. The second analyst was a strange guy who I think was also somewhat disturbed, in a different sort of way. Very brilliant. And he knew how to do analysis. It was not that long, but it was enough. And so I felt that I knew what I was doing, and I could go back over what I had worked on before. I felt a sense of knowing something.

I never really felt completely free until I had reconstructed that past for myself, remembered a lot about it; and from that time on I could feel a sense of confidence in knowing that if anything troubles me, I can go and I reflect on it; I get right back to my past, and it opens up and if I feel anxious in any way, it immediately dissipates. For years after my sister's death, I had anniversary reactions. Each time I had them, they would come as an absolute shock. I would suddenly have this feeling that I must be going mad. I would suddenly become very anxious; one of my fears was going crazy; and after a while I would suddenly realize that thing was coming up again. The madness was connected with the fear of retaliation. I would have the same kind of infection and lose my mind; I remember being restrained from poking my sister's eyes out as a child. It all came together in that way after her illness and death.

So I've gone off in a kind of discursive way, but I think it's pertinent. The analyst has to have had an analytic experience himself, and one that leaves him with the conviction that what he's doing is efficacious—because it has been effective and has changed his life in a very fundamental way. I think if you don't have that, you're moving and working at a distance from what you really experience as a truth. And I think if that is taking place, you're going to be at a distance from working really with your patients. Because you're going to be frightened about things you're unfamiliar with. And you're not going to let your patients experience what they have to in the setting that you're developing with them. And I think that once you've had the experience, you can prepare the way for the next person in a very different sense.

I see myself as being a helpmate. I told you a little bit about my life. I had a strong identification with my mother, and I think I work with a motherly—but a tough motherly—attitude. I also like to help others. One of the things that happened with the kind of background I have, where I was really neglected, is that it either makes you into a misanthrope or into a perennial optimist. I'm more the optimist. I like people. I'm more gregarious than many analysts, probably less solemn, although I developed a scholarliness in my forties, not before that.

With the transference neurosis, what the patient is indicating you often don't recognize for what it is. That's where the collaboration is so necessary. I'll give you examples. One patient had tympanic membrane invasions. This was a patient I liked very much. That's an important thing. I think he was afraid of me in the beginning, but I think we both liked each other. I looked forward to working with him, and he looked forward to working with me. But four years into the analysis something happened that shocked both of us. He went into panic reactions, only in the sessions. Panic. The first time it happened, it scared me. I am pretty unflappable, but he looked so terrified; and I found myself talking about what we had talked about before, and he calmed down. He had about eight or nine of these over the next four years. It's an interesting thing, it took four years for this to come out. They were related to the bodily experiences, and the panic reaction, basically, was the affective counterpart to temper tantrums he had in reaction to these invasions when he was a little child. The terror the child had was being enacted—neither of us understood it at that time. Finally we got down to that and it cleared up.

But before it could emerge and be cleared up, we got to a lot of other episodes in his life that were connected with intense anxiety, that he had never adequately worked with: the death of his mother, the death of his father, some difficulties in his work. At one time, the analytic room became the bathroom—his mother gave him enemas.

These were the affective counterparts to bodily experiences, which as a little child he was unable to conceptualize. And it was in the process of reconstructing what happened, my providing words, that those experiences became more understandable and actually meaningful to him. They took place in the analysis itself.

I couldn't recognize that until we had worked, and then it became clear that this was the affect the child felt without knowing what it was, that his parent ignored him, let him fall asleep in this exhausted state from this stress. And never said a word, that was the interesting thing. Apparently the psychiatric literature makes panic an organic and physiological substrate, but this was something that had—there were no drugs—this was something that came about I think because the analysis facilitated it, permitted them to emerge, and then permitted him to work on them.

Something I did unconsciously: when he went into the panic, I started to talk. Which was the opposite of his life situation. His mother had been silent during all these things. And that was very, very significant for him. Neither of us understood that.

Which is the other thing. I think that when you work, after a period of time, I work basically with my preconscious. I do not plan anything. What comes up is spontaneous. I find myself surprised at what I say, very often. But I have by this time complete trust in what is going on between us. And what happens more and more often is that the patient will say, well I was just thinking that. And that does something for both of us. And I think the more that occurs, the more I realize what Freud talked about the unconscious being tuned in. I think this is what happens. But I think the analyst has to surrender to his preconscious.

I do know that I find myself talking a lot more than I used to. I think I understand more. And I feel less constrained and less need to be silent. I mean, I wait for the patient's material, and the analyses are deeper. With more talking. Because I think the patient is able to let more emerge. I think it's the preconscious resistance that interferes with many patients' getting a deep enough access to their unconscious.

That's why I say if the analyst hasn't had this opening within himself or herself there are things that are going to block off the possibility of them ever really thinking about or being able to articulate what would be appropriate. It requires openness in the analyst. You really have to help somebody to surrender to what's within themselves and to let them begin to experience and explore it. But you have to provide a setting where they feel safe. I think that's the key. Now, how each analyst goes about providing that is an interesting question. Because we don't talk to each other about that. I don't think we know. I don't think we know. I suspect that it's different at different phases in the analyst's life, and in your experience. There are some colleagues who seem to grow, you know, they seem to continue to be interested and excited; and there are others who have stopped; you know, they've stopped long ago.

I think you have to provide the setting in which this can take place. And I'm not as distressed by the extent of the pathology as long as I have the feeling the patient is psychologically minded and can work with me. I'm working with someone now who went into a severe depression after many years of analysis. It was after the birth of a third child, and the severity was unexpected. The whole analysis was conducted with a negative transference. Everything I did wrong in my technique she picked up on. Actually, she has taught me a great deal. I don't think she's realized it, but I've changed.

I had pointed out to this patient that she was so depressed she had tried to injure herself when she was a child. She kept pooh-poohing it. Finally she began to realize that she *had* been that depressed.

What we dealt with after the birth of her third child was an abandonment very early in the preoedipal period. Her parents are still living. It was easier for her to deal with her hatred toward me than to deal with her hatred toward her parents, the opposite of what you generally see. I always had to push the other way, but it was necessary. What became apparent was that the tie to those parents was just so great.

I had to watch my countertransference with her. There was something about her sadism I didn't like, the streak of cruelty she had. She picked it up. I had to discuss with her that what we were dealing with had stirred up something in me that I hadn't been able to recognize. It cleared the air. I think we both felt more able to work. This depression was really very severe; early, very primitive oral material, preverbal stuff, came out. This is where a transference neurosis is so intense, with all of the hatred and with all of the pain.

She got much more than either of us bargained for because the early childhood depression emerged in the transference. On the couch. In respiratory symptoms, which were terribly painful. She was pleading for medication for them. I said that she could have it but we'd have to stop analysis, because I felt that was not going to do anything for her. Ten years ago I wouldn't have pushed the regression as I have. I would have gotten scared.

What we had been dealing with was the identification with her mother, which had been in the foreground, but it had been very difficult for her to recognize her mother's incapacity to be involved with her. Her mother was a woman who had been sick her whole life and had been nursed by the father, which had really been something that the patient couldn't tolerate. It became more and more clear, as she began to get sicker and sicker, that she was competing to see if I would take care of her the way her father had taken care of her mother. She began to develop more and more distress, and she was obviously having difficulty breathing; the mother had asthma, and she was developing the same sickness. At one point, she began to experience terrible wheezing in her chest. In talking about the pain, it began to be clear to me that she was confused as to who she was, whether she was her mother or herself. Instead of getting her out of it, I interpreted that she was trying to get me to care for her, now that she was like her mother and confused with her mother, wishing she had the father. With another patient, or if I wasn't sure where I was going, I would have tried to get her to defend against further regression because I could see the confusion. I interpreted that, also, that she really didn't know who she was at that moment. I'm not out of the woods with her yet, but I feel she has to face all of that. I believe she will have a possibility for a different kind of life than she could ever have had without going through that horror that she's been terrified of. She's hated me more for it!

This is where you have the opportunity with transference neurosis. If the analyst gets worried, he's going to close it off because he's afraid of the regression. Now, that can be a fear that is based on a correct perception of the patient, an incorrect perception of the patient, an incorrect perception of the analyst's perception. I think an analyst may very well not want the patient to go more deeply than he went. Or maybe get threatened at that. Loewald talks about the psychotic core. I'm not sure I agree with him. I don't think it's that. But I think it's an openness to the primitivity that's within us, which is different. This patient we just went through, she was really trying to drive me crazy with her picking, and then became frightened that she might. And she at the same time was feeling that I was trying to make her crazy by not permitting her to search out certain things she felt I squelched. But I think what's necessary is that especially in the midst of a regression, and in the midst of this kind of transference neurosis, there has to be the capacity to communicate between both parties. And I think that is only possible if the setting has been based on that kind of equality that is basically described by Loewald. I don't think you can make the setting into what you think it could be ideally if you don't really experience it yourself, feel it yourself. You have to recognize your own vulnerability. You always have to keep in mind the difficulties that you had yourself, and the limitations that are inherent in your knowledge and attitude, and to be able to enjoy the adventure basically. That's what's so great about the work.

But it doesn't work with every patient. There are some that I think can't do this, they are—I think this is also where there's a need to respect how far the patient is willing to go. You have to sense that too, and not make them feel ashamed if they can't. Because some can't. They can get a great deal out of what's going on, but there's a limit. You have to just be able to sense that and to have a certain amount of tact about it, too. Because the patient is also going to be able to pick up if you're disappointed.

Something happens where the patient is able to understand, and I've been able to give them a different level of understanding, but something internally has not been opened up for them that has permitted whatever it is to be reflected in the relationship with me. It can be played out in other relationships, but it's at a different level of intensity. It's enacted rather than experienced and worked out. I think there are some people where the damage may have been too much, [too] early. I'm thinking of a woman who had the feeling that her looks could kill. When I put her on the couch, she curled up into a ball. So I got her off the couch. And we worked together analytically face-to-face for about five years, and it was very, very helpful to her. But there was a level that she could tolerate and there was a level that she couldn't. And we were able to work out a comfortable awareness.

I don't know if I'd call it psychotherapy; it was psychotherapeutic in a way, but she had access to a great deal of material that she could rework. It really was quite deep, some of the stuff. But it was of a different order. I never had that involvement with her. I had an involvement, but there was an understandable distance between us, which I never could get beyond.

She was most like this other woman who was having this trouble with asthmatic attacks. In that the aggression was so great, the sadism was so great. Maybe if I had seen her now, I could have worked with her more. I may have been more frightened of her aggression myself. I didn't think of it until just now. I said she scared me and when she rolled up into a ball and became absolutely silent and couldn't move, and then I was afraid she couldn't get up from the couch. But I might have been able to get her back on the couch if I had been less frightened of her burden, which I think I would be more able to tolerate at

> this point. I think it's the sadism that is obviously my own that's more difficult, even though I recognize it, and I know that it goes back to my sister.

Transference Neurosis and Personal Freedom

Dr. A's central conscious preoccupation, like Dr. Z's, was with the best way to conduct an analysis to provide the patient the opportunity to explore as needed. Both saw the analyst's freedom as crucial to effective provision of this atmosphere. Dr. A, however, located the impediment in the external world, in the authority of institutions, and focused on the transference neurosis as a theoretical concept that had become too political. Dr. Z, perhaps because of his suffering, thought more directly in terms of his inner freedom from conflict. Dr. A wanted minimal encumbrance to his fluid listening from a stringent set of rules, was concerned about the effect of a rigid concept of cure, and was aware that the fact of psychoanalysis having made the transference neurosis its identity could have a limiting effect on technique and on the development of young analysts. He was particularly sensitive to the concept becoming a vehicle for a certain kind of suggestion often ignored. The technique in which everything is interpreted in the transference could, he believed, create a collusion between analyst and patient, obscuring conflicts more alive outside the transference. Moreover, he did not want the analyst to feel the need to submit to an external rule, nor did he want the perceived need for such a submission to cloud his sensitivity to the patient's experience or to the "countertransference neurosis," which he believed to be the reciprocal experience of the analyst to the patient's transference neurosis.

Dr. Z connected the acquisition of inner freedom with having had, in his second analysis, a profound analytic experience. This experience gave him the tools that allowed him to take the work further when confronted with a personal crisis. The continuation of the themes of his analysis in his self-analysis led to the affective recovery of memories of his childhood sadism toward his sister. This work itself and the fact that he was able to do it on his own gave him a sense of inner freedom. He associated the ability to continue the work on his own, the affective recovery of these memories, and the resulting experience of inner freedom with his conviction about the efficacy of analysis and particularly with the centrality of the transference neurosis.

One result of Dr. A's freeing himself from external rules was his ability to notice that the transference neurosis as he had learned the concept was not the only pathway to cure, or even always the best one in his own conduct of analyses. He nevertheless considered that the transference neurosis is an entity qualitatively distinct from transference manifestations. He described it in relation to a continuum that begins at the near end with transference manifestations. At the transference neurosis end of the continuum he saw a consolidation of transference patterns in the form of their increasing stability and continuity. This consolidation represented a reanimation of past patterns of object relations and past conflicts involving unacceptable wishes and defenses against them toward specific objects in the transference.

He considered the transference neurosis more than a regression. An entity that emerges out of the analytic work, different in manifest appearance for each analyst-analysand pair, it is partly a result of the patient's willingness to create a situation with which he can work with a particular analyst. It therefore constitutes a willing elaboration of central conflictual material in the service of cure. Moreover, it is a two-person phenomenon: the patient's deepest conflicts elicit the analyst's and engage his attention. A consequent reaction in the analyst reciprocal to the transference neurosis in the patient creates subtle and often hard to see interactions.

Both Dr. Z's personal experience and the vignettes he offered added up to a conception of transference neurosis as the affective revival of significantly organizing past experience in the transference. His version of the nature of past experience, however, emphasized specific traumatic events and their associated affects, wishes, and fantasies, which must be reexperienced and, when they are not remembered, reconstructed within the context of a new therapeutic object relationship. The emphasis on trauma, to which his own life experiences surely sensitized him, marks a difference in emphasis with Dr. A. The latter stressed the reanimation of characterological patterns, object relationships, and conflicts. The reemerging of the repressed traumatic past in the transference seemed a definitive criterion for the transference neurosis irrespective of the psychosexual stage of the conflicts attached to the memories and fantasies for Dr. Z. Although Dr. Z did not articulate an idea of a two-person organization in which the analyst's reciprocal conflicts were engaged as fully as did Dr. A, he tellingly illustrated it.

Dr. Z's account raises several questions. For example, he reported saying to his depressed patient that she could have medication for her breathing difficulties, as she was requesting, but that the analysis would have to stop. Since the patient could have obtained medication from a physician on her own, the request to the analyst seemed part of the reliving of the childhood scene at her mother's bedside. The usual procedure in that case would be to interpret the request as a reenactment of the early memory. But Dr. Z did not do only that. Was the intervention he made partially an enactment of the sadism he was struggling with in the reciprocal countertransference that Dr. A emphasized? Or was it an intervention he considered necessary given his understanding of the patient's very regressed reenacting of this early memory, an effort to remind the patient that she was not the frightened and envious little girl watching her mother being attended to by her father, nor was she the sick mother wheezing, but was reexperiencing a memory in an analysis? Whatever conflicts it might contain, the comment also simultaneously attempted something therapeutic, reminding the patient that her present suffering had an analytic meaning in the past and was in the service of the analytic work toward reducing her suffering.

Interventions stemming from engagements in a patient's deepest pathology almost invariably have something ambiguous about them, as Dr. A would agree, because they frequently touch on and revive the analyst's own deep-seated conflicts. Very often in the heat of such a reexperience, where a patient's childhood projected sadistic wishes predominate in the transference with a vividness that seems to the patient absolutely real, the analyst's sadism, in attenuated form, will be temporarily called forth. Its manifestations may reside in something as imperceptible as silence or in interventions that derail the patient. This evocation furthers the identity of the transference actuality and the past, which the patient already has confused and which makes analysis very difficult. Although an intervention that helps the patient distinguish the analyst from the object representation of his fantasy/memory complex is necessary, the temptation is to do so by emphasizing the *present reality* of the analyst rather than interpreting the transference and distinguishing the analyst from the patient's experience of the past in that way. The emphasis on the analyst's reality may constitute the analyst's need to disclaim the sadism evoked by the patient's transference and with which he or she is struggling (Levine, 1993).

Dr. Z's views on the patient's need for a reexperience of those early traumata with an object more helpful to the individual than the original one was Dr. Z's attempt to answer the question both he and Dr. A grappled with regarding what in the patient enables him or her to surrender to the analysis sufficiently to allow a transference neurosis involving very painful affects and memories to emerge. Dr. A mentioned the willingness of certain patients to create something new with the analyst almost but not quite as though it were an a priori ego endowment of the patient. Dr. Z talked about the need for the analyst to create a sense in the patient that he is a new and safe object at the same time that he is a transference object with whom the patient dares to reexperience the previously unspeakable. Neither seemed disposed to agree entirely with Freud (1920a), who solved this perplexing problem with the concept of the repetition compulsion.

The frankness with which Dr. Z talked about his own life also highlights the meaning of a respondent's choice of case. Respondents may frequently have discussed cases in which their own central conflicts were deeply engaged, without being entirely aware of the fact. One of the memories Dr. Z recovered in his second analysis was of his mother's psychotic depression and her attempts to harm him; this depression occurred during the pregnancy and continued after the birth of the sibling whose tragic illness later in his life precipitated a renewal of sadistic conflicts, which he discussed in relation to his self-analysis. The case that Dr. Z discussed was of a woman who developed a postpartum depression. Given the contiguity of his associations and his awareness that the patient's sadism was stirring something up in him, it is entirely possible that Dr. Z was in the midst of struggling with the revival of the emotional upheaval that his mother's depression had originally caused in him. That is, he illustrated the existence of those reciprocal, central conflicts touched off in the analyst by the depth of the connection between patient and analyst that Dr. A called a countertransference neurosis.

If we can extrapolate from Dr. Z's material, more than for most psychoanalytic concepts, the transference neurosis designates something so personal and central to an analyst's analytic experience and the reanimation of that experience in the analyses one conducts that discourse about it may be more consistently influenced by conflict and personal connotation than is true for many other psychoanalytic concepts. Concerns about the validity of the concept, about the political freight it carries, about whether it hinders technique or enhances it, about what the "right" way to do analysis is may all constitute, at one level, derivatives of these personal conflicts. At the same time, of course, they represent valid and important concerns about how to help patients.

CHAPTER FOUR

The Central Psychoanalytic Experience

The interviews I have cited are well suited by their personal and informal nature to illustrate the subjective experience of analysts as that experience has interacted with their understanding of the concept or as the concept's historical connotations have affected their learning, teaching, or technique. But because most of my respondents put themselves in the patients' position to the extent that they were eager to talk openly about their clinical experiences and to explore the meaning the transference neurosis had for them today without much previous reflection and intellectual control, their responses do not lend themselves as well to approaching directly a substantive issue, such as a theoretically rigorous definition. Instead, their responses illustrate the uneasy tension between the classical definition, remnants of which remain in individual analysts' understanding of the term, and modern views of structural theory and psychoanalytic process.

Despite that tension, or perhaps as an attempted solution to it, the concept has become a signifier for a cluster of clinical experiences associated with the essence of a productive psychoanalysis. Thus, one current meaning of the transference neurosis that emerged from these interviews was whatever was transferential in nature and seemed clinically central about a well-progressing psychoanalysis to that analyst.

In this chapter, I shall quote a case narrative that illustrates that meaning and captures something essential about the immediacy of an analyst's experience in a productive analysis. I emphasize the word *experience* because the nature of the interviews precludes the verbatim analytic material that would lend substance to an analyst's understanding of a patient's inner life and unconscious thoughts. It is useful to linger for a moment on the word *productive*, as well, because it is related to the conceptual tension mentioned above. That is, seeing the concept of the transference neurosis as designating an entity and seeing it as measuring the quality of the analysis itself is a result of its historical origins in a theory of cure that strongly influences the operative meaning assigned to it. Indeed, Dr. T, the analyst whose case illustration captures a clinical experience so well, prefaced the illustration with some general remarks that are instructive precisely in the light they throw on the interaction between the conceptualization of the transference neurosis and the pressure its connotations exert on the analyst who attempts not only to conceptualize it but to use it. I shall begin with these remarks before moving on to the case.

The transference neurosis, Dr. T began, "is a very important concept for clinical work, a metaphor for something which one strives to help the patient uncover and relive, but which has no meaning without the relationship to the analyst." Although theoretical rigor and its companion, grammatical precision, are never salient characteristics of oral discourse, lack of clarity sometimes suggests the presence of contending meanings in the speaker's mind. Dr. T's reference to the transference neurosis as a metaphor may indicate that, without quite knowing it, she partly thought of the transference neurosis as a figurative entity. If so, that attribution highlights a more widespread tendency to use the concept loosely as a signifier of central, mutative aspects of psychoanalytic experience. But she also meant the concept to indicate something more literal, a psychological entity that is anchored in the patient's dynamics and history and emerges during the psychoanalytic process. The central experience involved for her the reactivation and working through in a psychoanalytic transference process of pathogenic unconscious conflicts from childhood and adolescence that had been both expressed and defended against by well-entrenched character defenses.

Moreover, the psychologically literal entity is something with which the analyst can interfere. Dr. T moved almost immediately from an attempt at objective description to clinical concerns centering on the analyst's *interference* with the transference neurosis: "the relationship to the analyst impacts on its development, appearance, and existence to such an extent that it's something that I'm always conflicted and worried about. I mean this, for me, more in terms of aggressive than libidinal issues; that may be idiosyncratic to me, and doesn't necessarily have to follow."

These concerns quickly became her subject matter: "I'm never comfortable with the degree to which I'm facilitating the development of the transference neurosis by being sufficiently allowing of the patients' expression of their aggression, rage, and sadism, and not being too comforting or tender; versus what I have heard among colleagues, in case presentations, or which I've even done at times under the aegis of misperception or bad supervision, a kind of sadistic withdrawal which iatrogenically creates an enraged, regressive, sometimes paranoid state in patients—which isn't a true trans-

ference neurosis but which is a regressive state along with whatever transference neurosis is there. An iatrogenic creation. The art of helping achieve and find and keep a focus on a transference neurosis is the hardest thing we do."

She introduced, then, the idea of interference with the transference neurosis, intended here as a literal psychological entity, by acknowledging the impact of previous meanings of the transference neurosis on clinicians: that the knowledge of the centrality of this entity may encourage technique in the direction of an iatrogenic creation that is not only composed of the patient's conflicts but also of his or her response to unnecessary frustration in the treatment situation. Acceptance of the concept can lead to the imposition of a technique guided by a misconstruction of the transference neurosis concept itself.

Dr. T was not only aware of the pressures on technique that the concept exerted; she was raising questions about how to steer a course between the internal pressures those connotations generate and clinical action in the patient's best interests. Whereas Dr. A chose to solve this problem by regarding the transference neurosis as an optional occurrence disconnected from the quality (e.g., successful or unsuccessful) of the analysis and others rejected the concept because they associated it with incorrect technique, Dr. T distinguished between technique misguided by the concept and technique guided by the idea of its optimal uncovering. Clearly, she was trying to preserve the concept as a designation for something central that can be interfered with in the worst of cases and allowed to emerge in the best.

But adopting the term *transference neurosis* to designate central analytic issues that must be resolved to effect change imports a fuller lexicon with an already established conceptual apparatus. Dr. T designated the reactivated experience as the infantile neurosis: "The infantile neurosis *is* reactivated in the transference in a good, productive adult analysis." The invocation of the infantile neurosis brought up a conceptual problem: "The infantile neurosis is also reworked at other stages in life, in particular, in adolescence, so I don't think that we're reproducing, or allowing to come to life like a genie out of a bottle, something which was preformed in the infantile period and then went underground into hibernation, and then comes forth in the analysis as though the intervening ten, twenty, or thirty years didn't occur. That's foolish and simplistic."

Although she invoked the concept of the infantile neurosis, Dr. T changed its meaning. In her case description, conflicts contributing to the patient's problems will be seen to have come from a number of psychosexual and developmental levels and ages, from under two years through latency and well into adolescence. For Dr. T, the entity reactivated by the transference neurosis, which she called an infantile neurosis, is not the traditional pathological organization of particular oedipal content that was said to reemerge in the form of transference symptoms but a series of early conflicts shaped and reworked at various formative stages of development. These constitute the nidus of the transference neurosis because they compose the patient's neurosis: "Around the middle of a good analysis there are certain hard-core repetitive issues which are more and more focused in the transference, or more and more defended against coming out in the transference; these issues are the crux issues of the analysis. When they are resolved, you see characterologic change."

The alternative enunciated in that quotation is more crucial to her use of the concept than is at first apparent. If repetitive conflicts are *either* more focused in the transference *or* more defended against coming out in the transference, she is positing that both alternatives are allied manifestations of the transference neurosis. Thus, one form of this opposition would be that the transference neurosis might appear *either* as conscious feelings and/or thoughts about the analyst *or* as defensively motivated enactments, and another, that it might appear as defensively motivated hostile thoughts or feelings about the analyst rather than more guilt-provoking affectionate feelings.

It is hard to tell whether it is the quality of the analysis upon which the emergence of the transference neurosis depends or whether the occurrence of the transference neurosis is seen as inevitable. The uncertainty is built into Dr. T's description and reflects a tension between the transference neurosis as objective entity and the transference neurosis as entity emerging as part of a psychoanalytic process. The qualifier (good or bad) might better, for the sake of logic, be applied to whether the transference neurosis emerges from the clinical interaction in a form that can be analyzed and then is analyzed or not.

We might say, following her indications, that something happens between analyst and patient that is a sign of the pressure of material about which the patient has been least willing to know and to speak. He cannot, however, keep himself from demonstrating the pressure of that material in some disguised form within the relationship to the analyst. Since the transference neurosis is not a preformed infantile neurosis in the historic sense of the term—emerging fully formed like Aphrodite from the sea—it is a result of the analysis of resistance: "one can cull out the transference neurosis more than one lives it in a crystallized form." Its conscious manifestations, that is to say, are a result of analytic work on those actions, resistances, and defenses that constitute unknowing repetitions of the conflict itself or of the defenses against it. In describing her case, Dr. T laid stress on the analyst's proper technical contribution by emphasizing the need to remain neutral and interpret the patient's enacted resistance.

Although Dr. T appealed to the ideal of neutrality to solve the problem of what constitutes proper technique, in the heat of the clinical moment neutrality is not always self-evident. The result of this solution is that the therapeutic scene is divided into neutral and unneutral analysts. The division leads to a way of thinking in which the good analyst preserves and nurtures an objectified transference neurosis, and the bad one fouls that same entity by a sadistic withholding. The analyst's "interference" might be seen less perfectionistically as his or her inevitable contribution to the course an analysis will take (see chap. 8). The test would then be what can or cannot be analyzed by the particular patient-analyst pair and what form the patient's conflicts will assume in the transference.

Not only has the infantile neurosis changed meaning; the transference neurosis has as well. It is not, as Dr. T used it, an illness motivated by libidinal wishes from the oedipal period alone. It comprises aggressive components and conflicts from many developmental stages. It constitutes the reactivation in the transference of core unconscious conflicts from childhood and adolescence as well as of the defenses historically used to ward off those conflicts.

Although the idea of the transference neurosis she expressed was different from that of Freud, its enduring link to cure was evident in the continual association between the evolution of a transference neurosis and doing good analytic work: "That's what it's all about. It's an ideal toward which you strive."

Good work was also allied with affective intensity in the transference. This connection was inevitable given the way the crucial conflicts in question were seen to mobilize defenses for last-ditch stands:

> You see and feel a person who is fairly sensible in most of his life functions, but who comes to you troubled in selected areas of his life and becomes massively irrational toward you. For example, the very well-functioning professional woman, and good wife and mother besides, who is literally convinced, suddenly, that I will not step out of my role and make some kind of gesture beyond what I consider to be adequate neutrality in the direction of showing that she is more meaningful to me than just being a patient. The fury and desperate demand that that request be met overwhelms everything in an otherwise seemingly well-functioning human being, and it's rather startling! The transference neurosis is not something where one sits back and says, "Oh, here we are in the transference neurosis." You begin to get a lot of storm. It can have different qualities, paucity of associations, aridity, all the ways analyses seem to grind to a halt or blow up, or seem to be in jeopardy or disappointing.

The valorization of affective intensity led Dr. T to note the inevitable presence of countertransference responses. She thought this in part a function of the observation that although transference symptoms sometimes occurred in keeping with the original definition, another frequent sign of the transference neurosis was that character traits intensified. "The transference neurosis is probably an exaggeration of the character traits that one encounters at the beginning. The depressed patient becomes a blackmailer. The withholding and withdrawing person becomes more withholding, more silent. The transference neurosis is not a magical entity distinct from those traits." That is, in patients in whom character traits intensify, the pressure on the analyst to enact according to the defensive wishes of the patient increases. For every blackmailer there is a potential victim.

In general these remarks showed the interplay of aspects of the original definition and significant revisions that are not necessarily identified. The traditional assumption that the emergence of a transference neurosis is a measure of good work is evident both directly and in the analyst's preoccupation with the misconstruction of the concept facilitating interference with the process. But the assumption is theoretically inevitable since the core conflicts that constitute the transference neurosis are identified with what is necessary to resolve to effect desired change. The concept, however, has been quietly but substantially redefined through its companion, the infantile neurosis, so that neither required unconscious content nor prescribed developmental level of conflict is now a part of it. The imprint of the original understanding remains in the focus on the consciousness of transference experience and in the emphasis on affective intensity. The more modern influences of the structural theory and of the idea of the psychoanalytic process being a mutual creation are visible in the idea of the intensification of character defenses being included in the possible manifestations of the transference neurosis and in the weight accorded the analyst's contribution to the form the transference neurosis may take. The tension between these positions accounts for some of the ambiguities in Dr. T's introductory comments.

Case Illustration

> A man who's an activist has had a very productive but long and difficult analysis. Although he's in the ministry and teaches at a university, he solves conflicts through action—leading student strikes, picketing meetings. The ministry out here leaves lots of room for his kind of activism. Much of his action was productive, but there was a lot of impulse-ridden action that was not productive. Underneath that action were poly-perverse fantasies and attendant sexual and relationship issues. He was argumentative, narcissistic, entitled; he rationalized and manipulated. It was a difficult analysis because there was a dwelling on his own instinctual life that was not hard to come by, but there was very little observing ego turned on himself with regard to the ways he

obscured from himself what he was doing and how he was impacting on the people around him.

He talked a great deal about his instinctual life; it was a resistance. Early on in the analysis, there was a flood of material, lots of memories, lots of connections made, a willingness to talk about me in any terms, sexual fantasies about me were right on the surface. He could talk about wanting to "fornicate with me," and much less biblically, to "eat my pussy" or "suck my cock" a lot more easily than he could talk about concern that I should like him, or want me to care about him, or worry that I would not be there for him. He took any interpretation, ran with it, and blew it into its ultimate instinctual form as a way of not dealing with it.

Since most conflict was immediately channeled into action, the analysis was hair-raising. Beneath his apparent compliance and sexual wishes toward me, he was subtly, but always threatening me. He committed questionable acts that could have done terrible things to his life. I want to stress that he was a very productive, talented, well-endowed human being. He was driven to do terrible things and would just stop short of doing something irrevocable for his life. He would commit minor acts of vandalism and come close to getting thrown in jail, or suffer professional setbacks because of agitating with his superiors in an inappropriate manner. There were episodes of minor theft, misuse of his pastoral position almost to the point where criminal charges could have been pressed, but not quite. Lots of troubles in his marriage, all over the place.

His presenting symptom was an obsessional thought that he had a penis in his mouth. He'd go into certain professional situations with superiors in the church especially and he'd have a somatic feeling of having a penis in his mouth. Despite this man's willingness and ability to talk about instinctual things, it took several years of the analysis to uncover that there'd been two operations in early latency, an appendicitis and a surgical procedure for a hernia. The two surgical experiences were three years apart. Each of them had been experienced as the most hair-raisingly frightening organizers for castration anxiety. You would think that that's something that we would have dealt with throughout the analysis, but it was massively warded off. Real amnesia was also there for the organizing events, in a similar way. We knew that the mother had had lung disease and had died when he was an adolescent; and we knew that the mother had had a miscarriage. We didn't know that the miscarriage was right between the two operations, all of them in a one-and-a-half-year sequence; and that the appendicitis and the hernia operation were merged in his mind. So whose body is mutilated, how, and what happens to you if you object to things and protest and want things you shouldn't want, look what happens to you. It's an analysis in which the actual instinctual issues, and even their organizing events, weren't as available as you might think superficially at the outset. We heard about a bastard, controlling father, upright, moralistic, and rigid, and we heard about an idealized, wonderful mother who had died.

Yet that idealization didn't seem to fit. Because what was going on with me? After an initial idealization, gratitude that I wasn't telling him what to do, desire for me sexually, appreciation that I was not going to take hands off all the acting out either, what was increasingly apparent was an absolute onslaught, absolute overwhelming compulsion and need to criticize me constantly—done in the most subtle, sweet, supportive, church-"sharing," soul-saving, all for everybody's benefit way; but there was no aspect of the relationship to me that didn't come under scrutiny and wasn't somehow just corrected a little bit: how I walked, how I talked, how I sat, how I dressed, how I interpreted, when I intervened, when I didn't intervene and why I was silent, why I wasn't silent, how I decorated my office, how I didn't, whether I believed in God. And on and on and on and on and on. And wailing on the couch and controlling on the couch and crying on the couch. Years of hard work and many life changes came before the real crux of the transference neurosis.

The transference neurosis didn't come into the analysis for several years. It first made its appearance over the issue of fees. Rather than just raising the fee, I suggested that I needed a fee raise, wanted a fee raise, wanted to make sure it was manageable. This man would have been very glad to submit masochistically. He'd done little things of that sort in the past, but I took the position I wasn't raising the fee, I was inquiring about what was manageable. Period. We spent a year and a half on that fee and the whole issue of being made to do what I wanted. The wish to submit to me, and the fear of submitting to me, and the wish to make everybody submit to him, and the wish to get everybody to let him have his way with them began to come out in the transference toward me. For example, dreams were used very resistantly. I would be flooded with dreams. And then I would be castigated for not making use of them. He would come in and tell me, "Okay, we're going to raise the fee." And then he'd yell and scream because I didn't jump on it. How unappreciative and mean and withholding I could be! Then he wasn't going to raise the fee. But through all of this, a lot of the acting out stopped, and the promiscuity stopped. He had left the marriage. Eventually he formed another relationship that led to a second marriage. A lot of the acting out stopped and came into the analysis. It was incredibly stormy.

This man was somebody for whom social activism and Christian religious vocation were combined. Both his parents were highly devout pillars of the church, very aware of social inequality, and conscious of their Christian duty to work against social evil. Manifestly, he had a tremendous wish to save the victims and support the beleaguered, less-fortunate victims of the world. Victims of racism, of gender discrimination, of discrimination owing to the country of origin, everything. His parents, by the way, seemed to be people who wanted to save souls but could not be concerned with the welfare of the people around them. During this stormy transference neurosis, for the first time, he got the idea that the Ku Klux Klan, the sadists, racists, discriminators were really in him. Something I had hypothesized for a long time.

The insight emerged when he realized that he wished to rape me anally, and do God knows what else to me. It was over the fee that those issues came full force into the analysis. And then he wasn't talking anymore in a pseudo-instinctualized way. It was a terrifying wish to harm me cruelly, which included fears of being humiliated by me and being puppeted by me.

This man had a sibling born fifteen months after him. People who have siblings born before they're verbal have an instinctual onslaught that's always difficult to deal with. So that the sibling rivalry for him has been traumatic. And my hypothesis is that he wasn't old enough at fifteen months to find a verbal expression for his sibling rivalry and whatever else went on. In the middle of this first stormy, intense phase of what I really felt was a transference neurosis he ended up reenacting a memory that screened his very early, sadistic fury at the sibling, without knowing it, of course. That gives you an idea of the intensity of the rage over being dispossessed that was reactivated. There were lots of simultaneous transference symptoms, a urinary urgency before and after every session, for instance, as well as a prolonged depression and preoccupation with feeling failed in my eyes.

Now, that went on for about a year and a half. It broke, like a fever does, and then maybe six months to a year later, there was a new version of it: more refined, having moved on. During that period, the issue of sticking his penis in me, and wanting to do it in a raping, attacking way, and the fantasy that once he pulled it out, it would be diminished, was a key reconstruction I made about his castration anxiety. I've not finished this analysis.[1] I still do not know quite why that's

1. Several years after the interview, Dr. T informed me that the analysis had been successfully terminated. Two years after termination the patient was seen for one session and reported that he was doing well.

the fantasy. It's not something out of a textbook. It's what I reconstructed. I don't know what we're going to make of it yet. Certainly the herniorrhaphy is pertinent, because the hernia represented many things to him. He could push it out and pull it in. He would toy with making it protrude. So it was a phallus, and it was also a body cavity he wasn't supposed to have. It was a masturbatory displacement. He wanted it repaired because at the age of eight he was teased about it. When he was put in the hospital, however, and was put to sleep, and was terrified and had a fantasy they were cutting off everything, he felt he had brought this upon himself.

That was an organizing fantasy too, that he would somehow bring about his own castration in an attempt to solve his anxiety about it. In adolescence this man thought he was a woman inside. The original period of the transference neurosis, when he was fighting with me about the fee, and discovered the operations and the wish to attack me anally, and the understanding that he was a member of the KKK beneath all those rescue fantasies, it was in the context of this work that his symptom of premature ejaculation was resolved and has never come back. He had been episodically, and not always, premature. The prematurity was in a marriage. When we went into a promiscuous, unmarried phase, the symptom was related either to how sadistic he was actually being or to how claustrophobic he felt about the meaningfulness of a particular relationship.

Two things that came to light in this first period of transference neurosis connected to the premature ejaculation symptom. There was his question whether putting something in and taking it out was doing a good thing or a bad thing. It was related to the wish to hurt me with his penis, to toilet training, and to wanting to get rid of the sibling. The other thing that happened was that his claustrophobic fear of intimacy diminished. This fear was related to aggressive conflicts connected to separation, which were also being dealt with at the time. Needless to say, there was no one psychosexual level to any of this. It was anal; it had to do with separateness; it had to do with castration anxiety; it had to do with oedipal organization and wishes to possess me. Somewhere in there, I also knew I had to be a father figure. I had to be the homosexually threatening figure; but was I also the phallic woman? I sit with him not sure . . . am I the phallic mother or am I the father? Especially with a man who endlessly talked about wanting to suck my penis. By the way, that kind of talk has diminished a great deal as he has stopped using that thinking in a defensive way.

There's a recurrent wish to find something by which he has to have an operation. The most recent and I think the last of these—we're nearing an end, he's afraid to know it—he thought there was something wrong with his bowel. The organizer was: there will be something wrong with him and he will have to have an operation. And he'll have to relive the operations of latency. Or his mother's miscarriage. He saw her carried out bleeding when he was nine and a half. His operations were at eight and eleven. That's an interesting thing, too. These organizing events occurred after five. But the sibling's birth occurred at fifteen months. So there's a lot of theoretical things that don't quite fit.

In earlier episodes of sadomasochistic aggression and perversion, as well as of obsessional self-torturing symptoms, this man had a need to put himself at risk. He was the clergyman leading students in a sit-down demonstration who ended up joining with the rowdiest students throwing eggs at establishment figures, then mace at campus policemen who were called in to disperse the students. He appropriated hymnals and Bibles from churches and gave them to people who couldn't afford them. Things like that. The version of it at the time that the transference neurosis was more and more full-blown had to do with temptations to abuse his pastoral counseling functions. So that the acting out was more torturing for him, and at the same time the stakes were higher. For somebody whose life was a commitment to helping underdogs, there was also a promiscuity that rose to an unbelievable level, with increasingly degraded behavior with people he considered lowlifes. All of the symptoms and focuses and ambivalence and distortions were more accentuated.

With me there was, first, an overwhelming wish in the analysis to get me to feel that he was a wounded, fragile person, entitled to compensation, needing my ego support, needing my guidance, but not able to tolerate his own frustration. So many of his actions were presented as things he had to do, that he couldn't help doing. They were out of control. He would come and tell me about things as though something had taken him over. So while we were reconstructing organizing fantasies and uncovering significant memories, I was also confronting his ego attitudes: "What do you mean you couldn't help it?" In the simplest, most crass, nonsympathetic terms, "You talk as though you really had no control. You talk as though this thing happened and you somehow lost being the one who's in charge of what you are doing. What is this? Because . . ." I kept telling him that it wasn't a matter of symptoms, as he would have me see it, and behavior and thoughts that he couldn't control; it was as though somehow he tacitly and subtly gave himself over to this behavior, that he had a choice. I could show him how I knew he had a choice, because I could point out the difference between the times when he chose to exercise it and when he didn't, and how close to the line he let it go. He would say "How can you say that to me? I don't know what I'm doing! If I knew what I was doing, I wouldn't be here! If I could control this, I wouldn't be telling you about it!" Perhaps the most important thing was to deal not only with his feelings of entitlement but with this very subtle decision he made that it was okay to be out of control. That he had a special license to get away with things, cross lines, be lawless, and most of all, this idea that his body and his life and his actions were not his own domain.

We knew he had a father who although a respected figure in the business community and a pillar of the church was a madman at home. Threw things and made a lot of noise and frightened everybody to death, a very very very crazy man. So that was the genetic tie to the whole issue of one's decision as to when one lets oneself go out of control or when one doesn't. And about the exaggeration of that in the transference, you could say, this is a return of the repressed or you could also say, one is giving oneself permission to do these things. Because until there's a willingness to try to stop, you're going nowhere. Only later did I learn that in early adolescence, this man was so jealous when his mother went out with his father to dinner and didn't come kiss him good-bye that he slept with a knife under his pillow. He threw rocks at their car. And then much earlier he was very violent to his sibling. There were always ways in which we could eventually see the early antecedents and the characterologic traces of this permission he gave himself not to follow rules.

These memories often came back after there was a confrontation in the transference and a depiction of what he was doing to me or with me or that he wanted from me. This is somebody who thought of himself as a Good Samaritan. He's a very perceptive guy. Criticisms of me were usually fairly valid. A lot of the assaults were perceptive. But in the burgeoning of the transference neurosis, there was not a new human being, there was a more frightening, more frightened, more infantile version of the same person. All of the hints became manifest. We also had increasing ego to bring to bear on all this. And in fact, as there was more and more craziness with me, there was a more and more well-functioning somebody out there. Everything got better and worked out better. The second marriage seems much better. This man, by the way, has a terror of being devoured by little children and other needy people; not unsurprisingly, he is an exaggeratedly good father, a mother-father to his children.

Lately in the analysis, he has a new, intense wish not to be a little boy who's taken care of by me, or a frightening sadistic rapist, but rather of being sexually successful with me. That wish, occasionally accompanied by being erect on the couch, has been the hardest for him to talk about, in contrast to the early instinctualized resistance. All along the way, however, always recurring in different forms, are aspects of the resistance and the central issue of the transference neurosis: his terror of his wish to submit to a castration, whether it's the surgeon's knife, my supremacy, verbal assault, homosexual assault. That, in my opinion, is the organizing issue and explains his need to be in control.

The case description seems consistent with the meaning Dr. T attributed to the concept in her preliminary remarks. She described the transference neurosis in her case in terms of phases in which central childhood and adolescent conflicts reactivated by the psychoanalytic situation and acted out extratransferentially exploded in the transference. Those conflicts were aggressive as well as libidinal. Aggressive conflicts in particular raised the technical problem of allowing their expression without being sadistically withholding and producing an iatrogenic, quasi-paranoid reaction. Concern with the technical problem was also undoubtedly the point at which countertransference manifested itself. It would have been tempting to withdraw sadistically in response to the patient's intense transference hostility, rather than actively confront his acting out. These transference neurotic phases did not constitute a facsimile of an infantile neurosis in the historic sense of the term. Rather, selected core conflicts reworked in later developmental phases repeated themselves in various transference configurations. In fact, latency traumata became the locus of the reorganizing of earlier fantasies and memories in her patient.

An issue indirectly raised concerns the question of the patient's ego structure and whether, given his acting out and disavowal, what Dr. T described will conform to my conception of a transference neurosis. Dr. T's patient characterologically defended against castration and other anxieties through perverse action. The acting out increased, not randomly, but as his anxiety became intensified by the transference. It ceased when the conflicts were engaged by the analyst, especially by her challenging his disavowal of responsibility for his actions. The therapeutic result was a characterologic change in which perverse enactment no longer was depended on as a defense. The fact that the patient was not *conscious* of his ability to control his action and frequently acted as though he was out of control was motivated by his need to give expression to his sadistic wishes without experiencing the unpleasure arising from conscious guilt or the anticipation of punishment, both of which would have stopped him from his sexually gratifying enactments. Although the criterion of adequately integrated ego and superego structure, which I shall make a requisite of the transference neurosis, is not meant to imply good patient manners, an absence of passion, or the absence of focal outbursts of irrationality, it may be that the transference organization in this case conforms to what I shall call a transference perversion (see chap. 7), at least during the period Dr. T described. Since the transference perversion has not generally been elaborated, I am introducing a distinction, not criticizing Dr. T's broader use of transference neurosis. As I shall point out, in any event, the categories shade off into each other, and how one describes this transference organization becomes a function of how much emphasis one places on the shaping force of ego structure in the evolution of a transference neurosis.

Dr. T also saw the transference neurosis as occurring as a regression along the axis of maladaptive character traits. Her patient became more and more action-oriented, ready to submit masochistically, to enact sadistically. This observation is probably best explained as Freud (1926) explained it: "In proportion as the purely sensual and hostile sides of his love try to show themselves, the patient . . . struggles against them and tries to repress them before our very eyes. . . . [He] is repeating in the form of falling in love with the analyst mental experiences which he has already been through once before. . . . he is also repeating before our eyes his old defensive reactions" (p. 226). In Dr. T's patient the repudiated wishes included murderous wishes against his transference mother. Dr. T included two interrelated aspects of central childhood conflicts in her idea of the transference neurosis: the repetition of defensive patterns as they intensified, a sign of the growing pressure of more unconscious conflictual material reactivated, and the reactivated unconscious conflictual material itself. The transference neurosis Dr. T described emerged as a result of a technique that interpreted the defensive maneuvers enacted in the transference in terms of the conflicts they defended against. It required the analyst's ability to see beyond the surface and to take into account the derivatives in the patient's associations.

What makes these conflicts reactivated in the transference a transference neurosis for Dr. T is their centrality. It is signaled by intensifying character defenses. That is, she uses two different criteria in combination. One criterion, increasing affective intensity allied to a remobilization of character defenses, is manifest. The other requires a complex judgment by the analyst about the structure and unconscious content of the patient's psyche, neurosis, and/or character in order to identify what is central. Evidence particularly valued in the making of that judgment is the first criterion.

The appearance of central conflicts in the transference in an affectively intense form is desirable, though with a very important caveat about the iatrogenic effect of bad technique. The technique that brings about the good result is not specified in the preliminary remarks, but it is implied by the coupling of intensifying character defenses and core unconscious conflicts to include the identification, confrontation, and analysis of character traits that manifest themselves in the treatment as transference resistances. That activity is not otherwise conceptually related to the transference neurosis.

More generally, the extent to which a focus on the concept shapes discourse and thinking, particularly with regard to the elevation of material appearing in the transference over all other clinical material, is noteworthy. Dr. T made a statement that could be taken to reflect this shaping process: "Around the middle of a good analysis there are certain hard-core repetitive issues that are more and more focused in the transference." In the context of a discussion of the transference neurosis, it is difficult to avoid the perception that her implication is that an analysis in which the analyst did not continually focus these issues in the transference would be a bad one. Yet an analysis in which these same core issues appeared also in a variety of areas outside the transference and were addressed in that form as well might also be productive, as Dr. A reported. Moreover, the two views are not necessarily incompatible. If we can step away from the shaping process of the connotations of the transference neurosis, Dr. T may mean only that the appearance of these conflicts in the transference is inevitable if they are not otherwise addressed and that in a productive analysis their hidden transference presence is eventually recognized and addressed.

Dr. T convincingly described the usefulness for her patient of experiencing in the transference the hostility he had been enacting outside it and covertly expressing within it. As he recognized his sadistic fantasies through his transference experience, his acting out ceased. It does not follow from this productive work, however, that what is always called for is a technique continually laying emphasis on patients' conscious thoughts and feelings toward the analyst. In some cases the patient's focusing in the transference may be less a measure of productivity than a by-product of a technique shaped by the rhetorical influence of the concept and its connection to a topographic formulation of cure. Focusing on the transferential aspects of unconscious conflicts may, as Dr. A also noted, help sculpt an intense, conscious transference reaction as a measure of the patient's compliance.

Since an analyst's character and technique always influence to some extent the form in which a patient's conflicts appear, iatrogenic elements are an inevitable fact of therapeutic engagement. Where the concept of the transference neurosis is adopted as clinically useful, it will exert pressure toward a focus on transferential material. That focus inevitably interdigitates with the core conflicts that compose the patient's pathology. The modern awareness of this influence is a considerable factor in questions about the transference neurosis. Nevertheless, the transference neurosis continues to be used not only to designate whatever is central, mutative, and transferential in a productive analysis but to guide technique toward the optimum uncovering in the transference of those central conflicts.

CHAPTER FIVE

Toward a Clarification of the Concept

Preference for or rejection of the transference neurosis as a useful operational concept more often than not came down to a matter of how an individual analyst implicitly or explicitly defined it. Given their variety, moreover, definitions clearly represented personal choices. Thus they raised the question of what motivated those choices and not others. As was clear with the training experiences cited in chapter 2, with the two evolutions cited in chapter 3, and with what may be true for the use of theory in clinical situations more generally (W. I. Grossman, 1992b), the concept of the transference neurosis tended to represent various conflicts involving authority. The endorsement or rejection of a standard identified with authority was never far from the choice of definition even though that choice was ostensibly arrived at on clinical grounds.

If one leaves out the crucial factor of definition and concentrates on attitude alone, roughly two-thirds of the respondents were positive in varying degrees toward the concept and one-third more negative. It was notable that no one thought the transference neurosis, whatever they meant by it, inevitable or absolutely necessary. Those who, like Dr. Z, thought it most desirable were at the most positive end of a graduated scale. Others who, like Dr. A, considered a focus on transference only one of many forms a productive analysis could take or who had other questions about the concept, yet did not seem to regard it unduly negatively, occupied a middle ground. This middle category shaded off into respondents who were more and more lukewarm to the idea of the transference neurosis as a useful concept. At the far end of the scale, some analysts objected to it with few if any qualifications. Since some respondents who were extremely ambivalent about the concept (e.g., Drs. F and M) nevertheless offered clinical examples of it, allocating numbers to particular categories, even without regard for definition, is inevitably subjective. Some respondents simply had not thought much about the issue and searched their clinical memories for examples of what they would consider a transference neurosis without assessing whether the concept was useful to them or whether their conceptualization was theoretically logical. Where respondents attempted to expound a more articulated theoretical position, that concept was often theoretically inconsistent and tended to be influenced by subjective factors, whether they were aroused by the cases discussed, a historical relation to the concept, or dynamic forces reactivated by the interview setting.

I intend in this chapter to illustrate first the complex interrelation between attitude and definition that makes the concept so inconstant. I shall then attempt to forge a definition of my own, using the respondents' illuminating theoretical confusions and acute clinical perceptions.

Objections

Analysts who rejected the concept or found it rarely useful had a pronounced tendency to define it in a very narrow way. Once the transference neurosis was narrowly defined, the definition was used to show that the term thus defined did not fit clinical experience. That is, the assessment of value seemed determined by a definition shaped by a proclivity to reject the term. Case material attempting to substantiate the negative assessment sometimes illustrated another possible way to understand the concept.

Those analysts who rejected or found the term unhelpful generally emphasized one or more aspects of the original meaning. Their narrow definitions centered on the patient's conscious involvement with the analyst to the exclusion of most else in his or her life, the patient's conscious libidinal involvement with the analyst with all the attendant jealousy and frustration the reexperiencing of an acute childhood oedipal phase brings, the patient's involvement with one single primary object, the patient's conflicts at one single developmental stage, the development of a transference symptom, and the cessation of symptoms simultaneously with an affective focus on the person of the analyst. They chose not to extend or modify the concept to bring it more in line with the complexity of current experience, knowledge, and practice.

There were, however, major disparities in what they objected to. Some objected to the *neurosis* part of the term, assuming it mandated manifest oedipal conflict. Dr. I described a female patient she diagnosed as a hysterical character. "This was an individual whose reality testing was never in question, but as soon as she lay down on the couch you were in the nursery with every imaginable monster. She had this one area of regression to which she went first." The regressive material turned out to be associated with the birth of a sibling when the patient was in the preoedipal phase and with what the patient experienced as being handed over by her mother to the father for her exclusive care.

Although Dr. I thought the patient's character structure consistent with neurotic capacities, the fact that the patient began the analysis experiencing the analyst as a horrifying witch led Dr. I to reject the concept of the transference neurosis:

> There is a problem with the term *transference neurosis*. *Neurosis* means that you have to be in the oedipal period and be at the stage of resolving the oedipal situation. In the case of this woman, tremendous confusion in the preoedipal period interfered with the full evolution of an oedipal situation. She had obtained oedipal success while she was still wrestling with preoedipal situations. She already had a gender identity that was truly feminine, but she was in a very complex situation because there were preoedipal maternal attachments to the father, and maternal rejection and enormous rage against the mother that were all preoedipal; so when she arrived at the oedipal period, the whole thing was like scrambled eggs.

Despite her assessment of the patient's psychic structure, Dr. I assumed that the patient's manifest lack of awareness of the "as-if" aspect of the transference vitiated the possibility of her behavior being a piece of a neurotic conflict. Moreover, she equated neurotic conflict with its manifest oedipal content.

Analysts who objected to the *neurosis* part of the term preferred to think in terms of transference alone. Dr. J, for instance, said:

> When I was originally trained I thought analysis was as final as the development and resolution of the transference neurosis and there was a connection between the transference neurosis and the infantile neurosis. As the years went on what I found was that the intense and ongoing transference issues that a patient developed with me and that we worked on by and large couldn't be reduced to one transference neurosis. I would say that there were various transference manifestations. I don't mean trivial things. I mean significant components either of reproductions of the way they felt as children or defenses against those or turning around the other way and making me feel as they did, but it did not deal necessarily with one particular issue.

Those analysts like Drs. I and J who were opposed to the *neurosis* in the term continued to emphasize the transference.

Others, however, objected to the emphasis on the overriding clinical importance of the relationship to the analyst, that is, to the *transference* part of the term. Several analysts, for instance, discussed the analysis of an intensely neurotic marital relationship substituting for work in the transference (see Blum, 1983). To put his objection to an exclusive emphasis on transference most provocatively, Dr. O stated: "Suppose a person's chief and principal conflict was with her kid sister, and she goes to an analyst with a gray beard. He's sixty, seventy years old, and he smokes a cigar and wears thick glasses. Do you tell me that that patient's gonna develop a sister transference to this person?" The question of whether or not a gray-bearded analyst would become a young sister in the transference is not, of course, dependent upon the patient's conscious ideas. The issue can be resolved only through an examination of the derivatives of the patient's free associations.[1]

Dr. O was trying, however, to underline his objection to the transference being seen as the sole or even the best entry to the central unconscious fantasies that govern a patient's pathology. To emphasize his contention that there are other clinical pathways to the analysis of what is central to a patient's pathology and thus to change, he described the analysis of a young man who came into treatment after having failed to perform sexually with a prostitute:

> The most conflictual person in his life was his mother. The principal theme in his analysis had to do with a fantasy about a woman having a hidden phallus in her vagina. In one dream he was walking into very shallow water at the ocean's edge, and there was some little sea creature, a sea anemone, there that would bite him. There was a great deal of material about phallic women and the dangerous interior of the vagina. He was very apprehensive about dating girls, and he began to have some sexual experiences with increasing success and fell in love with this girl and married her.
>
> The work unrolled around the analysis of dreams, not of transference. He would come in and lie on the couch and free associate. He would bring in dreams and would tell me what occurred to him. By and large the central theme of his analysis had to do with his sexual experiences. He would have some experience with a woman and have a dream about it and be able to go back and look at what happened. He gradually became much more aware of his repetitive patterns and of

1. Dr. J provided indirect support for Dr. O's point. He noted that Dr. Edward Kronold once told him that when he reanalyzed many patients who had had a relatively satisfactory first analysis he was a different person in the transference neurosis than had been the case in the first analysis, most often a sibling. I have not noticed this observation reported elsewhere. The question of the degree of difference possible between the reality of the analyst and the conscious transference experience of the patient has been discussed most thoroughly in literature on cross-gender transferences. See Raphling and Chused (1988), Goldberger and Evans (1985, 1993), Lasky (1989), and Kulish (1986).

what the core fantasies seemed to be, and with that there seemed to be an erosion of the power of these fantasies to disrupt his life.

Although the clinical observations on the basis of which all these analysts chose to reject the concept were generally unexceptionable by themselves, the objections often followed from definitions that excluded the observations they were making. Dr. F, for instance, excluded character from the domain of the transference neurosis and then called the term "old-fashioned" and contended that the transference neurosis often did not appear in contemporary clinical practice. As an example of material that was not a transference neurosis he described the clinical manifestation of a characterologic, narcissistic defense.

To summarize his remarks in a little more detail, he understood the transference neurosis as a new compromise formation arising partly from childhood conflicts in the past and partly from the transference present of which the definitive sign was the development of a new symptom in the treatment. He described an analysis in which symptomatic neurotic compromise formation occurred in the transference with a patient who had an "unusual capacity for regression" within the session. Then he pointed out that Freud did not use the concept after 1920[2] and thought analyses different when the term was current because analysts tolerated more acting out and were not concerned with the patient's character. He saw no sensible theoretical reason to extend the term to cover manifestations of character. Given that position, his emphasis on the second part of the term, and his generally narrow definition, he was consistent in holding that we see many patients in analysis today who do not develop a transference neurosis. The term was not, therefore, particularly useful to him.

As an example of a contemporary patient for whom the concept was irrelevant he described an individual whose associations became very arid. He tried to catch the moment when the aridity began in the session, and each time investigated with the patient the function of this shift in his associations. A whole series of self-idealizing fantasies from childhood emerged as a result of this work, which defended against the disappointment that patient had felt in his father.

Although Dr. F did not make the point explicitly, the vignette illustrated his idea that there was no new transferential compromise formation and therefore no transference neurosis because the patient characterologically and defensively withdrew from direct involvement with the analyst. The patient, retreating into himself, became occupied with self-idealizing fantasies that had historically been an adaptive response to his father. Dr. F's position assumes that defenses employed in the psychoanalytic situation

2. The last mention of the term in Freud is actually in the lay analysis paper (1926b).

may be autonomous and are not necessarily indicative of the presence of impulses toward the analyst or the defenses against them. That is, in this case, at least, he excluded the possibility that the withdrawal itself might have a transference meaning. It is also possible that a different analyst, or the same analyst with a different patient, might come to a different conclusion. The disregard of the analyst might be seen to carry a meaning within a transference or a transference neurosis. It could represent the expression of a murderous wish, for instance. Such a viewpoint, however, would require extension of the classical concept to accommodate a wider range of intensely hostile urges within it. It would also separate behavior—in this instance the absence of conscious thoughts toward the analyst—from possible unconscious meaning. Moreover, it would be necessary to examine clinical process to decide if such a conclusion were supported by data.

Dr. Q also chose a definition of the transference neurosis that enabled him to criticize the concept on the basis of the definition he had chosen. Rather than the creation of new transference symptoms, the definition Dr. F adopted, he thought of the transference neurosis in terms of the cessation of symptoms. The term was a historical relic for him: "When symptoms had almost gone into abeyance or appeared only in the periphery, and when the analyst became the most important person in the patient's life, one could say that the transference neurosis was in evidence."

Not surprisingly, he found the transference neurosis according to this definition "overly limiting" and refutable by clinical fact. He mentioned a patient in analysis for nine years whose symptoms persisted until nearly the end of the treatment. The patient also denied the importance of the analyst to him.

Implicitly, Dr. Q also saw the transference neurosis as historically distinguishing psychoanalysis from psychotherapy. He advanced the concept of the psychoanalytic process as a concept better able to serve that function. He introduced the term *resistance* to show how the "old term," *transference neurosis*, relates to the more "modern term," *psychoanalytic process*. Resistance "is an inseparable covariant for transference. Linking transference to resistance explicitly places in italics that we're dealing with transference in a treatment context and that the resistance is not viewed as a resistance to the analyst as a person, or necessarily even to the process. The transference resistances, transference viewed as a resistance, still constitutes one of the keystone concepts of psychoanalysis that separates it from other forms of psychotherapy."

He conceptualized transference—though interestingly not the transference neurosis—as a compromise formation. "In the modern view of transference, we would say that there is never only a positive or only a negative transference, but these are always complex amalgamations of drive derivatives, defense, ego interests, and superego considerations."

Once he had identified transference as a compromise formation, he could somewhat modify its centrality in treatment. Unlike the historically derived idea of transference neurosis where, he believed, "everything that would be affectively meaningful to the patient had to be deployed through the evocation of transference experiences," transference, he said, is "one of the most if not the most important group of compromise formations one addresses in doing psychoanalytic treatment." Transference, however, "is not the only manifestation of compromise formation that engages the attention of the patient and the analyst."

By noting the pressure of the historical meaning of the concept on the clinician to behave as if everything of affective importance had to emerge in transference experience, Dr. Q touched on the rhetorical influence of the concept. His solution was not to correct that influence but to discard the concept. Thus Dr. Q was ready to think of transference as a compromise formation while continuing to define the transference neurosis according to manifest criteria that contradict the concept of compromise formation.

Furthermore, Dr. Q thought that transference neurosis, unlike the term *resistance* which better linked itself to the psychoanalytic process, evoked a "static" phenomenon that led even many "orthodox" analysts to overemphasize regression in a way he ridiculed, citing Arlow (1987, see chap. 1) as awaiting the coming of primary-process babbling as though the latter were a "therapeutic triumph."

> The analyst who's working correctly with the transference—correctly, that is, in terms of what seems most valid today—makes the effort to establish the various meanings for the patient of an experience, rather than to induce the patient to do anything at all. We are constantly trying in analysis to discover, first, that we are in some kind of trouble in understanding the patient; that we have been for longer than we knew; that we had not realized that we were not understanding something; and that there had been an emerging avoidance by the patient. And we're continually trying to delineate for ourselves and for the benefit of the patient what that avoidance consists of and what its functions are in terms of the concealed pleasures and defensive gains and punishment aspects; and we move from one position to another. It is the continuous and ongoing recognition, and the way in which those resistances are recognized often in the transference, perhaps even most acceptably, ultimately, in the transference, that concept is the psychoanalytic process.

Ironically, in the turning away from the transference neurosis as an acceptable concept, Dr. Q transferred its function as arbiter of good treatment to a different concept, this time one that implies technical action rather than passive waiting for the patient to produce a result. Dr. T saw passive withholding as a misconstruction of technique that led to an iatrogenic reaction easily mistaken for a transference neurosis; however, Dr. Q seemed to have identified the embracing of the notion of the transference neurosis with a technique in which such passive, sadistic withholding was the norm. In Dr. Q's formulation, analysis of transference resistance becomes the substitute signifier of good technique.

Dr. Q turned to a clinical example that in his view illustrated the superiority of making resistance the central tenet of the psychoanalytic process and thus made his case for relegating the concept of transference neurosis to the dust bin of history:

> A patient who was a bed wetter until his adolescence was in many ways encouraged by his mother to remain a bed wetter for complex reasons of her own. What was important in the analysis is that she always changed the bed for him, and in many other ways related to him as though he was an extension of her needs rather than attending to his developmental requirements. And he had many reasons in his development to adapt himself to her behavior by fitting together with her needs, and each of them utilized the other for gratification and, later on, defensive purposes. In the analysis, this man, who wet his bed until he was a teenager, became gradually discouraged and disillusioned with the analysis and with me, became passively hostile in a number of interesting and useful communicative ways, and began finally to tell me explicitly and directly in exactly these words: "When are you going to throw in the towel?" And his fearful inquiry about when I would "throw in the towel" had multiple and useful meanings for us to consider. The most obvious and immediately visible, of course, related to the mother changing his sheets each and every day. But it had a number of other meanings in a number of different transference positions. Some of them related to his father, some to his older brother, and still others to his mother. So his seeming to avoid painful affects by demanding that I do the work—change the sheets, so to speak, wipe his behind as his mother used to do while he would retain stool—although his behavior viewed superficially represented an opposition or, in the literal concrete sense of the word, resistance, it was a highly communicative form of behavior. And by viewing those communications as analytic advances, one could obtain a different kind of result than might have been the case if, in a nonanalytic way, the behavior was understood only as a repetition of the past to be circumvented or to be overcome. Had I done the following, had I said to him, in effect, that he was not helping himself by acting that way and that he was making my job harder for me, and if I had in some way implored him to do something other than what he was doing, I would have been

a very poor analyst—because it would have meant gratifying certain of his masochistic wishes; it would have meant reviving and continuing the complex struggles he had in his relationship with his mother; and it would have taken us in the direction of a stalemate.

The unstated implication is that an analyst thinking in terms of a transference neurosis would have fallen into the traps Dr. Q describes. But there is no particular reason identification of the patient's enactment in the session as the outward aspect of a transference neurotic conflict necessarily implies (1) that the enactment must repeat a conflictual involvement with one primary object only; (2) that that conflict must be limited to one developmental level; or (3) that treatment must involve persuasion rather than transference analysis. Dr. W, for instance, had a rather different idea:

> The transference neurosis is a focusing of the original neurosis upon the person or the persona of the analyst. It is not necessarily a mother transference neurosis or a father transference neurosis or positive or negative. It's a melding of all of these. There's no mistaking it. You know the old criterion that the patient is doing better on the outside and doing worse in the analytic sessions? I think that is a good criterion; I think that's valid. But that's only one of the criteria. There is also a sense of closeness with the patient, which arises out of a sense of intimacy between two people that had not existed in the prior work.

I asked Dr. Q why the enactment and the multiple meanings he attributed to it could not be considered a transference neurosis. He replied: "I really have no objection to anybody saying that's a transference neurosis. But it is important to point out that if I canceled appointments, he might cancel some appointments, before my vacation started, to go on a white-water-rapids trip with all of the allusions to his bed-wetting that that would entail. Well, he would not be treating me as though I was important."

If transference is seen as a compromise formation, manifest behavior cannot logically establish transference meaning by itself. Nevertheless, the concept of a transference neurosis is arbitrarily treated differently and not subject to the same rules of inference. The *behavior* in the context of the analyst's vacation indicated the patient treated his analyst as so important that he had to defy him without acknowledging his defiance. The problem is that the patient's conscious awareness that the analyst is important to him is used as a criterion for the transference neurosis, but not for transference.

Although such a criterion, a relic of the topographic theory, is theoretically inconsistent, its persistence is a function of the historical origins of the concept. It leads to discourse in which, in the case of the patient's seeming lack of involvement with the analyst, manifest behavior is equated with dynamic meaning. The best evidence on which to base a decision on the meaning of a patient's apparent lack of involvement is the patient's verbatim associations in the context of the session in which they appear. In the following material of mine, for instance, the importance of the analyst was quite clear through the negations.

> After my return from a ten-day vacation, a patient who never experienced conscious transference feelings reported that she had gotten the flu while I was away and that it was good timing since it had given her time to think about my absence. As was usually the case, she had not missed me at all. She worried about her lack of feelings, but she didn't feel anything. She knew I was coming back. If the analysis were ending, she would feel something—that's how she knew I had some meaning to her—but she felt nothing about my vacation. I intervened to remark that she had just told me that she felt guilty about having no conscious regrets about my absence. Her response over two sessions was to tell me about a movie that had terrified her in childhood and that she had watched on television during my absence. It concerned punishment meted out on a little girl by a terrifying angel of death. This was followed by memories of night terrors around the age of two. When I pointed out that that was her age when her brother was born, she remembered a childhood belief that children died in their mothers' stomachs and associated it with a miscarriage her mother had had before the birth of her brother, which she had just at that moment remembered knowing about. Subsequent analytic treatment concerned the working out of her terror of me as a retaliatory mother who punishes her for what emerged as a murderous rage toward the analyst/mother concerned only with making new babies, her belief that she had killed the lost fetus, and her violent fantasy wish to kill the brother born after her.

The session began with a statement that linked the patient's illness with my vacation and with her thinking about me by contiguity. This connection was followed by a negation. She didn't miss me—that is, she did miss me, and by a further thought that she worried about her complete lack of feeling, a worry promptly denied only to come up in the next thought: she would feel bad, she continued, if the separation were permanent. That may be translated "I was so angry that I wished you were gone forever," a death wish. If I were dead, however, she would feel bad. The conscious lack of feeling about my going on vacation with which that wish was equated also expressed a death wish. The patient's noninvolvement was her involvement.

When I pointed out her guilt over apparently having no feeling—that is, without my saying so, at wishing to kill me for being away—material emerged that connected these wishes with her childhood experience of being abandoned by her mother for other babies, her rage at her mother, and her fear of her mother and analyst being on the verge of retaliating for these impulses.

Dr. Q's patient's lack of involvement was the manifest sign of a transferential compromise formation, a series of unconscious fantasies woven around the object representation of the analyst. He not only scheduled trips in reaction to his analyst's absences, but the white-water trips had a clear symbolic import in relation to the childhood enuresis and in that way brought the childhood symptom directly into the transference (see chap. 9). One might easily consider the patient's question about the analyst's throwing in the towel the central manifestation of a transference neurosis, emerging partly as a defensive reenactment, and consider the sequelae of that question, the work that elicited meaning on all the different transference levels, as contributing to its resolution. The context of the patient's question indicated that he was waiting to defeat the analyst by the failure of the cure and was frightened by his negative impulses. The analysis of the wish to defeat the analyst and of his fear of acknowledging his wish to do so became central to successful termination. Thus the continuation of the symptoms throughout the analysis itself had a meaning that could be conceptualized as being part of a transference neurosis in the more modern way of thinking that Dr. Q adopts for everything but transference neurosis.

Although Dr. Q contended that the concept of the transference neurosis influenced clinical technique in such a way as to impede the psychoanalytic process, it would seem that the factor limiting to clinical freedom in the concept is more a result of meanings he imported with the concept's history. Implicitly and by his choice of definition, Dr. Q associated the transference neurosis with bad analysis and with countertransference enactment—for example, forcing the patient to give up a way of behaving and limiting interpretive possibilities. In order to be clinically free to do analysis, he needed to reject the term.

Favorable Opinions

If negative opinions about the transference neurosis were influenced by historically obsolete meanings of the concept that were not updated to make them consistent with modern structural theory, favorable opinions were no less inconsistent in theoretical conception and for the same reason: unnoticed contradictory criteria from contending topographic and structural models. As examples of what they considered a transference neurosis to be, proponents offered different, partly overlapping clinical constellations: a particularly intense reenactment of a central childhood, latency, or adolescent conflict, the re-creation of the entire childhood ego, including all the ways of adapting, a repetition of a central *cluster* of conflicts that are part of the original infantile neurosis, a repetition of oedipal conflict, the reexperience of childhood trauma, the reexperience of preoedipal conflict, regression and affective intensity to the point of psychosis, and the transformation of character trait to specific unconscious childhood conflict, all, of course, in the transference.

Where negative opinions tended to emphasize a narrow definition and show its inapplicability, positive opinions tended to isolate one commonly recognized aspect of the historical definition, generalize it into the definition of the transference neurosis, and show its applicability. For example, if affective intensity in the transference was chosen as the main criterion, then even a psychotic reaction (see chap. 7) would not seem contradictory and the transference neurosis would not seem a rare clinical occurrence.

Respondents had particular difficulty distinguishing transference neurosis from transference without recourse to topographic categories such as the patient's conscious involvement with the analyst or new symptom formation. Moreover, in a clinical context, what one referred to as transference (Dr. J) and another as transference neurosis (Dr. N) seemed indistinguishable from what a third intended by transference resistance. This confusing interchangeability was partly a consequence of not taking process into account, and partly a consequence of omitting the idea that conflict builds on previous conflict solutions. As the process unfolds, an important transference resistance often reveals itself to be a wish that turns out to represent a historically relevant defensively motivated position. In the transference, as genetically, this wish then defends against a central wish connected with a primary object. All of these positions, defensive at one level, wishful at another, are linked in the complex, multilayered organization of compromise formations that derive from specific, interrelated childhood conflicts. But it was also a result of the fact that topographic and structural formulations, unrecognized, were contending with one another.

The topographic theory speaks of regression followed by the partial lifting of repression and coming into consciousness of the infantile neurosis through the *inevitable* intermediary of a transference illness. In a structural theory formulation, regression is not a mandatory first step for insight and resolution of pathological compromise formations, nor is repression the only or major defense that requires attention. Moreover, transference is not an inevitable intermediary or necessarily an illness in the sense of a symptom formation related to the analyst. It is one possible compromise. Other interrelated and hierarchically arranged compromises that are transformations of and have transformed the childhood sources of the present conflicts also exist.

The concept of the infantile neurosis is an additional and interrelated source of confusion. In the early topographic formulation it was both a symptomatic childhood neurosis and a synonym for oedipal conflict. In more modern conceptualizations, the infantile neurosis has instead been seen as "a structural organization of the mind, characterized by internal conflict, affect regulation, and self-responsibility which takes place through differentiation, organization, transformation and reorganization of a variety of interrelated systems" (P. Tyson, 1993, ms. p. 10).

Since the conflict solutions of the infantile neurosis integrate previous conflict and in turn significantly influence subsequent conflict, they are best seen as amalgams of content and structure. Neurotic-level functioning in transference configurations may occur with a variety of content, and oedipal conflict may occur within a less integrated structure. Structure, however, can reflect content. That is the case whether the presence of a superego is taken to imply a resolution of oedipal conflict (Freud, 1923; Milrod, 1993) or whether the superego is assumed to exist independent of oedipal conflict but its coherence and consistent functioning is taken as the sign of oedipal resolution (Tyson and Tyson, 1990). Moreover, content can reciprocally express structure. An oedipal fantasy, for example, can vary in content in a way that reflects a more narcissistic character structure or a more neurotic one (Arlow, 1961, 1969). The infantile neurosis may be seen to manifest itself through the integration of ego and superego structures and through the form that a transference takes, but it also manifests itself through the transferential emergence of core conflicts from a variety of developmental levels (see chaps. 7, 9, and 10).

Many analysts favorably inclined toward the transference neurosis thought of it, too, as a structure that reflected a developed psyche. They used modifiers such as *crystallized* and *compact* to describe it. The modifiers reflected a tacit sense of a patient's relatively integrated ego and superego structure, particularly an ability to synthesize. The assumption that the transference neurosis required psychic structure capable of neurotic conflict was more explicit in Dr. B's statement: In a transference neurosis "somehow the personality structure is substantially engaged in the analysis in the context of another person, the analyst, without the dramatic qualities of the old narrow [symptom] neurosis. The problem was that there is not much talk about the character structure of developed people."

Dr. K, describing the transference neurosis as a "complex molecule" unique to each person and his or her specific history, also implied the necessity for integration. In addition, he touched on the complex relation of primary object representations and the transferential representation of the analyst. "The complexity means that there isn't just one figure, but that the analyst is aware of playing different figures. They're limited, however, not infinite, and they are made figures. The analyst would also have to be aware of the various interrelations among those made figures and the patient."

The modern emphasis on structure and on the object representations of the analyst as complicated compromise formations ("made figures") at the expense of access to consciousness and symptom formation, however, meant that the transference neurotic crystallization could no longer be easily identified through reference to manifest criteria. It would not be all at once conscious and could not be considered to involve one identifiable *manifest* change, for instance. Although affective intensity in the transference, a concentration of conscious conflicts on the person of the analyst, a transference symptom, oedipal conflict, or other manifest criteria were often cited, they prove on closer examination to be either theoretically inconsistent, unspecific and too general, or too narrow. Affective intensity in the transference is insufficiently specific and far too inclusive by itself. It is historically related to the idea of libidinally intense, transferentially reactivated oedipal strivings of childhood. Without the concept of adequately integrated ego and superego structures, it is difficult to think how one could contain intensely hostile conflicts within the transference in a workable form.

The analyst's observation that core conflicts are present in the transference and easily accessible to consciousness depends too heavily on the topographic criterion of access to consciousness and omits more veiled, less conscious signs of transference conflict, such as conflicts that are enacted. As a requirement, manifest oedipal conflict omits both significant and shaping precursors, overlooks its possible defensive function, and disregards the possibility of its regressively disguised presence. Moreover, it confusingly condenses oedipal content with a capacity for internalized conflict and the establishment of a superego, signs of structure that can give rise to neurotic conflict. The confusion is understandable since, where earlier solutions to conflict make it possible, oedipal conflict integrates previous conflicts and occurs at a developmental apex. Nevertheless, integrated ego and superego structure—whether always visible or not in the heat of a specific conflict—involving the capacity for integration, object constancy, internalization of conflict, and the assuming of responsibility for one's own behavior and wishes are usefully distinguished from manifest oedipal conflicts themselves.

The transference symptom, historically linked to the idea of transference illness, also proved too narrow. It was acceptable only to those ready to discard, or severely limit, the concept like Dr. F. Dr. A's comments in this regard were typical:

> The symptom definition binds; it's too tight for me. There are these marvelous circumstances in which a patient describes a symptom, and let's say one of the first consequences of the analysis is that the symptom disappears. Wonderful—the patient feels I'm cured, everything's fine. And then as the analysis unfolds, that symptom comes out in the relationship, or some component in the relationship to the analyst. I don't mind that. It can be a common occurrence. I could not make that

the definition. It's very hard to distinguish in a precise way or describe in a precise way the difference, say, between habitual reactions in general and transference reactions. We're not up to the transference neurosis yet. But somebody comes in and has a habitual reaction. Let's say a character reaction. I'll give you an example. A patient comes in and wants the analyst to describe very precisely and in great detail what is likely to happen in analysis. Perfectly reasonable: he doesn't know what he's getting into, what this procedure's about. He goes on and on about more description, more precision, and so forth. And the difference, let's say, between somebody who does this habitually in all circumstances, somebody who does this some of the time but more of the time in certain kinds of anxiety-laden situations, or the patient who does it habitually but is doing it at this moment out of an intense anxiety which is countered by this reaction, those are difficult enough to spell out.

And then we have the further difficulty. Some regression takes place. We do see reactions that get more and more specific and idiosyncratic and are shaped by the past and the present, and we call that a transference reaction; not just a habitual reaction, but that this reaction, whether it's habitual in its global form, now has taken more specific qualities, been built anew, and is in reaction to some lead conflict that's emerging. So all that can't even be put in the linear form. But then we say, All right, so now we've got these transference reactions. They're not just habitual. And they come, and they go, and they get more intense. What is the point when you're going to call it a transference neurosis? I mean, not only can I not say at a point where a symptom develops, I can't name ten points at which that happens. Although I can say it does seem to happen with some people that things go well and that there is a new creation: something that seems more elaborate, more intricate, more intense, and more consistent with the tension between emerging primitive impulses and counterimpulses; and intentions to analyze; intentions to look at, to communicate, to learn something about; and when it gets rich enough I'd call it a transference neurosis.

But I don't know what rich enough means. I've thought about it a great deal and I can't gain any more precision. I can't even describe it.

Not only is Dr. A's perplexity illustrative; he accords regression the major role in changes from habitual to transferential attitudes, implying paradoxically that even more regression is necessary in order for the complex organization he describes as a transference neurosis to evolve. Yet regression can be a defense against the habitual becoming specific and is not necessarily a pathway to useful revelation. The analytic situation inherently focuses on and intensifies the patient's conflicts, introducing a figure in the person of the analyst who upsets through verbal interventions, especially those that identify habitual defensive constellations, the patient's dynamic equilibrium. If aspects of these shifting and reorganizing conflicts emerge directly in relation to the analyst, habitual attitudes become specifically transferential whether regression occurs or not. Shifting compromise formations and with them shifting internal equilibrium, not regression per se, are necessary ingredients of a transition from habitual to specific.

The recourse to a topographically influenced view of regression led Dr. A deep into the paradox just adumbrated: "The transference neurosis is a curious situation in which the regressive forces, which are pushing toward gratification of a much more primitive kind, are stronger. And at the same time, the progressive forces are stronger." Dr. A had an idea in mind, such as regression in the service of the ego, that implies a structural point of view and is at odds with his description of regression being the motive force for the habitual becoming transferential.

The idea of transference neurosis as a topographically defined unconscious crystallization was nevertheless evident. Dr. M:

> What I would call transference neurosis today are many clusters of transference linked to well-organized structures. The analysis of these structures permits the patient to acquire knowledge of something very central which organizes the nature of his or her experience. One recent patient came to me suffering greatly after an interrupted analysis. She first thought that she couldn't go into treatment with me although she liked me and had heard good things about me. She was sure that she would feel very competitive with me and extremely criticized by me. In fact she did and the feelings intensified. But that was only the outward sign of a very complex inner situation of which she had absolutely no conscious knowledge: when she was thirteen her older brother had become psychotic; although her brother recovered, the patient forever after remained in a relationship with him in which he was still decompensated. That is, she solved the problem of working successfully by never getting friendly, never having a family, always remaining in a state of nervous tension. As long as she experienced herself as criticized, she felt less, not more, successful than her brother and believed she was preventing him from further regression. She did not realize what the function of feeling criticized by me played in relation to the unconscious and ongoing relationship with her brother.
>
> The analysis of the transference was the analysis of that structure. I was many people for her. I was herself at her best so at least one of us would be free from the tyranny of the sick sibling. I was also the criti-

cal brother, father, mother. I am less interested in the immediate manifestations than in analyzing the structure that supports it.

It changes nothing—almost nothing, very little—to analyze the transference by identifying manifest object relations and saying, "you see in me your critical father." That doesn't deal with the truly important thing: the structure sustaining those attitudes. Unless you have an extraordinary reading of the unconscious, you can't help patients to change. You get there through dreams and behavior too. You don't find it at the level of the woman feeling criticized by me—there, the problem was what function that transference played in her overall unconscious organization. Yes, we could have said that she was severely criticized in her family. She was—but why of all the possibilities offered by their behavior did she pick out that one? Because it had a function in relation to her psychotic brother, to her guilt, to her compassion, to her unconscious fantasy of her function in the family. I could have analyzed for years "how critical your parents were." Nothing would have changed. *If you do not get to the level underneath that, analysis does not work very well.*

Dr. M seemed to be describing an unconscious organization in terms derived from topographic theory rather than a compromise formation conceptually derived from structural theory. Addressing consciously available transference manifestations is not a technical mistake as long as one moves from the surface manifestation, through the transformations of defense, to trace the connections between surface manifestations and unconscious, defensively protected sources. That is, seeing the analyst as critical and identifying that imago with a particular primary object does nothing, as Dr. M notes, because identifying a manifest aspect of a compromise formation and merely changing its nomenclature does not constitute an effective intervention. Clinically, one must ask "critical of what?" An effective intervention in this situation requires that the analyst connect the consciously experienced criticism and the unconscious guilt that motivates it. If the connection between manifest material and its unconscious sources is not made, no meaningful dynamic shifts result.

Despite her rhetoric, Dr. M was conceptualizing the conscious manifestation as part of a larger, more complex and multifaceted central conflict. It was the sign of the patient's guilt over the sibling's psychosis. We do not have enough information to know the fantasy connected to her guilt, although in similar cases agressive wishes toward the sibling that antedate the actual falling ill create enormous guilt in the so-called healthy child. Dr. M's topographic rhetoric, however, separated the conscious manifestation from the unconscious aspects of the constellation rather than emphasizing their interrelatedness. Thus the transference neurosis was identified with an underlying or "sustaining" unconscious organization and the manifest feeling of criticism was seen as a separate, less valuable, "transference."

Two Observations about Change in the Psychoanalytic Process

Since objective criteria seem unsatisfactory, if inevitable, residues of the topographic theory, analysts turned to observing changes in their subjective experience. They recognized two interrelated subjective criteria for a change in process and connected them to the idea of the crystallization of a transference neurotic organization. Both come under the general heading of a change toward greater "intimacy": (1) an increase in the analyst's understanding—that is, a growth in his or her understanding of the unconscious meaning of the patient's surface behavior and manifest language that is the parallel of analogous change in the patient; and (2) an intensification in the analyst's emotional involvement, parallelled again by a greater immediacy on the part of the patient or an intensification of the struggle against it.

Dr. S will exemplify the first:

> The case that comes first to mind is a woman who would probably be described as a classic hysteric who clearly is in the midst of a transference neurosis as I understand it. An hour begins with my opening the door and this person coming in darting a somewhat apprehensive glance at me. I'm aware of her clothing, which is little-girlish as well as designed to discourage attention to herself. This has been something I've been aware of since the beginning of the analysis.
>
> However, now I'm aware of it in a different way. Part of what I mean by the transference neurosis is my own awareness. I'm aware that she's frightened. I'm aware of the fears of some kind of attack, that she tries to deal with by being both seductive and infantile. It may be that she fears her mother's possibly psychotic rages when she was young. I think about how quickly I heard about that and how long it took to hear more clearly about her father. He, too, is a very frightening person and someone who might rip into a child.
>
> As she's walking to the couch, I'm apt to be reminded of these puzzles. Some of them upset my preconceptions, one of them being that I would have expected to hear more about how frightening her father was to her mother. I'm wondering about her wariness.
>
> She will begin to fill me in on all that's happened, and we'll run through a number of things that have been the focus of a lot of work over the past few years, maybe a lover she feels is tormenting her, whom she is failing to break off with and finds herself going out of her way to get together with. She then carries complaints to a whole series

of women friends about the way the man is treating her, so that they say "Why don't you leave him?" Once a month we can relate this to her complaints about me and about the frustration she feels in the analytic situation.

She was in analysis before. She presented her previous analysis to me as sarcastic, angry, and belittling. I don't know him, but what I know of him, he couldn't have been as sarcastic, belittling, and demanding as she describes. She's now occasionally getting people to tell her that I'm a son of a bitch, but she protects the analysis to some extent by inducing people more frequently to tell her that her boyfriend is exploiting her, as I described just before. I am now aware that the provocation involved is sexualized and I don't get so angry at it.

I've never thought of it till this minute. She used to irritate me. It was so hard to understand and interpret these patterns of complaint; they seemed to be like a huge series of reverberating circuits that maintained her in a steady state in her life. She was so indirect for so long. Now, although she's doing the same thing, I have a clearer understanding of what she's doing. I can break into it much more helpfully.

She complains to friend number one about her boyfriend, not exactly complains but talks about her interaction in a naive way that invites the friend to say, "Oh, for God's sake, can't you see, he's not serious about you." Then, simultaneously, she gets involved in something with friend number one where I find myself thinking, "why is she putting up with that with friend number one?" She then goes to friend number two, who tells her, "your boyfriend is just terrible," then to friend number three, who says, "maybe you've got a chance with the boyfriend and you know, if I were you I'd really stick it out with him; but why are you putting up with that from friend number one?" This has been her fight, going back to having neighbors who probably saved her from some very difficult things that were going on in her own house as a kid.

Learning how to point out this pattern was a first step, because for a long time, my awareness of it had stopped at just being able to point out her friends' reactions. She complained to them about not being able to respond sexually, about being afraid of losing a man. I had been hearing this in terms of her fears of depending on a man, and her fear of an eternal transference, but now I understand that what she was describing was that it was very important for her to be telling all her friends that she had no sexual satisfaction.

It's as she is able to show me in finer detail what she does with this huge supporting cast of characters that I feel I am able to make an interpretation a little more often. And she is able to accept its relation to what's going on in the hour in a specific way. I'll say to her, "you told

> friend number one about how your boyfriend seemed to expect you to make dinner for him and then wanted to go Dutch treat to the movies, and you described how indignant she became about all of that, but you don't say anything about how you felt at the time, how you came to offer him the dinner." Then we hear how she came to offer him the dinner and to offer paying for the movies, and then I am able to point out to her that she's recently been very annoyed at the thought of the fee she has to pay me—she's thinking about how nice it would be to not be paying me so much. Before the transference neurosis, such issues might have come up but wouldn't be very richly elaborated.
>
> The transference neurosis certainly has at least as much to do with what is going on in my mind as it has to do with what's going on in the patient's mind. She is a good example of a transference neurosis. I'm sure this would pass muster with anyone who has to present a transference neurosis. But as I think about it, I don't think this is just a matter of a woman who is finding her thoughts, impulses, and fantasies increasingly focused on me and her neurotic behavior taking shape more and more in response to the analyst. It's an analyst who understands and is more able to relate to these interactions. The great change is not in terms of a neurotic structure; the great change is its accessibility to interpretation.

Reciprocal understanding, then, refers to the analyst's deepening grasp of the patient's conflicts in relation to the manner in which they are expressed and to his or her deepening grasp of the specific meaning of the signifiers provided by the patient's history. In addition, it refers to the patient's growing self-understanding and *willingness* to become involved in the process to the end of self-understanding.

Dr. S insisted on a qualitative change. So would, in the next vignette, Dr. R. Analysts were associating the transference neurosis with a felt and relative *quality of transferential object relationship*. The patient makes a mature choice in the direction of self-revelation. The relation to the analyst is less defended, more intimate and engaged, infused, whatever else is going on, with a libidinal quality that takes in interpretations in ways that, earlier, were not possible and permits the engagement of hostile conflict as well. This change both results from and leads to the analyst's greater integrative vision. Phenomena that might now be included in a complex transference neurotic organization of dynamically multivalent and shifting elements might have been seen as discrete resistances only at an earlier stage of the treatment. That knowledge enables the analyst to respond in a different way that allows the patient's experience and insight to deepen. Of course, the subjectivity of the criterion is a potential limiting factor: it does not necessarily follow that a new organization was not present before the analyst understood, or that his or her understanding is determinative.

The second criterion, the analyst's reciprocal involvement in the transference, referred to this same intimacy as well as to potential overinvolvement. That is, it referred to the activation of the analyst's conflicts, optimally in their signal capacity, as well as to reactions that exceeded that signal capacity.

There was more than a suggestion that the excess, itself, might be a signal of a transference neurosis.[3] Dr. A thought of the transference neurosis as so entwined with strong subjective reactions in the analyst that at one point in the interview he repeatedly referred to *countertransference* instead of to *transference neurosis*. Dr. W mentioned being so empathically involved with the patient that "I would close a session with a patient, go to my desk to make some notes, and realize I couldn't remember the last name of the patient. I was so intimately empathized with the patient that there was no real necessity for a distinction." Dr. R relied similarly on a sign that others would use to indicate a countertransference: the patient entered his dreams.

> Today, I find myself much more attuned to the way in which the process and the experience of the analysis itself contains the transference. There's something about the way in which patients behave with you as they're doing the analytic task that they don't usually comment on. There's something about the way in which they listen to what you say and experience what you say and experience what they say, which is very subtle. You have a feeling with certain patients when their sensitivity to you and the treatment and their reactivity to it is heightened; and their willingness to let derivatives come more into consciousness increases. How you tell the difference between an hour in which it's more present and less present, when the issue isn't how many times they talk about having important feelings about you in treatment, is a very difficult thing for me to define.

He described a woman with a hysterical repression for an attempted seduction by her stepfather in adolescence. In one session the patient reported experiencing a great deal of anxiety and pain, thought the feelings must be connected with the attempted seduction, and asked the analyst to tell her what he thought. He responded to her request by saying that what was going on wasn't yet clear, but if she continued with her associations they would eventually understand. A flood prevented the next day's ses-

3. Interestingly, Skolnikoff (1993) has recently proposed that the analyst's overidentification is an inherent part of the middle phase of an analysis, not, as Arlow (1985) has written, an avoidable countertransference.

sion, the last of the week, from taking place. When, at the start of the subsequent session, the analyst did not express sympathy for the patient being left in such a painful state for so long, the patient stormed out of the session. "I felt totally taken by surprise. I thought, 'How could I have underestimated the level of pathology?' She ultimately came to tell me that she doubted whether I appreciated her, was with her, and knew what was going on—like the mother and father."

Dr. R wanted to emphasize a difference: at the beginning of the analysis his patient used to say, "I don't know whether I can trust you; you might misuse me." After three years of analysis, when the situation described above came up again, as it periodically did, the patient reacted by saying, "I'm very angry at you, and I feel like you don't want to listen to me, and I must be having a transference reaction with you, because this is very much like what I felt with my mother." He was relating this difference to the transference neurosis.

> What's different is a quality of alliance and also her capacity to contain these conflicts herself. The last time we went around this particular issue, she was berating me for not knowing. She's furious at her mother for not knowing the seduction went on, or if she did know, for not saying anything and stopping it and protecting her, and she's asking me to do the same. She's a grown woman, a few years older than I am, with grown children. This last time she says to me, "Why, if you don't do it, I'll have to do it myself!" This is now a possibility for her. She's not relating to me solely as if she were helpless, as if I were the expert analyst and she wasn't good enough to join the club.
>
> This is a very important issue in the transference; it represents the culmination of a lot of work, of issues in the transference and from the years before the age of three when she had a big loss, as well as of oedipal issues about competition with men and with women. She hasn't gotten to it but she knows enough to know, what if she liked it, encouraged it? So this reaction has all these different meanings.
>
> But does she have a transference neurosis? She says that the sessions are very important to her. She drives a long way to get here. That's dedication. But she drove in the beginning of treatment too, in order to have an analysis, when she was telling me how I was too young and couldn't be trusted; although that too is part of the transference, it's both the transference to the untrustworthy stepfather and the father and it's the defense against the transference and the longing for the stepfather and sexual attraction.
>
> Somehow it isn't the same. Now, instead of feeling "who is this strange person?" inside myself, I have all these feelings of very intimate involvements with her, the way you do with all patients when the

treatment goes well and you reach that point where you know that affectively you are very much involved in each others' hearts and souls.

Now, call that "transference neurosis"; but I don't know how to describe it from the outside. I mean, I don't dream about patients about whom I'm indifferent. I dream about patients at the point at which they are worrying and preoccupying and encompassing—you know, "I've got you under my skin." And I assume that they have me under their skin at that point too; otherwise they wouldn't make me dream about them, as I think unconsciously they do.

The criterion of intimacy is not meant to advocate an unnecessarily supportive, nonanalytic stand. Indeed, it is worthwhile considering the effect of Dr. R's not answering the patient's request for help. Because he acknowledged the patient's wish to understand without responding as the patient wished, the past anger at the mother emerged in a workable transference present. By speaking as the patient wished, Dr. R would have joined in a wished-for enactment defending against that reexperience and lent himself to an ongoing, regressive libidinal transference resistance. Such an ongoing enactment, unknown to the analyst, is not necessarily destructive. It may even, at times, be necessary. It is certainly, at times, inevitable (see chap. 8, Dr. N). If it had occurred, however, it would have had eventually to be analyzed or would have led to a stalemate. An analyst misunderstanding the transference neurosis as necessitating the patient's conscious libidinal involvement, or one concerned to rectify developmental trauma, might easily have colluded consciously with this invitation to an enactment and never have considered its unconscious meaning.

When the transference neurosis is engaged, it is not a conscious, libidinal overinvolvement with the analyst that is the issue. Dr. R spoke, instead, of a "quality of alliance" that is different. His patient not only experienced unconscious conflict in the transference but *willingly undertook to explore the experience and identify its sources*. That undertaking involved the application of the integrated adult ego to the task of understanding reactions now identified as belonging to the past and to the more infantile ego available at that time.

The criterion of immediacy, intensification, or intimacy in Dr. T's sense is something noted as a *result* of productive analytic work. Dr. W saw it also as characteristic of the work itself. He believed the immediate experience of an ongoing transference neurosis was of a subjective struggle for intimacy in the context of a shifting group of conflicts in which the analyst represented those primary objects most centrally involved in the way the patient's original neurosis had become structured.

For analysis to be successful there has to be a struggle—not necessarily in terms of violent emotions expressed and certainly not on both

> sides but there has to be a resistance that takes the form of a struggle between the two participants in which the analyst, it is to be hoped, retains his objectivity but the patient is almost entirely caught up in what he is struggling against or for or toward.
>
> While the patient is so caught up, the analyst has an empathic awareness of the other person which involves a certain regression on the part of the empathizer, momentary and fleeting, a trial identification in which you know the other person, but knowing what he or she is trying to struggle with and to say does not lead automatically to an interpretation. There has to be an integration of what one has perceived empathically with what one knows generally about the patient, an application to a larger template of what the patient is about.

Thus from the analyst's side, as well, infantile conflicts are engaged, so that the adult ego may apply itself to them.

Like its companion, reciprocal understanding, the criterion of reciprocal affective engagement poses problems owing to its subjectivity, its connection to countertransference interference with the analyst's analyzing capacity, and to countertransference enactment. Accounts of the latter, particularly, invite scrutiny as to the reliability of the analyst's understanding. Nevertheless, as mentioned above, analysts observed a change in the experiential quality of the object relation with the patient and an internal change in the experience and understanding of the patient in many productive analyses. Moreover, they commonly linked those observed changes with the concept of transference neurosis.

Further, the greater affective mobilization recognized in both parties to the dyad is related to the concentrated distillation of conflict encountered especially in later stages of a well-progressing psychoanalytic process through which central conflicts emerge in the transference in less defended, more immediate and integrated configurations. The quality of intimacy is not, therefore, mysterious, but an understandable result on the analyst's part of better empathic identification facilitated by a change in the patient. On the patient's part, the change occurs because of a working through of defensive layers of central conflicts, including those that are more ego syntonic and thus more associated with compromise formations related to character. This working through results in greater accessibility to interpretation in part because the adult ego's capacity to work and to understand has been strengthened.

Reprise: Toward a Definition of the Transference Neurosis

Although the topographically conceptualized "learned" version of the transference neurosis continues to carry emotional authority, it does not correspond to current clinical usage. Analysts today use the concept to designate a qualitative change in the transferential relation reflected in increased reciprocal emotional involvement, increased reciprocal understanding, and increased willingness and ability to work at understanding in the crucible of intense affective experience. That recognized qualitative shift can be ascribed less subjectively to a shift in defensive organization in the patient. The transference neurosis therefore denotes a structural reordering.

Since topographic thinking misleads analysts into emphasizing criteria influenced by access to consciousness and into erroneously equating transference neurosis with symptom formation, I propose a reformulation that will take structural concepts and psychoanalytic process into account. The reformulation involves ego and superego structure, the concept of object representations as fantasy constructs, the qualitative change observed in the course of the psychoanalytic process, and the concept of a transference or transferring process that I distinguish from transference neurosis. The reformulation will be further developed in chapter 7 where I contrast transference neurosis to other possible transference organizations.

Structure

To begin a redefinition of the transference neurosis, it is necessary to assume a psychic structure that includes an integrated superego and ego. Signs of ego and superego integration include cohesive functioning within and among systems, affect regulation, self-observation including the capacity to notice contradictory actions and feelings, reality testing and adaptability, object constancy, the ability to differentiate among self and object representations, the capacity to relate to objects in a way that takes a differentiated other into account, sustenance of a signal function in respect to anxiety so that id impulses deemed unacceptable are not primarily acted upon but rather give rise to conflict, and a capacity consistently to accept responsibility and to act with intention so that moral considerations and ideals influence behavior.

These rather general signs are further complicated by the fact that any area of functioning can be disrupted by specific conflict. Disruption of integrated functioning must be judged against the overall pattern of ego and superego functioning. Neurotic-level conflict may give rise to impulsive and ill-considered action, for instance, without the action indicating structure inadequate for a transference neurosis to evolve. Action can be frenzied, chaotic, and executed by an individual who cannot reflect or observe himself in any matter, or it can invite punishment as part of a conflict in an individual who is capable of reflection and self-observation and, when the conflict is understood, of restraint, for example.

Clinical criteria are hard to specify since the psychoanalytic situation encourages the partial externalization of internal functions and fantasies, including fantasies of and about objects and frequently results in regression to earlier stages of functioning. Nevertheless, experienced analysts can describe general differences between neurotic and more disturbed patients that can be ascribed to differences in the relative integration of ego and superego. When an analysis is progressing well, the patient neither willfully disregards the analytic relationship nor obsessively scrutinizes it. Interest in the analyst and the analytic relationship tends optimally to issue from the patient's adult curiosity and integrated adult personality. Renik writes about the increasing willingness of neurotic patients to explore their relationship to the analyst as an "elective focus that complements, rather than replaces, the patient's attention to transference elsewhere in his life" (1990, p. 198), and Stone, emphasizing the "symbolic" centrality of the analyst in relation to the patient's experiencing ego, continues, "There is a free-observing portion of the ego also involved, but not in the same sense as that involved in the transference regression and revived infantile conflicts. And there is, of course, always the integrated adult personality, however diluted it may be at times, to whom the analysis is one of many important, realistic life activities" (1967, pp. 94–95).

Moreover, because of the synthetic capacity of a more highly integrated individual, his or her verbal derivatives throughout a session often reflect aspects of a conflictual compromise fairly constantly and coherently. He or she can also more easily work collaboratively on the conflict. A patient with a less well integrated ego structure is liable to mention something troubling in an unguarded moment and then deny it in a categorical way that speaks both to the absence of self-observation and to enormous difficulty with the regulation of certain affects. The structural necessity of maintaining the denial (in order to ward off extreme destructiveness, for instance) interferes with collaboration and self-observation.

A clinical example of the latter situation occurred with a patient who complained briefly that her husband, an extremely withholding and sadistic man, never gave her anything, whereas she was constantly doing things for him at considerable time and effort to herself. When asked to say more about her feeling, she insisted that her husband was emotionally generous and only materially ungenerous. When pressed that she must have feelings about this latter quality, she denied it with tortuous reasoning. When I began gently to explore the reasoning, the patient intimated that I must be crazy not to accept her reasoning as obvious. The patient could not allow herself to recognize that there was a contradiction in her thinking because maintaining the contradiction allowed her to isolate her murderous rage, concentrate it on a "materially ungenerous" split-off representation, and maintain a connection to an idealized "emotionally generous" object. The rage then manifested itself in defensive form in a paranoid transference.

Conflict resolution in this case interfered with structural integration. In a patient with a capacity for transference neurosis, conflict could be handled among integrated structures rather than within them (Rangell, 1963) at the cost of their integration.

In an early paper, Loewald grappled with the interrelation of conflict and structure from the point of view of defense:

> Defense, in the sense in which we speak of it when dealing with neurotic mechanisms, is based on the development of the ego as a specialized structure within the psychic apparatus, and, correspondingly, on the formation of and interaction with libidinal objects. A certain degree of ego structuralization and of object structuralization has to have occurred to make defense processes and operations possible. Ego structuralization and object formation occur to the extent to which synthetic-integrative processes can proceed relatively undisturbed. (1951, p. 24)

A developed and integrated psyche capable of neurotic conflict presumes as well and is the result of an infantile neurosis in the more modern structural sense that I have discussed earlier in this chapter. It is useful to recognize that oedipal conflict is an essential organizer of this development as long as one neither neglects the distinctive preoedipal shaping of these later resolutions nor forgets that an oedipal conflict is never *only* instinctual, but one that includes the attainment of ego integration and the ability to relate with differentiated object representations in ways that go beyond need satisfaction. As Loewald continued:

> Since by the time the Oedipus conflict has fully developed, the ego has gained considerable strength, and since in fact, oedipal development can take place in full realization only under circumstances that permit sufficient solidification of the ego and a differentiated configuration of mutually related libidinal objects, defense structures typical for neurosis can largely be understood in terms of oedipal and post oedipal development. For the understanding of psychotic and related phenomena we have to have recourse to the pre-oedipal phases where neither ego nor reality are as yet sufficiently organized and differentiated from one another to make defense processes possible. (1951, p. 25)

Structuralization depends first on the establishment of the difference between outer and inner. The establishment of this distinction occurs through what Loewald, in a later paper, called the "boundary-creating processes" of internalization and externalization. These processes are carried over into conflict where in addition to their newly acquired function of defense they continue to contribute to the essential differentiation of self and object representations:

> The relinquishment and internalization of oedipal objects . . . must . . . be seen . . . as a resumption on a new level of boundary-creating processes. Ego, objects and boundaries of and between them—at first nonexistent, later still indistinct and fluid—gradually become more distinct and fixed. . . . Side by side with object relations, processes of identification persist and reenter the picture in new transformations representing resumptions of boundary setting, differentiating processes, notwithstanding their prominent aspects as defenses against loss of love objects. (1962, p. 266)

Once the development of structure is taken into account, and with it the differentiation of objects, the specific *content* of the transferential compromise formation no longer needs to be used to determine a transference neurosis. The transference neurosis depends on the comparative quality, including object relatedness, of the transferential expression of all central conflicts—preoedipal as well as oedipal, as that quality reflects structuralization and integration.

Object Representations as Fantasy Constructs

The establishment of differentiated object representations is necessary because the process of transferring requires a point of origin and a point to which something is transferred, with the former being the object representations of the primary objects and the latter the multifaceted object representations of the analyst.

The historically derived explanation that ascribed the essential qualitative shift to the libidinal cathexis of the analyst alone (Glover 1928, 1955) concealed a tendency to treat the analyst as objective entity. All object representations are, however, constructed by various intermixtures of drive and defense mediated by fantasy. Thus the representations of the analyst are most productively considered compromise formations. Moreover, they are always compromise formations composed of previously hierarchically interrelated compromise formations. The latter are the result of childhood conflict and its later additions organized into unconscious fantasies.

As a result of the ego-mediated transferring process, these fantasies contribute substantially to the object representations of the analyst as they evolve through shifting compromise formations in a transference neurosis. But the relatively structured ego and superego necessary for a transference neurosis to evolve are also capable of differentiating fairly consistently the representations of the analyst from those of primary objects. Ongoing work increases that ability by increasing understanding of the propensity to confound past with present while it deepens the experience of the past in the present at the same time. The transferred similarities are thus perceived in the context of a growing awareness of difference, a paradox that by itself testifies to the ego flexibility and observing capacity necessary. That increasingly concentrated amalgam constitutes what we might call the compound/complex compromise formation of the transference neurosis.

The specific fantasies involved in the transferring process change according to the psychic equilibrium of the patient at any given moment. That is, at one moment superego influence may be a more shaping force; at another, various defensive processes of the ego; at still another, more intensively experienced id demands. The variability of these fantasies is, however, limited to a range characteristic of that particular patient and his or her unconscious conflicts as they have been structured in the infantile neurosis and in later compromises. Thus, the number and organization of transferential compromise formations are varied but not infinite.

Qualitative Change

At earlier stages of the psychoanalytic process defensive, filtering, narcissistically enhancing fantasies, not centrally painful, experience-near versions of central conflicts, will play a dominant role. Assuming a relatively integrated ego and superego, the analyst is first perceived *according to* the integration of perceptual data about him or her with core-drive–defense–fantasy-derived *constructed* object representations from childhood and adolescence dominated by the filtering defensive fantasies mentioned above.

When the qualitative change that analysts identify with a transference neurosis occurs, however, one can say partly metaphorically that the series of variably constructed object representations of the analyst has become *entwined* with the network of core organizing, experience-near, perceptually influential fantasies and memories from childhood. The word *entwined* connotes both a greater proximity of core fantasies to moment-to-moment experience and the strong presence of a libidinal component to the transference. The libidinal component allows the expression not only of itself but of intensely hostile and humiliating aspects of conflicts. The experience is one of immediacy and intimacy. Accompanying these changes is a greater *voluntary* application of adult understanding to the revived infantile experience.

The difference in the two stages is not absolute. The second depends on the reduction of fantasies functioning characteristically and defensively to ward off the more immediate and painful aspects of organizing unconscious conflicts. The analyst, as well as the entire external world, is always perceived and constructed to some extent *according to* various unconscious conflicts and fantasies active in the patient. Those that underlie ego syntonic character defense will be most accessible. The representation of the analyst is therefore always a construct, or more precisely a variable, though limited, series of constructs dominated at first by those fantasies functioning defensively to ward off intensely painful aspects of central conflicts. The difference between the constructed object representation of the analyst perceived *according to* a variety of defensively dominated fantasies and the object representation of the analyst more thoroughly *interwoven with* core unconscious organizing fantasies characteristic of a transference neurosis is the proximity of the latter to the most anguishing and unmentionable aspects of childhood conflict reactivated in the present. Thus, the struggle on the patient's part to avoid the pain, guilt, or anxiety aroused by the transference reactivation of these conflicts, which Dr. W also associated with the transference neurosis. Thus, too, the changed, libidinally suffused "quality of alliance" (Dr. R) or "intimacy" and "immediacy" experienced when the analysand reveals his or her inner pain, humiliation, anxiety, and/or guilt-ridden passions and memories in less self-enhancing or distancing ways. I hasten to add that the libidinal quotient does not preclude intense hostile expressions and conflicts; rather, it makes them possible.

The greater degree of self-revelation is certainly addressed to a variety of beloved, desired, and hated primary objects or wished-for primary objects, defensively displaced onto the analyst. Differentiated aspects of the object representation of the analyst, however, also compose some part of the configuration. Although many classical analysts will concentrate only on delineating the former, leaving the latter to be identified by omission, the separation and identification of those different components are also part of the working through of the transference neurosis. That is, the greater the adult ego's integration, the greater the part played by its well-functioning perceptions.

A brief example from my practice illustrates the difference between the two stages I have delineated. There was a marked difference in the depth and scope of the transference experience of one patient's perceiving me, like all women, to be a betraying whore according to infantile fantasies originally elaborated about his mother and his later, experience-near fantasies of me in the illicit embrace of successful male colleagues. The first experience had a self-righteous, narcissistic quality and was dominated by a defensive fantasy of knowing better and being a condemning judge. This configuration represented a character defense against certain painful aspects of oedipal defeat. The second, with the fantasy embodying the character defense much less prominent, increasingly recaptured in the present experience the immediacy of the painful humiliation, crushed love, hurt, frustrated sexual wishes, sense of castration, and frightening reduction of a sense of masculinity associated with the childhood defeat. The difference in the two stages extended to my experience as well. The patient was more removed and distant in the first, more willing to risk showing his pain to me in the second. Whereas the second still represented a defensive formation, one against remembering his wishes toward his mother, the latter were more readily available.

From a comparative standpoint, the transference neurosis is a compromise formation organizationally different from those from earlier phases of the transferring process, but one that gradually, not suddenly evolves. Defenses against acknowledging and revealing the pain, humiliation, and guilt and the illicit wishes to which these affects are connected both to oneself and to someone other than oneself do not disappear or melt away; they have to be worked on and with. We may then say that the qualitative change observed is a result of the sequential analysis of more defensive compromise formations over the course of a productive analysis and that it follows that the transference neurosis could be defined as the *transferential dimension of that observed progressive change*.

Dr. B spoke of analysts too often parroting the received "truth" that the transference neurosis was the core of the analytic work and not knowing its wisdom. Dr. W spoke of the patient and analyst both "understanding so as not to know." One might take their distinctions as emblematic of the difference between the first and second stages I have described and extend them to say that the concept of transference neurosis is caught in the difficulty of distinguishing between the first and second stages. To define the transference neurosis, we extract criteria from highly charged experience, and in attempting to objectify and codify that experience, we lose it. Each reader must resupply the missing affective dimension both from personal analysis and from clinical experience.

No one can bring what he or she has not experienced to a reading that requires the contribution of experience. The person of the analyst and the extensiveness and depth of his or her analyses influence the understanding of self and patients and shape both personal clinical experience and the ability to know transference neurosis from highly abstract definitions. Dr. Z's struggles (chap. 3) ring true not because he accurately described a transference neurosis—what he described so honestly is a countertransference—but because his continuing self-examination allowed him to remain open and thus allowed for the possibility of a transference neurosis.

Transference Process

The delineation of the concept of transference neurosis can be furthered by distinguishing it from transference. That distinction is, in my opinion, best made according to function, I consider the transference neurosis as a phenomenon of the psychoanalytic process in patients with an integrated ego and super ego structure. Transference is both a more general term and one that involves internal transformation.

To make the distinction more cogent, a prevalent ambiguity in psychoanalytic discourse needs to be recognized. Many psychoanalytic terms suffer from transformation from verb to noun (Boesky, 1990), and *transference* is among them. In its reified substantive form it condenses the active verb process of *transferring* and the transferred result. One meaning or the other predominates depending on the context.

That condensation could be reversed by separating process from result. Transference or transferring would then be considered linearly as a process of transformation, and transference neurosis one possible result of the transformatory process. That is, transferring is the general, multifaceted, and shifting process within the patient in which the variable object representations of the analyst are constructed as a result of the analysis of previous compromise formations. Transference neurosis would be reserved for the result of that process as, shaped by a relatively integrated and advanced ego, it moves progressively toward the core structuring infantile fantasies that compose the redefined infantile neurosis as the latter gradually deploys itself in the less defensive, more immediate, more crystallized form mentioned above.

Not every phenomenon of an analysis is thereby encompassed. Narcissistic phenomena that are regressive reproductions of earlier experience in the context of a continued capacity to sustain the object representation of the analyst and the capacity for internal conflict would be considered part of that evolving transference neurosis (e.g., Dr. Q's case). Situations in which the relatively sustained "as-if" object representation of the analyst discriminated from primary objects and the corresponding capacity for internal conflict are questionable would result in a parallel process (transference perversion or transference psychosis) reflecting different ego organization (see chap. 7). That process could, of course, modulate into a transference neurosis where the treatment first fostered greater integration.

This distinction between transference as transformatory process and transference neurosis as a result of that process seems to me to be implied by Freud (see chap. 2). One of the semantic functions of Freud's delineating a new transference illness was, after all, to emphasize the intermediate *result* of the transference of the repudiated wishes of the childhood neurosis onto the analyst. A structural theory version would replace the idea of illness by the idea of an organization reflecting compromises among agencies and encompassing the fantasy/memory content of interrelated conflict solutions.

The two terms would then imply different perspectives and operate at slightly different levels of conceptualization of the clinical process. Transference neurosis, were the application of the process appropriate, would subsume what earlier would appear as the interplay between resistance and transference. Any cross section (including an apparent stalemate) in a generally well-progressing analysis might be identified, although only perhaps subsequently, as comprising part of or deriving from the more encompassing transference neurosis organization. I shall call these segments *specific transferences* to distinguish them from less delineated and more habitual reactions to the analyst. In an evolving analytic process, specific transference configurations later in the process are likely to have more and more characteristics of distillation, condensation, affective intensity, and integration associated with recognized qualitative change and thus with the transference neurosis.

If we do not make the distinction between process and result of the process, transference neurosis overlaps transference as further unqualified compromise formations (Brenner, 1982). If we do, we can say that a transferring process within the patient with requisite ego capacity may eventuate in a transference neurosis as a particular kind of organization in the patient that is shaped by the patient's ego structure, specific history, and attendant fantasies as well as by the character, conflicts, and understanding of the analyst. The process may take a long or a short time to develop depending, among other factors, on the narcissistic component of the patient's pathology. It may not, in some cases, become *evident* until the termination phase. It will comprise conflicts from different developmental levels, but it will bear the stamp of the ego capacities characteristic of the oedipal stage resolution: of internalized conflict, of differentiated object representations including that of the analyst, and of the superego. The new organization becomes visible to different analysts at different stages of its progression, depending on technique and on individual criteria. It can be recognized partly as a comparative difference in the quality of the therapeutic object relationship.

Object representations of the analyst need not be entwined with core unconscious organization in a transference neurosis for analytic work in general to progress. Indeed, since a transference neurosis is a possible result of earlier work on defensive aspects of conflicts and character, a transference neurosis cannot itself be considered necessary for the progression of an analysis. Substantial benefits can be derived from an analysis before its crystallization.

It is inconceivable to me, however, that in a well-progressing analysis of an individual with the requisite ego organization the qualitative shift in the relationship with the analyst discussed above not occur to some degree and in some form, however muted. Such a shift could conceivably occur and work could proceed on central conflicts extratransferentially, moving from these to work on primary objects and memory. Dr. A described such a case (see chap. 3). I would not consider that a transference neurosis was necessarily absent, however. *The organization need not be conscious in content or the major subject of discussion for core conflicts to be activated through a transferring process and for intense and immediate work on them to occur.* That is, transference neurosis, as I have defined it, need not be seen purely as a resistance in the way of remembering and a stage that must be traversed before remembering and major resolutions can occur. It can also be a barely perceptible facilitator of the latter. In making this statement I am assuming that the analyst knows how to differentiate between intellectual knowledge and emotional understanding. The immediacy and mutuality of the work may be the major conscious transference signifier. Termination would then be the phase in which the meaning of the transferential dimension would be addressed and resolved because it would be the phase at which the approaching loss of covert gratifications associated with the mutuality of the work would make those gratifications, or the search for their replacements, appear more overtly in the derivatives of the patient's associations.

Transference neurosis is variable in appearance and quality as well as in content and organization from one patient to another. The patient's conscious experience of the analyst and the mark of the core psychically organizing conflicts from childhood may differ in the immediacy and clarity of their relation to each other according to the character structure of the analysand (see chap. 6). Nevertheless, given adequate psychic structure, in a transference neurosis, the constructed object representations of the analyst become integrated with the core psychically organizing network of fantasies from childhood and their later editions into a new organization. When the extent of that intertwining either becomes the subject of discussion or facilitates relevant memory and both participants are consciously emotionally engaged with a degree of immediacy and intimacy, we may agree that a transference neurosis has evolved. Such an immediate engagement, the growing mutual sharing of language and affect, of hatred and love, of the discovery of central unconscious meaning, shapes each analyst's experience and thus his or her description of the transference neurosis.

CHAPTER SIX

The Relation to Character Structure

Historically, aspects of character were not considered relevant to the concept or subject of a transference neurosis unless, through analysis, the conflict of which they were a part was mobilized and they became transformed into symptoms. The possibility of a broader manifestation of character in the transference neurosis was entertained in a major forum only with the 1968 panel contributions of Blum (1971) and Loewald (1971).

Despite these contributions, however, the concept of character is often still conceived of as being in opposition to the transference neurosis for several reasons. (See Dr. F, chap. 5; Kepecs, 1966; Cooper, 1987). The concept has often retained its historical meaning as a symptomatic illness; in addition, the term *character* subsumes the idea of differences in ego development, so that it is frequently not clear whether the reputed absence of a transference neurosis in "cases of character," to follow Glover (1955) in using a term that begs the question, is being attributed to chaotic ego organization or the absence of ego dystonic symptoms. I shall here concentrate on character structure organized around neurotic level functioning and postpone to the following chapter a consideration of more diverse ego structures.

Rather than seeing character neurosis as a nosological entity that excludes the transference neurosis as a pathway of cure, character structure and allied neurotic pathology can be seen as opening up the range of possibilities through which infantile conflict can manifest itself not only in adult mental organization but in a transference neurotic version of that organization. Dr. E elaborated on variants. At one end of this range is a character structure that he believed allowed relatively rapid access to organizing ego dystonic, originally childhood conflict, and at the other, a character structure that ego syntonically incorporated, transformed, and diffused that conflict. From a perspective within the transference dyad, these extremes translated as a relatively direct transferential appearance of the core organizing conflicts composing the structuring infantile neurosis, warded off only by a "pseudo-adaptive" character defense, on the one hand, and a surface behavior toward the analyst much more distantly connected to discernible core unconscious conflicts, on the other.

As Loewald (1971) pointed out, failure to take into account the interrelation of core conflicts and characterological presentations may lead too easily to mistaking character traits functioning as resistance for a more immediate transference expression of core, originally childhood conflict. Manifest content can conform to a content definition of a classical transference neurosis while representing a major character resistance particularly seductive by virtue of its conforming to acceptable criteria. Consider, for example, the following clinical situation from my practice.

A businessman presented all the signs of a classical transference neurosis. The transference was highly instinctualized. He experienced an intense sexual attraction to me that he connected to his childhood attraction to his seductive, yet frustrating mother. He developed a transference symptom related to a regressive wish to get even with me for frustrating him sexually. He was terrified of being in the room alone with me because he thought that a man he occasionally encountered at the bus stop near my office building whom he took to be my husband and who took on the characteristics of his father would interrupt us and kill him.

As a trauma was worked through and paralyzing anxiety over competitive wishes somewhat diminished, I began to be aware of his manner of speaking. Over time, its staccatolike machine-gun quality had become more marked, particularly when he described his intense erotic attraction and his fears of my husband's imminent attack. When I made this way of speaking a focus for analytic exploration, he became furious and very frightened and threatened to leave the analysis. I was "poking holes in him," he declared with great anxiety, and he would not put up with it.

This man had been appeasing the imago of a very frightening, envious, castrating, phallic mother by conforming to his idea of what a "good" patient in analysis should feel and express. He had even consulted a prominent textbook to inform himself of how a classical analysis should proceed. The important transference element at that moment was the defensive wish to please me, a wish with a multitude of genetic and dynamic roots. Ultimately, we discovered that a narcissistic identification with this terrifying maternal imago defended against hostile wishes associated with an early separation. These had been manifested by the staccatolike machine-gun bursts of his speech. Only after this constellation was addressed could oedipal conflicts be meaningfully and feelingly engaged.

Before the immediacy of this crisis, this man's feelings toward me and fear of his transference father were used primarily in the service of self-protection, not self-knowledge. What looked like a classical transference neurosis was a characterological behavior in the service of obscuring an important transference: what we were seeing was behavior directed toward the appeasement of a terrifying maternal object representation, behavior that had become a central part of his character. My questioning of his manner of speaking opened up an important phase of work.

If we are to apply the concept of transference neurosis to this material, we do so not on the basis of the manifest oedipal content but because of a theoretical idea that characterological behavior such as my patient's pleasing me forms a transferentially defensive part of a core conflict and that it is therapeutically beneficial to posit such a connection. Using the concept of transference neurosis hypothetically connects the attempt to please me with an originally unarticulated transference anxiety the content of which turned out to be a childhood fear of a castrating, phallic mother. Further, it assumes that the relevant, originally infantile anxieties form part of a structuring infantile neurosis as that concept has been redefined (see chaps. 5 and 9). The florid oedipal material my patient produced in defensive form to placate me was not irrelevant to his difficulties; it was simply not the relevant dynamic issue at that moment in the treatment. The dynamic issue had to be engaged through the resistance. Placating and pleasing me was part of a character defense mobilized to ward off more pressing hostile, preoedipal derivatives.

This example is of technical and theoretical interest for another reason. Had I held a concept of transference neurosis that included manifest criteria conforming to those the patient was producing as well as an idea of cure requiring the transference neurosis as described, the treatment might have become prematurely focused on derivatives of unconscious oedipal fantasies without my paying sufficient attention to that aspect of character structure and attached conflicts against which the oedipal material was defending. Prematurely addressing derivatives of infantile conflicts that are being used in the service of buttressing more immediate character defenses and the more immediately important impulses that those character defenses hold in check becomes an ineffective academic exercise. Unless we agree to consign the concept of transference neurosis to the dust heap, including manifestations of character within it seems less a choice than a clinical necessity.

When an aspect of an organizing infantile conflict is reactivated, revived, formerly repudiated wishes become more insistent. The character defenses that genetically have held them in check and continue to do so intensify. Such an intensification occurred in my patient, alerting me to the defensive function of his behavior. That then allowed me to observe a significant resistance and to analyze it. This interaction constitutes the dynamic behind Dr. T's observation (see chap. 4) that the intensification of character traits was a signal of the formation of a transference neurotic organization. As with my patient's speech, the character traits in question increasingly reveal the instincts warded off.

Not all character traits remain so directly linked to instincts, however. Some are observably more distant from core unconscious conflict and may stand at the basis of a clinical position that no longer holds character structure, whatever the underlying genetic givens, to be a product of structuring conflict. Dr. E believed that these ideas about the nonconflictual origins of character structure, with which he did not agree, were confusing current concepts of transference and transference neurosis.

> There are two broad categories of transference: one is the historical model of transference; the second is a modernist, even romantic concept, and it is related to the notion that one doesn't see transference neurosis in patients with character problems. Those who hold the second believe that everything experienced by the patient is transference. They make no distinction between aspects of character that still have dynamic roots in repressed material and those aspects of character that a patient needs to accept—perhaps with the analyst's help and after some clarification—as a part of how he or she reacts to immediate interactions with all people in the exigencies of life.
>
> Character traits are partly derived from the ways the person is trying to deal with the infantile neurosis, but they can be conceptualized either as character defenses that still have the dynamic connection with unconscious urges or as givens that cannot be changed. In the first case, where there is still a connection between the character trait and its dynamic root, character traits take the form of behavioral and affective equivalents. They represent an insufficiency of repression. They have moved into an area in which characteristic behavior is itself a derivative. This behavior disguises meanings of an early childhood conflictual nature. When it is lived out in every relationship, as it often is, it represents an attempt to buttress a repression that has failed.
>
> In the second case, the character traits have been severed from their infantile, dynamic roots. Character traits of this sort represent behavior that is so adaptive that though one might be able to say it is derived from a particular historical period of conflict, it is a late result and cannot be remobilized into its origins, even in the most searching analytic situation. These character traits are an inheritance—developmentally, genetically—of earlier experience, and now they've become taken up and so integrated, both for cultural and adaptive reasons, that one wouldn't think of them as transference; at least I wouldn't want to include them in the category of transference.
>
> The romantic view of transference leads to a neglect of reconstruction of the unconscious determinants and genetic origins of certain aspects of character. It encourages the concept that character-disordered patients do not develop a transference neurosis.

For Dr. E, then, the analysis of transference and ultimately the transference neurosis involved a process through which defensive strategies, whether those of repression or of characterologic "action," would yield to the rediscovery and experiencing of those infantile conflicts that contributed to their formation. Dr. E spoke of those core conflicts as "those constellations that have retained qualities of their origin, their infantile aims and modes, combined with the defenses against them, the fantasy elaborations of them, and the superego contributions of guilt that make it so difficult for the person to bring them out except in derivative form."

This definition implies that certain organizations of the personality lend themselves better than others to a psychoanalytic procedure defined by such a classical idea of the transference neurosis:

> The patients who are able to use analysis best are those who have not had the need to utilize secondary and tertiary characterological behavior to solve these infantile conflicts, but have had the ability to make some kind of segregation of unsolved infantile problems, that segregation then sparing the rest of the personality to develop and mature relatively unimpaired by these unsolved problems. These unresolved conflicts then may take the form either of symptoms or of certain kinds of character defenses that are pseudoadaptive, but nevertheless still have a defensive buttressing function to keep the unconscious fantasies from having an even greater pervasive effect.

A Taxonomy of Character Structure

It seems possible, following Dr. E, to elaborate a rough taxonomy according to which a category of character structure would give rise to a particular form of transference neurosis. The first of these, closest to the traditional symptom neurosis, is a character structure where the defensive character traits are "pseudoadaptive." This form lends itself best to the unfolding of transference according to Dr. E's definition because these pseudoadaptive character traits allow core unconscious conflict from childhood to remain relatively sequestered. Such character structure is unencumbered by secondary and tertiary adaptive characterologic overlay. The second and third categories in this taxonomy would be defined by the nature of the subsequent character defensive layering—that is, the mode of adaptation and degree of integration into the ego of character defenses originally connected to infantile conflict. The conflict has not, however, remained linked to pseudoadaptive defenses and sequestered by them and is therefore not attainable in such a relatively pure form.

The first type of character structure would lead rather directly to the efflorescence of a more classical transference neurosis; the others, to more attenuated types. Dr. E offered an example of the first type:

> One patient, a promiscuous woman, was intent on seducing me just the way she had seduced every man she came in contact with. This seduction was her character defense. It was a compromise formation, still active, and there was a compulsive quality. She had to do this. If she didn't do it, she would get anxious. This is what happened in the analysis: when she couldn't seduce me, she had to do something because her equilibrium, which was maintained by the seductive manner, could not be maintained. She would come into the office, get anxious, and have all kinds of symptoms, derivatives of anxiety about what she saw was a dangerous sexual situation: she had mastered it in a characteristic counterphobic way before by being the aggressor who seduced, partly as a way of keeping at arm's length any kind of intimacy, any kind of feeling of herself as being intimately involved and therefore masochistically vulnerable. When that was no longer a tenable defensive posture, the next step was to feel that she was coming into a situation that was out of her control, sexually dangerous, that she could be set upon and raped—and this was the bold and brassy woman who before had been the aggressor sexually. So that transformation is, to me, a very good example of what I would see as the development of a transference neurosis: a new kind of experience, and a special form of transference neurosis.

The third category would be one in which character represents such an adaptation to and integration into the ego of the original infantile conflicts that the link between manifest behavior in the analysis and the unconscious conflicts is extremely difficult to metabolize in the treatment. In Dr. E's terms:

> There has been a much more complex process of reaction formations, displacements, behavioral efforts to solve infantile problems. The process has pervaded the personality, coming to a kind of relative calcification of the character along the lines both of the direct-line molding effect, but also to the much more complicated, typically neurotic kinds of mechanisms of reaction formation, displacements, projections, perhaps symptom formation at some point. But those symptoms then themselves are taken more into the character, so they're no longer ego dystonic, but ego syntonic late modifications of symptoms that have then acquired, perhaps through cultural rewards, a fixity; they have become adaptive.

An example: a small girl tortured by a hand-washing compulsion. Such a symptom, would, of course, already have been the compromise outcome of various unacceptable urges and defenses—say, for instance, of masturbatory impulses and fantasies, themselves based on various sexual and aggressive conflicts toward primary objects. Dr. E emphasized the fate of the symptom, already the representative of illicit wishes, in relation to the development of her character. Progressively, it is integrated into her character; she becomes a very clean little girl. Cleanliness is not

> just limited to the hands. Everything has to be clean, controlled. The parents see this as a fine development—after all, she's being very good, clean, not causing any trouble; she's progressively more dutiful and controlled and obsessional about her schoolwork. All of this becomes so much a part of her character that she doesn't need the symptom anymore; she has settled it and found a place for herself in relation to her parents and progressively the broader cultural scene, and is now just a very obsessional little girl who has sacrificed some degree of her flexibility and access to her inner life that might have been easier to maintain if she had had just a symptom.

When a transference neurosis develops with such a patient, it will take a more affectively attenuated form at the far end of the spectrum Dr. E described more fully in connection with the second category, its major sign being some intensification of these very character traits of cleanliness and control. Even in these most attenuated cases, the idea for Dr. E was to mobilize the anxiety and guilt underneath the character defenses. With one obsessional man, the major sign was a change in language from very stilted speech to his eventually using "shit" and then observing that he was doing it.

The second category lies on the spectrum between the first and the third: the links between character and infantile conflict are both adaptive and ego syntonic, on the one hand, and maintain some segregation of the infantile conflict, on the other. Dr. E. continued:

> The character defenses are Janus-like. They are not only adaptive efforts at making the psychopathology work for you and still avoiding the anxiety. They serve a still-active defensive function against infantile conflicts and are still related to the original regressive material through a process of displacement, reaction formation. The character traits embedded in this kind of character disorder have therefore not become so entirely ego syntonic or adaptive or useful, nor have they lost their defensive function. Sometimes, in the analytic process, their origins can be tapped again; they can be loosened up and instead, perhaps, of a still somewhat ego syntonic obsessionality, they may be turned back and experienced in the transference neurosis as a more dystonic obsessionality that is related to the analyst. For example, someone who is very dutiful comes into analysis, wants to do very

well, is always punctual and respectful of the analyst. This behavior is ego syntonic. Gradually there may develop departures from that very dutiful obsessional analytic goodness. Maybe some lateness. Maybe bringing in some mud on his feet and messing up the carpet or the couch. And then being perhaps guilty about it and very apologetic and distressed by it.

These things are signs that here is a loosening up of the mode of character defense that made the person feel relatively comfortable; progressively he becomes anxious, not able to control his hostile wishes and impulses toward the analyst quite so well by his obsessional character defenses and behavior; he may then become more aware of problems in paying his bill. He may start to pay close attention to every detail of the bill, going over the charges very carefully, and whereas he might have paid the next day after getting the bill, now he begins to delay a little, wondering whether perhaps there has been a mistake made, has the analyst not taken into account the holiday, or he had told the analyst he wouldn't be there that day so he shouldn't be charged for it; so it becomes now instead of just a kind of controlled assumption of things always being good and in control, now they've become out of control and engaged in the analytic relationship. The analyst then becomes a partner in the patient's mind in the question of whether he is under control, being messy, getting too offensive in some way, to the analyst.

The obsessional patient really becomes obsessional with you; he externalizes his obsessionality, making you the superego. You are the one he has to answer to. He is still obsessional in his character, in his behavior with you, but it's a more anxious kind of personalized thing that makes him see you as an opponent or a judge. You are telling him how he should conduct his life; you are demanding that he come on time and pay his bill regularly; and he in his sharpened-up and more personal kind of way sees this as a conflict between you and him, where you're definitely now representing one side of what had been mainly in a less obvious way played out with other people, where he has involved wife, employers, children perhaps, other members of the family, in an obsessional system, and in many cases gotten their collusion to go along with him in certain ways. When the analyst doesn't, it becomes still an obsessional struggle, but there are many more qualities of interpretable material that teases apart drive and defense; whereas with the usual relationship where obsessional character defenses are used, it is just accepted as a given. This is the way he is. And you go along with it or you don't. Here the analyst doesn't go along with it, but he does something else: he sees where there's a break in that, and where his determination not to collude makes for the possibility of a touch of anxiety, a little more evidence that this is something that can't be easily repeated over and over again in just the same form. Now it's repeated, but in a way that the analyst and eventually, through clarification and interpretation, the patient, will need to see how he has organized his environment in terms of his inner conflicts, his need to have a controlling hand in all of his dealings, to keep him from being too instinctualized, to keep from being too guilt-ridden. Now guilt, anger, and frustration become experienced in the analytic situation with the analyst, and you can get a wedge in there for interpretive intervention.

So this, I think, is often what happens to that intermediate category where patients don't have any symptoms when they come in, except perhaps in the form of being depressed. They come in because they're dissatisfied with their life. Then their typical character defenses intensify. In the early part of the analysis they have to rely on these typical character defenses as their major line of resistance to the development of transference.

This line of defense itself, these very qualities that are resistant to the development of a more mobile transference, they themselves, through their intensification, in my way of thinking, become the transference. They may then lead to new derivatives that are more clearly related to the analyst and less character traits that may apply to all people that the patient has any dealings with. That is, they may become more individualized and perhaps new. Sometimes they bring, in this new transferential form, a rather upsetting and startling experience for the patient. They are upsetting precisely because they represent an earlier ego state more closely related to infantile drive derivatives and defenses against them that had been transformed into the more acceptable character defense that the patient started with in analysis.

Contrary to the first category where pseudoadaptive character traits lead relatively quickly to the appearance of sequestered infantile conflicts in the transference, this more muted intensification of character traits followed by recovery of earlier ego states is these patients'

equivalent of a transference neurosis. And if one doesn't see it in that way, the analyst is assuming in advance that there may be some impossibility of ever analyzing it. In my experience, that more attenuated transference neurosis usually is accompanied by a progressive lessening of those character defenses in dealing with the rest of the people in the individual's life. It does, in fact, become more concentrated in the analytic situation even though there isn't the qualitative change to a new kind of, more florid, infantile type of experience. Such patients may dip down temporarily, metaphorically speaking, into more infantile things, but usually this is covered over rather quickly, and the emphasis still is on, in the case of the obsessional, the anxious obsessionalizing of the relationship with the analyst.

The idea that the transference neurosis involves symptoms that have to be related to the analyst has to be clarified, too, because it's not just that one sees symptoms, such as phobias or obsessional traits, or compulsive rituals that are experienced in the analytic situation, there can be new derivatives that are much more personalized.

When other people talk about character-disordered patients and say that they don't develop a transference neurosis, I think what they are saying is that they don't develop one so obviously focused and their transference experience is not so different from their characterological experience. True character-disordered patients very often don't develop the transference neurosis Freud had in mind when he said that we regularly turn the patient's neurosis into a new kind of neurosis. Some patients do stick with their character defensive qualities through the analysis. That *is* their transference neurosis.

Three Clinical Accounts

The following three cases fall at different points on the spectrum just described.

Case 1

Dr. E described an operating room nurse in whom a phallic, controlling character sequestered a relatively unchanged organization from the infantile period. Infantile sexual conflicts centering around the patient's father were organized into a phobia which the phallic and controlling character protected.[1] The patient had dealt with sexual conflicts through a marriage in which she had been able to limit the sexuality and exercise a great deal of control. After she divorced, she had many affairs and other contacts with men all of whom were unacceptable either because they weren't right for her or because they were married.

Despite her education, her professional experience, and her intellectual sophistication, this woman was extremely naive in quite extraordinary ways, including ignorance of her own female physiology. She did not understand how the penis was attached, how it came out of the man;

1. Owing to a mechanical failure, the second part of Dr. E's interview, which included this case, was not recorded. The account here was dictated by me within three hours of our interview.

where the clitoris was in relation to the urethra; and she couldn't imagine where the urethra was in the male. That same kind of naïveté informed her attitude toward the transference neurosis. She would say, "Well, what's the use of having these feelings toward you? You're married." She had been a tomboy and continued to prefer to wear blue jeans and sneakers. The first manifestation of a libidinal note in the transference neurosis was her wearing very subdued but more feminine shoes. When her attention was drawn to the change in her attire, she was very embarrassed to talk about it. She thought people in general, or her analyst in particular, would laugh at her.

Her transference neurosis emerged as an obsessive wondering about whether her analyst was married or not—no other affects, just a wondering on and off about whether he was married or not; maybe he was divorced, maybe he was widowed. When she found out that her analyst was married, she immediately felt nothing toward him. Her attitude became "what's the use if you're married."

This conscious situation persisted until she went away for a brief vacation during the analytic year and then came back and reported that she had had no feelings about the separation from the analyst at all. However, she had had a great yearning for the man who had taken her to the airport, and she had actually called him when she was on vacation to keep up the contact. Dr. E asked her when she had called. When she realized that she had called at exactly the time of a missed analytic session, all the yearnings for the analyst came flooding back in a much more intense form. These yearnings were accompanied, however, by a repeated insistence on "what's the use, you're married."

This material aptly illustrates the particular way character defenses function as an ego syntonic resistance to the transference neurosis. As Dr. E described in his taxonomy, in his first category infantile conflicts remain relatively sequestered and ready to appear in the transference neurosis. The maladaptive character defenses intervene between the transference experience and the recovery of memories, fantasies, and impulses toward the primary objects to construe a situation in which, in the treatment, the patient is supposed to give up "impossible" wishes in reality. The clinical issue, of course, isn't simply that the patient has to give up the wish for the analyst; rather, the "impossibility" of the wish for the analyst is used to prevent affectively remembering the past conflicts around primary objects—here the forbidden wishes for her father. Resistance, however, does not only signify obstacle. The patient's attitude probably also repeated her childhood defensive attitude toward her father, and thus also brought an important aspect of the past to light.

Case 2

Dr. S discussed a man whose analysis might prove to fit the second category. Entrenched obsessional character traits had begun to yield in the most subtle way to transference enactments accompanied by changes in affect. It seemed possible that these ego states would be linked to early unconscious conflicts so that character change would ultimately occur in tandem with the analysis of clusters of uncovered infantile conflict:

> A professional man in his late thirties came from a very unusual background; he is very bright and had been a child prodigy in a remote part of the country. His father had been a brilliant young person in his field and had come from a metropolitan area, but he isolated himself in that backwater. My patient had been brought up in this provincial backwater town where he was the leading scholar of a large area and had easily gotten into the best university he'd applied to, which was a very good one. For the first time in his life he wasn't the smartest, most interesting person, and, more important than that, he didn't get acclaimed for knowing everything better than everyone else, a kind of perfectionism he'd been able to live with all his life. When you've been to a really third- or fourth-rate public high school and then are put into a good college, you find it's impossible to learn everything, on the one hand; and there's not a group of people sitting around waiting to applaud you just for being smart. He got into terrible trouble; wound up going to a very poor graduate school, which he felt he had to do to please his family, the rational thing to do. He ended up in a very inferior kind of position—this man who had spent all his life trying to make sense out of things, trying to follow his father's precepts of being fully rational and never allowing himself to be carried away with feelings.
>
> There's a strong rabbinical tradition in the family. An ancestor was a very famous rabbi. This man sought me out for analysis after hearing me speak at a meeting. He worked for an unreasonably demanding boss who insisted his staff put in an inordinate number of extra, unpaid hours. He not only accepted these demands but also succeeded in making sense out of some of the rather irrational programs that were developed. The two of them together made a pretty good team. This guy could make sense out of anything. He made good sense out of his parents. His whole life has been an unusual adaptation.
>
> In the early stages of analysis, it was really very hard to listen to him. He was chronically tired; he was still, at thirty, dressing the way his mother had dressed him, in ill-fitting bargain clothes. He'd been working just to support himself and his rather demanding wife; then he had a child. He sacrificed. He would be involved in working many

hours, far too many, and on top of that he would stay up late, being sure to cut all the coupons out of the paper to save money on groceries.

It's very hard to listen to someone drone on about what the coupons were, and how he would schedule time to get to the supermarket so he could cash them in before the expiration date because some expired on August 31 and others expired on September 5. His need to make sense out of things was overdetermined by the nonsensical behavior of people around him—as in making sense out of two different sets of rituals and traditions because of his parents' different religious observances—but it pervaded every area.

In the early years of the analysis, all I could do was to point out to him what he was describing. He felt these demands were enormous and inescapable. There were no loopholes. Even if he'd been in therapy, you couldn't have said, "Well, why don't you do such-and-such?" because he, of course, had anticipated all of this in terms of his values, goals. Again, just consistently pointing out what he was saying led him very slowly, once in a great while, to be able to acknowledge some discomfort other than that of being tired or feeling blocked. Though I wasn't aware of being able to get more into the detail of what he was doing, there began to be some evidence of change.

In the first years of the analysis, whatever changes there were seemed to be in reaction to changes in his life, in his professional work, in having a child. It was only as he began to change in being able to tolerate an awareness of his own discomfort that I began to get an idea of the meaning of clipping coupons. The event that signaled it for me was when this man allowed himself to buy a computer so he could be more productive. It seemed like a silly thing to do—he was committed to working so many hours to earn a living—but he had some dream that maybe then he'd be able to write.

I remember the first thing I was aware of was what folly this was, but this was a new kind of folly. He was spending megahours figuring out the best deal on this and that piece of computer equipment. Then he got the computer, and for the first month that he had it, he'd stay up till three or four in the morning working on the computer. But he'd find himself playing games. It was overdetermined by the brother who's a computer expert. I knew nothing about computers. It took me weeks until I suddenly realized: *My God! This guy's playing games!* He's never played a game in his life. And I don't think he's ever done anything gamelike since he became a prodigy and gave up being a child.

From that time, I began hearing the little room for play in his life. Clearly in response to a change in him. I don't think I'd ever made any interpretation that directly had to do with the issue of play. I just pointed out what he was saying. It was in response to growing spaces in his life, little activities that had not been there before, either revivals of old activities or new things: he was planting a garden, and then his wife had a baby, and he was fascinated with the child. A space became available in which these things that he was doing began to make more and more sense.

The opening phase of the transference neurosis with this obsessional man had the form of playing a game with me. It began to be that of clearly checking whether I would notice what he was saying. Only in retrospect did I learn that he had started and elaborated a subtly different pattern of paying—I've forgotten it exactly, but it was something like a day or two later one month, three days later another month, then two days early the next month. And this came up after about a year very indirectly, initially, in association to elements of one of his rare dreams. And what emerged was an incident that I was quite prepared to hear but hadn't been aware of all the time. When he was a child, his parents were eager that he give concerts at the age of five and six on the violin. By the age of nine or ten, he was wondering whether his parents really did give a damn about his playing. And he got so he would go into the room where he was to practice. He found he could turn the television on very low and his mother couldn't hear it, and he could saw away at his scales while really watching his cartoons on television. And so he'd been playing around with me in that way for a whole year.

As we began to talk about his playing around, there was a fairly big symptomatic change. He began to use the computer to turn out a torrent of papers. It's interesting, I hadn't thought of this. In terms of other words, there's some symptomatic change that clearly has something to do with the analysis. Once that change happened, new behaviors that express somewhat similar themes emerge that are much more accessible to interpretation.

Dr. S was emphasizing the experiential and manifest shift from habitual character pattern to character defense that carries the sign of a reactivated infantile wish. He did not specify the childhood wishes that the character behavior, as it took transference neurotic form, might have been both expressing and concealing; however, for the purposes of speculation, we might note that Dr. S first described that the patient began to play, then mentioned his computer-expert brother, and then his sense of a "space" opening up. He continued by noting that the patient was planting a garden and immediately followed with a reference to the patient's wife having a baby and the patient's fascination with the infant. He next noted that the patient began to play with him—the analyst. The "secret" game involved paying later or early by a number of days and was connected to the story of playing at practicing so that the patient's mother would not realize he was watching cartoons on television. Playing a game with the analyst was followed by the patient writing a "torrent" of papers. One infantile dimension of the playing, then, may have involved enactment of erotic, identificatory, and hostile wishes toward the analyst/mother genetically related to her pregnancy and the ensuing birth of the computer-expert brother. This speculation does not, of course, exclude the likelihood that other childhood wishes toward other primary objects also lie behind the obsessional character of this patient.

Case 3

Dr. C described the early stages in a case that may turn out to exemplify the third category:

> A psychologist who functioned perfectly well, so-called normal—everything about him was perfectly all right, married, some problems with premature ejaculation but they were not concerning him or his wife—ended up coming to see me in consultation and started analysis with me about a year and a half ago. The relevant history is that his father who was also a psychologist died when the patient was nine. The patient remembers practically nothing about his father except that on one occasion during his father's debilitating illness he and his brother were out in the street laughing about one of his father's symptoms and about how ridiculous his father was because of it. It's kind of a "fixed" memory. When his father died, his response to it was embarrassment and shame. As though there were something "different" about him and something ridiculous about him, that he had no father. Very striking.
>
> In the course of our work, he has been noticing the absence of any feelings about his father. There's also been a total nontransference. Very interesting in terms of the question you're raising about the forms the transference neurosis takes. He says that that means that he's not getting anywhere, that he's not a good analytic patient. He says, "I haven't gotten anywhere in this analysis"; at times he says, "Am I almost through?" And the most striking thing is the absence of transference except for tiny hints—probably the most important is when he talks about how negatively he responds to his patients' expressing a need for him. If the patient calls him up at home, and he's busy with something, he tries to hide it, but he's very angry that his patients are so dependent on him. And with me, he talks about how "You go on vacation, that's time off for me. I don't miss you, I don't notice you." But the hints are he saw my son who's pushing ten, my son being the

age he was when his father died—when I coughed, he wondered if I was getting sick, just a tiny hint. But what is palpably absent is the potential feelings of dependency; he just can't feel them. And I guess what I think about is that it's going to take a long time. And I think very, very slowly over time. Like on this vacation, he said, "I have been thinking about the fact that you're missing. And that's different from last year, when I never gave it a second thought."

That's all. But I think the feelings are so intense that he can't get to them. It's going to be a long slow analysis. I don't see an alternative. He's somebody who could pass for normal in that he has no symptoms. And he could easily talk himself into being normal and not needing any treatment. The treatment feels like an intrusion on an otherwise normal life.

I talk about the striking absence of feelings; we both talk about it. And intellectually he understands. "That must be because of my father. But I'm afraid I will never get to those feelings, because it's painful and I don't want to get to them. And nothing is going to make me do that." So although I comment on the absence of feelings, I pay particular attention to what we can see together in terms of feelings that are present. He's looking for feelings or dreams. He is so thrilled when he has a dream that he can talk about. He says, "You know, I don't have any material. I hear about all these other patients who give all this interesting material. I'm a very boring patient; I always think of what I can say to fill the hour, because if I just wait until I think of something, I won't think of it." We've talked a lot about the meaning of his being normal. I think his fantasy is that I will be so bored by him that I will end the treatment, and say, "Well you're not analyzable." He ended his previous therapies. The idea that I'm going to end this treatment I understand as a transference phenomenon: the treatment will end because of me. That is the analogy to his father's death. And he believes that with such conviction that he is trying to make it come true.

He's enacting. It's certainly not conscious. But I think—now that I talk about it—that he has in mind boring me to death. He had two older brothers, and he was raised by his mother to be independent, to take care of himself. And he adapted by high-level functioning. And was smart. Studied well. So that he is accustomed to being rational and functioning effectively without feeling. Doing what has to be done. Very respected for his testing skills, like his father. And people like him because he's so helpful. But there's an affective side that he doesn't have available to himself.

It is fascinating to observe Dr. C's passionate involvement in his patient's apparent lack of feeling. That is the patient's character-pervaded transference engagement. Dr. C realized that this example is a case of a non-transference being a transference, I think, but he did not discuss the hostility motivating the affective indifference except when he realized that the patient wished to bore him to death.

By observing the contiguity of Dr. C's discourse it is apparent that he associated many aspects of the patient's behavior and character with conflicts organized around the death of the patient's father, although the extent of the interrelations seemed often to be at the edge of his clinical thinking about the case. For instance, it would be possible to understand the independent, capable, apparently emotionless aspects of the patient's character as an identification with a defensively fantasied figure of the father as abandoner. Such a fantasy would ward off the painful, frightening, guilt-provoking, and disillusioning experience of seeing his father as sick, debilitated, and humiliated. The persistently denied symptom of premature ejaculation might be an identificatory reference to that premature death. There is a long literary tradition in which death and intercourse are treated as identical (Shakespeare, Donne). Such a formulation would suggest that the patient might leave the treatment prematurely as he had already left psychotherapy treatments.

At the moment at which he spoke about the patient, however, Dr. C was gradually formulating the idea that the patient was engaged, beyond adaptive character traits, in a covert enactment: he was trying to bore the analyst to death. The possible and multiple unconscious meanings of the enactment were not yet clear. The patient might be trying to defeat the analyst (as oedipal rival), thus punishing himself at the same time for his competitiveness, and/or his boring the analyst to death might be his way of controlling the fatality rather than experiencing the helplessness and humiliation of the loss. Or the patient, by being deadly boring, might be enacting an identification with his dead father and in so doing in fantasy keeping his father with him. The technical problem will be that the characteristic form of the enactment makes analyzing it extremely difficult. I asked Dr. C how he envisioned the analysis of the enactment taking place: "He brought up the idea of being boring. I was very interested in his view of himself as boring. It won't be a big step when the time comes to suggest that he may have in mind that he's going to bore me to death. Something I couldn't do now, but I could do in six months, having established—with his bringing up that he's boring. Working with that for a while. There will come a time when I can make that transference interpretation. And the meaning of boring me to death will be apparent."

From the point of view of the relation between transference neurosis and character defense, the question will be how intensively or intimately the patient will experience in the transference the past wishes and feelings that this enactment both expresses and defends against. One conscious manifestation of the transference neurosis may be the intensification of these habitual modes of independent adaptation. That does not mean that the organizing unconscious fantasy related to the father's death is not imbricated in the intensification. Rather, the intensification speaks to a greater need to defend against the related affects and wishes. According to Dr. E, that intensification, itself, might be seen as a sign of the transference neurosis.

On the other hand, in the course of the development of and analysis of this enactment, the psychologist may reexperience ego states in the transference linked to his feelings and conflicts toward his father, which existed both before and after the latter's death. Such a development signals the possibility for greater characterological change. The crucial point here, if one follows Dr. E, is that such developments are not uniquely a product of technique. Rather, the degree to which the infantile conflicts have been interwoven with and integrated into the adaptive aspects of an individual's character is determinative of the form, though not necessarily of the presence of the transference neurosis.

CHAPTER SEVEN

Transference Perversion and Transference Psychosis

Once we enter the realm of severe character pathology, identification of the transference neurosis becomes less a matter of recognizing clinical subtleties and more a matter of maintaining a focused definition. The definition of the transference neurosis risks being enlarged and blurred beyond recognition because, as the sine qua non of psychoanalytic cure, it is particularly prone to categorical expansion. Since the transference neurosis was deemed essential to every successful psychoanalytic treatment, the widening scope of psychoanalysis presented clinicians with a dilemma. Any specific definition of the transference neurosis had the potential of depriving certain individuals who could not meet its criteria of beneficial treatment. In fact, the danger of the concept being used to exclude patients from treatment was an argument that Dr. Q marshaled against the use of the concept.

Delusional Transference Neurosis: An Oxymoron

One solution to this dilemma was and still is an overly inclusive definition of the transference neurosis. Dr. Y's unusually broad definition was representative of this solution. He described the transference dimension of a psychotic regression as a transference neurosis. He arrived at this result by limiting his definition to a regressive transference and thinking of its manifestations as affective intensity over time: "The transference neurosis is different from the transference as I use it, in the sense that the latter is much more fleeting, or obvious, or general, or it doesn't have the real bite to it that the transference neurosis has." He recognized, however, that with a borderline patient both the progression and nature of the transference was different from that of a neurotic patient: "Healthy neurotics take their time to develop a transference neurosis. They have a nice, friendly, reasonable, more controlled, reserved, defensive posture. They don't get into the middle of this craziness the way many borderlines do." He saw no contradiction, however, in ascribing a trans ference neurosis to the latter: "I don't agree that borderline patients can't have an organized transference neurosis."

Since the outcome of the case he described was successful, one hesitates to quibble with his designation. But the case is of interest to us precisely because of that designation. Even though the patient was psychotic for a long stretch of time, the analyst felt the need to describe the transference as a transference neurosis.

> For the first three years, one patient was almost in a transference psychosis, a lot of projection and of sadomasochistic conflicts and a need to control me and a fear that I was controlling her, discounting her. It was very clear that it was a maternal transference neurosis, to the point where she was suicidal and acting out in a very crazy way. After three years, in the middle of this craziness, she signed herself into the hospital. I thought she did it to remain my regressed baby; but it turned out that I was also her secret father! She went to the hospital secretly to find her manic-depressive father, something I had completely missed in the transference. Missed the whole time! Never crossed my mind once in the three years I was caught up in this crazy situation! One of the other problems with sicker patients is that transferences shift around very fast. I don't think, as Kernberg does, that this has to do with a pregenital fusion of the parents. There are oedipal meanings as well. There are very complicated shifts that go on between the different parental images, and the patients' egos aren't very well organized.
>
> I sat her up four times a week to begin with and conducted an analytic psychotherapy. It has gone on for nine years, four and five times a week, and is now terminating. For the first four years, there was this almost unmanageable suicidal acting out, masochistic, depressive behavior, with lots of material that related to separation, wishes for fusion, wishes for mutual destruction, wishes for sexual union and merging, all with a maternal figure. Tremendous anxiety and self-destructive fantasies about heterosexual fantasies with me. I mean, her masturbation fantasy included heterosexual activity but then always ended with her being violently destroyed, even dismembered: the degree of punitiveness for separation from the mother was tremendous. I think that is one of the things characteristic of borderline patients. This patient brought an ice pick to the sessions and walked into the ocean in January to get herself hospitalized and became psychotic when she saw one particular horror movie. At any rate, the transference neurosis, as it was manageable, was intensely maternal. She was tremendously attached to me, felt that I was constantly criti-

cal of her; she was totally unaware of her projection, totally unaware of how critical she was of me and how much she was like her mother, and how her suicide was a threat. And that lasted for about three and a half years. Very wearing, very taxing, a lot of countertransference problems that we're all familiar with.

That, I felt, was the transference neurosis, my definition; almost transference psychosis, in the sense that there was no reality testing; she didn't behave as she was supposed to in the treatment. But after her hospitalization, and after some of the material began to emerge about her search for her father and the paternal transference, she began to settle down. After the fourth year, I put her on the couch. And from then on, she continued to work mainly with the paternal transference for a period of time, and then, toward the termination, it was the usual shifting, you know; some more of the maternal transference, a lot of the negative Oedipus reemerged in a more dramatic form, although it had been interpreted earlier in the treatment as part of the chaotic picture; the real desire to be the man in the family, to be the mother's lover, etc., evolved very clearly; the fear that she could never satisfy me because she didn't have a penis; but I was the mother at that point and no longer the father; evolved along what you would expect to be straightforward neurotic lines.

What I look for are repetitions of patterns and fantasies around the person of the analyst. That's how I think about transference neurosis. So that would be an example of the evolution of a transference neurosis in the borderline, not so different from a neurotic except that it was much more flagrant and wild and unmanageable from the beginning, which you wouldn't expect to see in a neurotic.

Beyond its success, Dr. Y's case is interesting because he broadened the category of transference neurosis so extremely. The phenomena he included went beyond both the transferential and the neurotic, passing even a widely accepted definition of the transference psychosis as "a term which should be reserved for the loss of reality-testing and the appearance of delusional material within the transference which does not affect very noticeably the patient's functioning outside the treatment setting" (Kernberg, 1975, p. 84). The first three years of the treatment Dr. Y described as a transference neurosis seem rather to have involved a more generalized psychotic decompensation.

Dr. M also had a definition of transference neurosis that allowed her to accommodate the successful treatment of nonneurotic patients within its expanded scope. As a definitional, though not, I suspect, as a practical matter, she excluded manifest behavior from her concept. Judgments about whether particular transference manifestations were neurotic or psychotic did not, therefore, enter into her assessment. She thought of the transference neurosis as an unconscious organization underneath intense conscious transference (see chap. 5). Dr. M illustrated her concept of the transference neurosis with the case she began to treat when she was a candidate (see chap. 3) in a very difficult supervisory situation:

> Although the institute had given this woman precise instructions on where my office was, she lost them, had to look in the telephone book, and ended up in my apartment for her first appointment. Obviously, she had a great need for comfort and symbiosis. Her mother, who was alcoholic and terribly depressed, had had seven abortions before she was born. During the treatment, she identified with her mother and became alcoholic, too. She was detoxed and began to drink again. And again. This woman also had very masochistic relationships with men, whom she ended up hating and beating up. She had eating and drinking problems. She had terrible difficulties with her bosses, by whom she always felt criticized.
>
> During the analysis, there were two phases of transference neurosis accompanied by envy, distrust, and despair that were very painful. The violence, rage, and sadism were extraordinary. The technique asked of me by my first supervisor made her reactions much more intense and painful than they needed to be. I couldn't stand her suffering. Also I was desperate because, more often than not, I wasn't doing what I thought I should be doing. Fortunately, after two years, my supervisor thought I was doing a superb job and didn't want to continue. I did quite well for another two years and then, because the situation was so difficult, I went to — for supervision. The analysis continued on after that supervision for many years.
>
> In the first phase, something happened that made everything seem very coherent. This woman asked me to call her by her first name. My upbringing makes it extremely difficult for me to call a patient by a first name. I always keep a distance with patients. This patient was absolutely desperate about it and would not continue in analysis unless I called her by her first name. I never did. Through that first intense transference, we discovered that her mother forgot her name, did not even recognize her, when she was drunk. Through that she recovered stuporous states of mind, moments in which she herself forgot everything. It was like going back to Breuer! All this was in the transference first. This was not the transference neurosis. Every session was like this. If she was like that spontaneously, you can imagine how difficult the task was made for a patient by an analyst remaining rigid.

When I got pregnant, the level of her hostility was unbelievable. She wanted to trample on my body with high heels, kill me, burn me very slowly. I had the feeling that the only thing that saved me and saved her then was that that was the time I terminated the first supervision. Before, following the demand of my first supervisor, I interpreted her intense hostility, with no support from where the hostility came from. Those were very painful moments. This was very much against anything I had gone through in my own analysis. When I had trouble doing this, my supervisor told me that I had terrible problems with aggression. There was no way I could come out clean. This technique was terrible.

The manifest hostility was not the transference neurosis. What I was supposed to interpret was on the surface. The intensity was attributed to the aggression; while, in fact, what motivated the rage was the intense wish to be part of my body. As a matter of fact, she did not have many ego resources. She practically had to be part of my body. There was no other way out, for her, at that time. I knew that she was very capable of developing differently, but at that point, I was the link to love. So I started interpreting how much she loved me, and how much she wanted to be part of my body, and how tremendously afraid she was that after my baby was born, I would say good-bye to her. She realized how much she wanted to be the fetus and be my child. She wasn't so jealous of my being pregnant as she was jealous of the fetus. She had a tremendous fear that, involved with my own baby, I wouldn't think of her.

Now, the interesting thing was that when this intense desire to be accepted as a child, which she had not been at a crucial part of her life, was understood, she brought in a photograph. She trusted me enough to bring me a photograph of herself at about eighteen months sitting on her mother's lap. In the photograph, her mother was holding her at this distance. This was very interesting for me, because I had been telling my supervisor for a long time—he took it as my intimidation—that when she would come into the session, I would feel very rigid. My body would go into a spasm, especially my back. It even sometimes hurt. I didn't feel intimidated. When I saw that photograph, I knew that through projective identification, I was enacting the mother. I could interpret, then, what was going on through me to her, and that was extremely helpful. It made her start talking about the mother whom she adored. Then came a phase of recognition of the inadequacy of this mother; she remembered a very difficult family situation, besides the alcoholism. Before, she had only said how extraordinary her mother was. She didn't remember her seven years with an alcoholic mother. All of this had been repressed and came out in a very explosive way.[1]

But the biggest trouble was still to come. The second phase of transference neurosis was far more difficult. It had to do with what the child had constructed to survive, in terms of an infantile neurosis, with all of what was going on around her. It explained her enormous difficulty in separation. We learned that she had constructed a fantasy that each time she closed the door, she killed everybody behind it. It was her vengeance; it was her way of constructing a better world with other things, with next-door things. It was an extraordinary desire for her parents to go away and leave her in peace. However, this fantasy was transferred to every situation of parting. In every situation, she became a murderer and then she had to sacrifice herself in the same way. When all the pieces of this could be put together—which took an extraordinary amount of time, motivation, on her part, pain on both of our parts, because in the course of things, I had to become her, in the sense that she became as sadistic with me as the parents had been with her, until I understood what was going on and could interpret it. It was a very difficult situation, where she would come every day to mistreat me. For instance, she didn't pay me for six months. She criticized absolutely everything I did. She went to see many people in consultation. She spread word around to everybody; she left; went to another analyst; came back; everything you can imagine. I was trembling for her life because at that time she was suicidal.

I have a feeling that were this patient in analysis today, with a technique I developed after her and another two very difficult cases, this work would have been done with less pain for her and with less commotion.

This patient ended her analysis when she felt very ready for a relationship with a man. She has done very well. She wrote to me: she married and a few days ago had her second baby. She was very proud. She married when she was forty because she was in analysis for fourteen years.

To tell you about that transference neurosis. At the end of the analysis, she said to me that she wanted to use the last months to relive her analysis. And for four months she recalled every transference that she had gone through. Especially these two transferential crises, close to psychotic. Her memories so fitted with what I had lived through that I was astonished. She did not have a different version than I. They were the same. Which doesn't happen very often.

1. This material presumably is the first phase of transference neurosis to which Dr. M referred.

I had the feeling that in the course of this analysis, she achieved a level of object relations that she had never had the chance of exploring before. There were things that were new. That were not related to the past. Knowing this was extremely important for the patient. I could only interpret toward the future. I couldn't interpret in terms of conflict in the past.

For instance, I never saw the passage from symbiosis to separation-individuation more clearly. Although she did not know Mahler's theory, by the way she left, I thought of it. There was one dream that I want to tell you because by it I knew that this was the beginning of the ending of the analysis. She had had a time of intense happiness followed by insomnia. I knew that it was about not wanting to accept the fact that the analysis was ending. She treated the insomnia with narcotics and became addicted to them. All this happened in the course of a month and a half. She left for a week for a detoxifying center, fearing that she was going to become forever addicted to narcotics. While she was at this resort, she had a dream. I still remember it. She dreamed, she said, "I was with you. And you were sitting at a table in a restaurant. You were with a child who must have been two, two and a half. And it looked like me, when I was a child. And the child was running around the table in the restaurant, and you let her go! And I was thinking for myself, what a lovely relationship you have with this child, that you aren't afraid that she's going to leave. You let her go and come back." All this was happening in a Chinese restaurant, which had meaning too. She decided to leave the detoxifying resort early and come back to tell me the dream. She realized that in having this dream she had understood everything that I had interpreted about the sequence of events that led to her becoming addicted. I had said to her that she had to drown herself in narcotics in order not to think. Thinking meant being very clear about the state that she was in. This was the last phase. This was like facing individuation. The last two years of analysis happened in a very agreeable atmosphere. This was the last crisis before the end. Severe, but not necessarily a crisis with me so much as a crisis with the destructive inner aspects of her personality, and a last wish to abolish meaning through narcotics.

Thus, perhaps to deal with what was taken as a mandatory interrelation of transference neurosis and cure in a very successful treatment, Dr. M arrived at a definition of the transference neurosis that excluded manifestly psychotic *behavior* while including the unconscious reasons for the behavior.

Dr. Y designated as transference neurosis transference phenomena that were part of a more global psychotic regression; Dr. M similarly described as a transference neurosis a transference psychosis that probably recapitulated an infantile psychosis. The material they both observed included a great deal of projection and introjection and interchanges among and instability in self and object representations. The abundance of these phenomena is characteristic of transference processes without the ego and superego structure that makes possible neurotic conflict. To ascribe psychotic transference behavior sustained over several years of analysis to a transference neurosis in order to maintain the treatment within an overly narrow definition of analysis and its cure seems to me to be forcing material to fit a theory.

Such an oxymoronic use becomes unnecessary if the transference neurosis is not seen as the exclusive pathway to cure. If analyzability is not held to be synonymous with the capacity to develop a transference neurosis, the concept does not have to be enlarged beyond its boundaries to accommodate such cases as Dr. Y and Dr. M describe. There is no particular reason to assume that where the conditions do not exist for the evolution of a transference neurosis, patients cannot be worked with analytically to their benefit. Nor need the patient's proclivity to regress and disrupt the analysis of transference rule out its eventual analysis. In certain patients, the reorganizing of compromise formations in the direction of greater integration may allow structuralization to take place during treatment. Others may benefit from analysis even if the requisite ego capacity does not entirely emerge.

Indeed, the patients described by Dr. Y and M appear to have reorganized during their very successful analyses to such an extent that one can speculate about structuralization proceeding to the level at which neurotic conflict became possible. Their later transferences may well have met my criteria for a transference neurosis at least to the extent that the transference process reflected a more integrated ego and superego. Without detailed process, however, it is difficult even to begin to answer a difficult question: How can an infantile neurosis be *revived* if it had not existed? Perhaps in some instances childhood conflicts and their rather fragmented solutions emerge in a more integrated form as newer conflict solutions reflect a greater capacity to synthesize. The lucid remembering of the transference psychosis that occurred in the last few months of the analysis of Dr. M's patient might then be understood as a reworking and integrating of that childhood material in a new form. In other cases, a more organized childhood conflict solution (e.g., an infantile neurosis) may have existed even if fleetingly, before regressive processes disrupted it. This solution then reemerges when the treatment reduces the present strength of the regressive processes.

But Drs. Y and M designated what seems to have been psychotic material, not the later more neurotic material, as transference neurosis. Perhaps their designation was influenced by the retrospective knowledge that the unconscious meaning of the psychotic behavior was affirmed by the clearly reorganizing effect of the interpretation of its unconscious transference components. In neither case have we verbatim data, so we can do little more than speculate. It is my impression, however, that the interpretations that connected the patients' florid, psychotic, and self-destructive transference behavior to its underlying unconscious fantasies fostered ego integration. For Dr. Y's patient to understand that she was attempting to be hospitalized to find a manic depressive father and for Dr. M's patient to be told that she acted toward her analyst the way her alcoholic, abusive mother had acted toward her and, in addition, was maintaining these primitive object ties to ward off a magical murder of each parent associated with the closing of doors contributed to each patient's ability to differentiate between primary and transference object representations. Presumably, identification had replaced an object tie in each case, and an object tie to the analyst became possible as the wishes for love behind the hostility of these traumatized patients could be verbalized. Since genetic interpretation is so often, though erroneously, said to interfere with transference (Reed, 1993), it is useful to note that in cases where primary and transference objects are very tenuously differentiated, such an interpretation fosters the transferring process rather than hinders it, at least if and where the patient can hear and begin to use the content of the interpretation.

But analysts do not stretch the category of transference neurosis out of shape only to accommodate patients who might otherwise be considered unanalyzable. They sometimes stretch it in order to work effectively. That is, they use the transference neurosis as an operational concept that implies the possibility of a successful analysis in patients with less apparently developed ego and superego organization. The analyst working with patients who develop psychotic transference often needs to have a sense that organization sufficient eventually to contain conflicts, impulses, and split-off states, to hear interpretations, and to work on them is coalescing in order to weather the hostility, despair, and pain that the analyst both witnesses and is subjected to. The analyst may integrate discrete urges, actions, defenses, and delusional beliefs into an unconscious fantasy and assume it belongs to the past and has been transferred to the present, even though the patient cannot distinguish the analyst from primary objects. The organization described is not a transference neurosis. It may not even be a transference psychosis in the narrow definition quoted above. The analyst, however, may think of it as a transference neurosis because it always carries with it the potential of resolution. The idea that the patient's regressive transference is a transference neurosis is, from this point of view, the embodiment of the analyst's hope. The analyst's synthesis of such an organization may function usefully to organize the patient, but it may be the idea of the patient's *potential* that enables the analyst to keep the analysis going in the face of massive provocation or discouragement.

Of course, the analyst always fulfills an organizing function to some degree. For many patients transient regression temporarily precludes the capacity for self-observation and for recognition of the illusory quality of transference experience that enables the analysand to work on his experience with the analyst at the same time that he experiences it. Indeed, Dr. T described the transference neurosis as frequently occurring on the very edge of that recognition and its loss. Nevertheless, these processes are characteristically different when ego and superego organization is more evolved.

Transference Psychosis

In distinguishing transference psychosis from transference neurosis, it is important to remember that transference as it evolves reflects the ego structure in its overall form, not in isolated ego functions or their failures. Reliance on any one manifest criterion in isolation thus risks oversimplifying and misleading. For instance, Kernberg's (1975) definition of psychotic transference, which I quoted above, seems to rely exclusively on the presence or absence of reality testing in the transference. Yet even there, the boundary between transient irrationality and "delusional material" within the transference is not entirely clear and may involve a judgment about the length and extent to which a patient is inaccessible to interpretation. I would not consider the reaction of Dr. R's woman patient to his failure to sympathize with her missing the session because of a flood to be a transference psychosis, for example (see chap. 5).

The emphasis on reality testing as the major criterion for distinguishing transference neurosis and transference psychosis is logical, given the necessary capacity for the analysand to maintain a sense of the transference as "as-if" or metaphoric so that its analysis can take place. Patients' exaggerated perceptions or misperceptions of their analysts, however, often seem "real" to them until the transference significance of the perception is understood. Moreover, transient, apparent loss of reality testing within the transference, by itself, may be the sign of the past actuality of the memory being enacted, a temporarily reduced capacity to modulate affect as a result of acute conflict, or an iatrogenic result of the treatment, to name only some possibilities. What is more, such transient loss may be more apparent than actual when the patient, in a negative transference, is unwilling to reveal his or her more rational assessments to the analyst.

The affective dimensions of repressed traumatic memories and concomitant organizing fantasies are frequently reexperienced in the transference as affect storms for which the stimulus is some "real" characteristic or action of the analyst, its connection to the memory unrecognized (see also chap. 9, case of Dr. D). The affective intensity of these storms and the encapsulated belief that, for example, the unfeeling analyst imposes an unbearable reality on the patient/victim may be one aspect of a transference neurosis if the overall ego and superego structure in the patient is well integrated and developed. I would not expect that the misperception be maintained for a long period. Rather, given a generally well-functioning ego, I would expect a relative accessibility to interpretation. The loss of the capacity for transference illusion is not in isolation a criterion for identifying such disguised, repetitive transference events with transference psychosis or with the organized disavowal of the transference perversion I shall discuss later.

Where such storms are intense and do not easily yield immediately to interpretation, the sequences in the process that lead to the disruption may reveal that it is the specific stimuli for the disruption that carry analyzable transference neurotic meaning. A clinical example will illustrate the idea that transference meaning can be located in the fact of the disruption itself and consequently be more accessible to analysis than it at first appears.

Occasionally, after an analytic intervention, Mrs. S became distressed and furious, wanted to cover her ears, and could barely restrain the impulse to throw objects around the office. If she talked at all, it was to report through clenched teeth in a strained voice that she was so angry she could barely keep from killing me, or she might shrilly and stridently accuse me of being a blundering incompetent and want to leave the treatment. When she calmed down somewhat she could say that she was afraid that I might "really" be ineffective and that she might be in "bad hands." But she also felt anguished by the idea that she would be better off leaving. These sequential reactions and her accompanying inaccessibility to analytic work would continue for several days and diminish in intensity only with my repeated attempts to explore her subjective experience of the transaction.

These incidents were puzzling, seemingly unconnected with the content of any particular intervention, and in contrast to much else in the analysis. During the initial rage reaction, however, no attempt at transference interpretation was possible without her construing the attempt as hypocritical self-justification. Gradually, the reactions themselves became less syntonic and the patient, her curiosity engaged, began to notice that she reacted during interventions that were not parsimonious. The longer the intervention, the more intense the reaction. The reaction turned out to be connected to a trauma. Longer interventions reminded her of the "long-winded" manner of speaking of a surgeon who had been responsible for a frightening medical procedure in her childhood and was seen over a period of years for dreaded follow-up visits. The rage in the transference was a heretofore repressed affective dimension of this trauma, which also defended against intense anxiety. When the connection became clear, the reaction was no longer accompanied by a loss of the as-if quality of the transference, and the unconscious fantasies connected to that event could be explored.

A transference psychosis occurs in ego structure prone to sudden structural regression. Individuals with character structures dominated by drive discharge and characterized by rapid and unpredictable shifts of affect, ideation, and organization corresponding to Kernberg's (1976) third level of character pathology, for instance, show the inapplicability of the concept of transference neurosis most starkly. The moment excitation increases, ego functions are overwhelmed and the patient is unable to perceive the analyst as different enough from primary object representations, themselves the product of fantasy-motivated perception, to experience the analyst as part of a new organization shaped by the past. This rapid dedifferentiation differs not only from the more flexible and less prolongedly catastrophic reaction in the transference neurosis but also from the disturbance of reality testing in the transference perversion I shall presently describe. Patients in the latter category sacrifice a portion of the as-if quality of the transference to preserve the whole, a maneuver that repeats their organized childhood solution to conflict. In the more character-disordered or borderline patients I am now referring to, the sacrifice of reality testing and discrimination among object representations is not part of a circumscribed conflict solution, but rather of a more massive and global process.

In such a patient, the only possible locus of the recognition of an evolving transference is the analyst because only the analyst's ego is flexible enough to experience and observe at the same time. Given the necessarily dual role of the analyst as interpreter and more than ordinarily alone discriminator among subjective experiences, such a transference may frequently manifest itself as a countertransference in the broader meaning of the term.

Dr. L described the ongoing attempt at analysis of a man whose pathology she considered to lie on a severely narcissistic/borderline axis. His ego disorganization precluded an organized transference neurosis from occurring. Based on the data she offered, we could say that the clinical situation was one of a consistently hostile transference in which the analyst was seen as the abusive parents whom the patient wanted to kill. It seems that he could maintain a distinction between those parental object representations and that of the analyst only occasionally and only if the analyst took infinite care. The lack of distance Dr. L mentioned was a sign of that inability to discriminate. It short-circuited into the delusion that the analyst and the primary objects were identical.

> In the office, there are barely containable impulses to act out. And fifty-minute silences. It's almost impossible to interpret anything. You approach him as though he were a baby of eighteen months who'd had

a high fever. You can't touch him. You can't offer him milk, you can't do anything that doesn't get him furious. Scathing, bitter, sarcastic, denigrating. Or silent. Enraged. You can't do anything.

The last thing he said to me before the break the summer before last was "You're going to have to really try if you're going to do away with this trust." He meant to say "mistrust." That slip was my only encouragement.

He transfers to me an entire abnormal childhood. He was treated abysmally. He wasn't physically abused, but he was abused in every other possible way. He's an example of soul murder, a production of his mother, created to satisfy her, and steamrolled by a father. He never thought he was worth anything. I'm all of these people to him. Whatever I say is taken as a power move; he has to counter it with a self-protective power move.

Most of the time, I ask him how he's feeling. Because he's been silent a good ten or fifteen minutes, I say, "This is a long silence. How are you feeling?" And he will respond either with complete silence, not even emotion, or he'll say something that wipes me off the face of the earth. "Why can't you ever think of anything to say?" "You should know, you're the shrink." And: "Look it up in your books. You can find out what I'm thinking."

He's repeating a desperate hiding. He fears a terrible attack and he received many attacks. In fact, his brain, which is very agile, was overpowered by his father throughout his childhood. The only area he ever won at was in playing chess. So our sessions are chess games. Only I'm not playing. And he's gradually coming to realize that I'm not playing chess.

The only way he does any work at all is by playing around with an idea, with me as the audience. One day he had an idea about colors. He said, "You're always asking me that fucking question, how do I feel? I don't know how I feel." That was one session. The next session he said, "There's an idea that I had about colors. If every color is associated with a feeling, you could give a person a color chart . . . "; very elaborate system, but it ended up that by picking colors, you'd be able to indicate how you felt. So it was on the tip of my tongue to say, "You're telling me this because you want to be able to answer my question, 'how do you feel?' " I didn't say it. Because by then I knew he was just going to shut up. Or get mad at me and leave, and that would be the end of that. So I just said, "That's an interesting idea."

If I'm interested, then he's threatened, too. Because he thinks I'm admiring him, and then he has an erotic fantasy. But that's become a little more manageable. So we can go on talking now if I say something's interesting. He went on with the color fantasy and figured out a

> way of coding using children's first associations with colors. They would be the purest. And he could work out this whole system whereby people could convey all their feelings simply by denoting the colors. Then he said, "What would happen if a child were trained in a certain color system and could communicate his feelings through these colors and then someone switched the colors? So red meant something else? Blue meant something else?" And then I was able to say, "That's what happened to you" without his getting furious.
>
> His lack of distance paralyzes me. You can't make any kind of an interpretation. I think that I'm getting awfully angry, but I remember that he's really in pain all the time.
>
> His impulsiveness and tendency to act rather than putting something in words and getting any kind of distance make this very difficult. Distancing is an ego ability. You need it to analyze character, but the impulse threatens us all the time. He loses distance. In fact, he never has distance. Any emotion can rapidly build up into an erotic fantasy, whether it's anger or pleasure or curiosity, anything. Anything can excite him to a danger point.
>
> There will never really be a transference neurosis. There's something transferred, but it's so chaotic and so immediate for this patient that I really doubt he will ever be able to analyze it. If I'm really lucky, he'll do a certain amount of changing and growing. And then he'll leave, probably in a rage that I couldn't do more for him.

The analyst could not work with the patient's hostile feelings as transference. In a neurotic patient, genetic interpretation of a hostile transference contributes to the differentiation of the object representation of the analyst necessary for the transferring process to deepen. But where the analyst loses his or her interpretive authority because the patient's ability to differentiate is so tenuous, his or her words themselves may be experienced as present malevolent actions from an object perceived as dangerous. Projected rage toward primary objects too quickly and thoroughly takes over the experience of the present and obliterates from the patient's mind any representation of a more neutral analyst that might have existed. The fragile awareness of the differentiated analyst needed for perspective on the past and for communication in the present vanishes. The patient cannot perceive the transference process in a delusional transference. The lack of differentiation among object representations makes perception of the transfer impossible.

Thus the structural marker of the clinical interchange was that a mutually perceived transference process did not exist. The result of Dr. L's awareness of this danger was that she focused instead on technical modifications that would enable the patient to perceive her as different from his representations of primary objects. She tried to maintain the fragile present connection to her to create a contrast with the past, which in turn could be used to discriminate past from present experience. But such a careful, conscious attempt to build up a connection simultaneously allowed the patient to enact his vengeance on his parents/analyst. If one listens, one may have the impression that Dr. L feels her patient moving in for a checkmate, cornering, frustrating, and intimidating her so that she can barely move. "If she is lucky" the patient will "do a certain amount of growing and changing" and then "leave in a rage." And if she is not so lucky? The analyst's present experience may be the closest reproduction to the patient's subjective interpretation of his past.[2]

Such an enacted reversal, also present in Dr. M's case, is frequent in transference processes verging on the psychotic. In such cases, there is only one observing ego. Only the analyst has the capacity to discriminate and create the awareness of transference, which is also its possibility. It is the analyst who must attempt to separate present from past and subject from object through interpretation. Interpretation creates the space, if anything can, between analyst and primary object representations so that the patient can perceive the fact of the transference.

The transference evolution in a potential transference psychosis may begin with the analyst's sense of constraint and need for great care in intervention, but must move on to the analyst's noting that constraint, discriminating his or her subjective reactions as those are evoked by the patient, and ultimately using those reactions as the basis of interpretations until the patient begins to know himself and his wishes and memories and is able to discriminate them from his perception of the world around him. What must happen, then, is enough ego integration to allow a therapeutic split so that core conflicts from childhood and earlier psychotic transference conflicts may be reexperienced and reintegrated with the more integrated structure now available.

It is possible to delineate other transference organizations reflecting distinct, though less dramatically shifting ego structure. Of course, an argument can be made for extending the transference neurosis to encompass a greater number of solutions to childhood conflict, even some that involve an obvious structural element. For example, I am about to describe a transference perversion the organizational signature of which is contradictorily functioning ego structures. Instead of holding that these structures are a sign of a different organization of the ego, one could contend that the core

2. Several years after the interview, Dr. L told me that she had indeed been lucky. The patient has terminated the treatment on friendly terms with her, better able to carry on relationships with the people around him and somewhat less uncomfortable within himself.

conflict the transference neurosis needed to reach and resolve is that expressed by the contradictorily functioning structures. Certainly there are cases on the boundary where it does seem more apt to think only in terms of conflict and not also of ego structure—Dr. T's minister, perhaps (see chap. 4). In many cases, however, it seems to me that the concept of the core conflict would become too broad, the specificity and helpfulness of focusing on the contradiction would be lost, and we would reenter a world of oxymoronic categories.

My argument applies equally to the arguments advanced by those analysts who follow Brenner (1982) in preferring to minimize technical vocabulary and discard the concept of the transference neurosis in favor of more general analyzable transferential compromise formations. They too would probably consider the analysis of the central conflict organized around a defensive splitting of the ego, which I have made central to my definition of transference perversion, as no different in concept from the analysis of any other conflict. It is consistent with that position that Brenner (1992) has argued in favor of jettisoning the structural theory and its ego/superego/id conceptual apparatus. It is worth noting that the serious doubts (e.g., Shapiro, 1992) this formulation has raised include the question of how, without an idea of agency, one could account for diachronic consistency in conflict solution.

The Transference Perversion

Certain patients with narcissistic pathology and concomitant disturbances in their object relations engage in a rather consistent, often sexualized undermining of the defining aspects of the psychoanalytic situation. The development of the treatment, more repetitive than progressive, differs from a transference neurosis in that, in these patients, childhood conflict solutions common to perversion alter the ego in ways which impede the synthesis characteristic of neurosis without the disorganization of psychosis. It seems possible that such an ego-altering conflict solution may give rise to a distinctive psychoanalytic process to the extent that we might consider risking unintended judgmental connotations to denominate a transference perversion parallel to a transference neurosis. Etchegoyen (1991) has done so from a Kleinian perspective, making consistent "ego dissociation" and the attempt to perpetuate an "illusory subject-object unity" (p. 197) cardinal features of his clinical description. Following Joseph (1971), he also emphasized underlying sadism, oral/genital confusion, and the eroticization of the transference through projective identification.

By utilizing Freud's late and extremely creative thinking about mental functioning which he first enunciated in describing the operations of fetish formation (Freud, 1927), it is possible to integrate recent emphases on narcissism, (part) object relations, and preoedipal pathology into the conflict model. Relevant allied work includes Renik's (1992) description of certain patients' use of the analyst as a fetish, Coen's (1992) concept of perverse enactments in pathologically dependent patients, Chasseguet-Smirgel's (1984) characterization of the transference of perverse patients as lacking the space for alliance, and McDougall's (1985, 1986) emphasis on the intermediary category of illusion in "neo-sexualities."

It is important to underline that I am discussing patients with character structure the essence of which is its patterned changeability. These analysands shift rapidly but not chaotically from more advanced to more primitive structural configurations. That means, for example, that they can move, in short order, from relating to whole objects to treating the other as a fetish or part object. If I emphasize that the perverse solution to conflict is organized around castration anxiety, I do not mean castration anxiety to imply stable triadic whole object relations or neurotic-level psychic structure. On the contrary, object relations tend toward the narcissistic end of the spectrum. The perverse solution to conflict organizes anxieties at all levels and permits their coexistence by creating a structure characterized by rapid shifts in its composition.

The transference material I have in mind has in common a repetitive, sexualized enactment that is often hard to discern. The enactment is used to avoid facing either castration anxiety or castration depressive affect (L. Grossman, 1992) as well as anxieties and conflicts from earlier developmental levels related to object loss, separation, and destructiveness, which inform and make more intense those involving castration (McDougall, 1985). The avoidance and the sexualized enactments utilize defenses common to conflict resolution in the perversions: disavowal, the substitution of something contiguous common to fetish formation, and a splitting of the ego. Since I wish to emphasize commonalities among patients different in gender and the specifics of their enactment, I shall describe several cases in succession.

Dr. Paola A

The obvious aspect of Dr. Paola A's enactment was a concretization of thought processes that annihilated the analysis. It proved to be connected to an unrecognized transference submission. A foreign-born research physician, she had a preanalytic history of attachments to wealthy men of questionable business ethics whom she took pride in "pleasuring." Although they openly engaged with prostitutes in her proximity, she never noticed, but instead saw herself as different and her relation to these men as special.

She worked hard in individual analytic sessions, associating, responding productively to interpretations, and in general, trying to understand herself. Then, suddenly, her voice would become hard and angry and she would talk about wanting money. It was as though all previous insight was annihilated, that we had never discovered specific unconscious meaning, nor realized the relevance of any of her extremely difficult life experiences to her current experience.

Many patients, of course, defend, sometimes tenaciously, against the acquisition of insight that will ultimately involve their experiencing anxiety in the course of surrendering a protected position; moreover, as an analysis progresses, new compromise formations emerge, some of them in the nature of an enacted struggle. But generally one has an inkling of an incremental acquisition of insight. In this case, however, the annihilation seemed impervious to process; it was sudden, persistent, and for many years apparently unchanging. The concreteness of the thinking that accompanied it left no "space" for analytic exploration (Chasseguet-Smirgel, 1984).

Dr. Paola A's sudden and massive disregard of acquired insight engendered feelings in me of frustration, impatience, and criticism to which I had a tendency to react countertransferentially by reminding her of the forgotten or disregarded insights at which we had already arrived. When I began instead to inquire into her experience of the analytic situation, it became clear that my assumption of collaboration had been misguided. The seemingly productive work had involved a fantasy of submission. The consulting room was a place to which she daily came anticipating humiliation and punishment. Even my attempt to investigate her experience of the treatment situation was experienced as an inquest with intent to inflict pain. If I pointed out that she seemed to need to forget the hard work she did, she experienced my observation as a chastisement. When I asked whether she had any inkling of why she seemed to need to experience my inquiries in this way, she felt similarly accused. My linking her forgetting to her need to experience the analytic situation as a humiliation was another humiliation. In short, except for the periods in which she turned the tables by wiping out the analysis and me, what I said was experienced transferentially as coming from a condemning, all-powerful judge.

A silent fantasy of submission is not by itself surprising in a vulnerable patient, of course. Dr. A's mother had become incapacitated when Dr. A was a child, and my patient had been lonely, frightened, and left prey to the attacks of a seemingly sadistic, considerably older stepbrother. Analytic work had revealed the penis envy beneath her conscious envy of her stepbrother's superior strength and intellectual prowess. As a child she imagined that his maleness brought him their mother's obvious preference and that her femaleness was responsible for her mother's abandonment of her when the mother withdrew to a sickbed. But neither the interpretation of this constellation, including her guilt over her wish to take his penis from him, nor additional work on rage at her mother for not protecting her and ensuing fears of object loss or on other issues related to early guilt over a belief in having made her mother ill and to separation anxiety made inroads into the concreteness she reverted to over money in the transference enactment.

Significantly, however, after I stopped reacting to her concreteness about money by reminding her of forgotten insights and began to explore more fully her experience of punishment and humiliation, she had an anxiety dream in which a hermaphroditic figure she associated to me had a bloody wound in place of a penis. Dr. A associated the wound to previous work we had done on her sense of herself as a vulnerable and wounded female and on her envy of her stepbrother's masculine strength. She further thought of an amputation her mother had undergone as a result of her illness. Women, she remembered fearing, got cut up and hurt. She next thought of her childhood fears of being raped, mutilated, and murdered by a male intruder, of her fears of what her stepbrother would do to her, of her growing sense that her mother had preferred her stepbrother, refused to see his viciousness, and never protected Dr. A from him. If she had been a boy, she thought, she would have been loved and protected. This led her to memories of desperate attempts—since she couldn't be a boy—to get her parents' love by being and looking good. She thought about wearing pretty dresses to please them. "The dress became the thing," she remarked, "not their love, just the dress by itself or, now, money. Money will buy a dress." Her voice became steely and hard and she began to berate her current male friend for his failure to provide that money and to berate herself for not exploiting or remaining with one of the wealthy men she had left.

The thought crossed my mind that now that Dr. A did not experience me as her stepbrother attacking her, she was attacking me, that her action was a phallus equivalent and represented the enactment of a fantasy designed to allay her childhood fears of being female and vulnerable. It was difficult to keep my insight in mind, however, for, hearing her tone of voice and knowing that she could continue for the rest of the session in this manner, I was aware of shifting from a sense of involvement and active listening to a sense of impatience mixed with despair. My hope of analyzing the dream was gone, the idea of mutual work was gone. I felt aggravated, deprived, and frustrated. If for Dr. A the fantasy of having acquired a phallus and attacking me had replaced analyzing, the power and concreteness of her prostitute-enactment made me feel helpless about intervening.

Deciding to use my reaction as a way of approaching her disavowal of her vulnerability, I asked Dr. Paola A if she were not trying to make me feel as deprived and unprotected as she had felt as a little girl. She began to cry. She did feel deprived. She was silent and then reported that she was becoming angry. If I didn't have answers to give her, everything became confused. She needed something to hold onto, money or anger. Anger was like being her father or stepbrother. They were frightening. They had guns and knives and used them. She remembered once forcing herself endlessly to put hooks through fish eyes as her stepbrother was doing, pretending it didn't bother her to watch him. If she were like him, she wouldn't need money or protection, certainly not pretty dresses. She was seeing her mother's scar in her mind. She had frequently been asked to dress it. How horrible that had been! She hadn't realized at the time how frightened it had made her. The same thing could have happened to her, could happen to her at any time. I could then tell her that in order to feel that she was not a vulnerable girl who could be sadistically attacked and mutilated by males like her stepbrother or father as she believed her mother had been, she turned on me and annihilated the analysis. Then she could imagine herself as male as her stepbrother was. She could both feel safe and wreak vengeance.

Such insight did not preclude the continuation of the enactment. The annihilation of insight, like the dress, disavowed the female state that she equated with the traumas visited on her. By annihilating recovered affect and memories of her physical vulnerability, she both acted as though she had procured a magic and protective phallus and prevented herself from seeing her mother's scar and all that it unconsciously stood for: her lack of a penis, her vulnerability, her rage at deprivation, and her terror of ensuing object loss. Only steady interpretation of her disavowal and the significance of the particular circumstances that each time heightened her anxiety and motivated her shift to concreteness began gradually to modify the absoluteness of the annihilation of insight. Very, very gradually she came to recognize and need less the vengeance she wreaked on her transference stepbrother and mother each time she annihilated the analysis.

Professor Morton B

In Professor B's case the transference enactment also appeared as an undermining of the analysis. It duplicated anonymous perverse encounters and functioned to disavow anxiety-provoking perceptions and to lend reassurance for the disavowed anxieties at the same time. A slightly built economist in his early forties, popular with undergraduates because of his personableness and willingness to be helpful to students in distress, Professor B led a fundamentally lonely life. As the treatment he reluctantly engaged in nevertheless helped him become more successful in his scholarly work, he began increasingly to seek out anonymous sexual encounters with men. His pleasure came from controlling his partner by exciting him into desire for his penis.

Nor surprisingly, in the transference, he would make significant connections, raising my expectation and interest in the continuation of the work, and then undermine the continuity with a series of absences. While

regulated her excitement?

exploring the meaning of the sexual encounters, for instance, Professor B gradually saw how controlling men by exciting them both bolstered his fragile sense of his masculinity and reassured him that he could control them and thus prevent them from attacking him. He then remembered, with great anxiety, how his father would accost him in fits of rage and threaten to castrate him. I would feel pleased with the insight he had achieved and anticipate further productive work. Professor B would then cancel several sessions and come back and describe the anonymous sexual activities with which he had replaced his sessions. I took up both his need to avoid looking at his anxiety over his father's threat, and his turning of the treatment into a duplicate of his reassuring sexual encounters with men. Professor B welcomed the insight, connected it to the previous insights about his fear of his father and the harm he feared his father would do to him if he were successful, and then missed more sessions. I began to address Professor B's avoiding looking at his anxieties by questioning in a variety of ways how he thought he might work his fears out if he continued to subordinate our work to maintaining the transference seduction and control of me. He knew his behavior made no sense at the same time that, at the moment of acting, he avoided knowing.

Avoiding knowing or looking at reality was endemic to him because reality, as the following sequence illustrates, had the unconscious meaning of the female genital as a sign of castration (Arlow, 1971). Professor B remarked one day that he had picked up the check for a large group of people in an expensive restaurant the night before. He did not want to think about his depleted checking account balance or how he would pay his credit card bill. He went on to connect his need to be a big spender with wishes that I look at and admire him. He reported an urge to expose himself to me so that I would see how big his penis was and be impressed. I linked these wishes to his anonymous sexual encounters and to his preferring to arouse a man with his big penis than to look with me at how frightened he was of losing his. He thought about not wanting to visit his mother and mentioned that he had felt intensely anxious coming to my office that day on the subway. The thought of the subway made him shudder. It was dirty, dark, dangerous, sleazy, filled with germs. I pointed out that he'd made a connection between losing his penis, coming to my office, not wanting to visit his mother, and feeling frightened of the subway as a dirty, underground place that was dangerous and germ-filled. That sounded like a vagina, but he did not want to think about all that, he said dismissively. The way he didn't want to look at his bank balance, I started to say. Professor B interrupted me to tell a joke about the wife of a dictator who bought an astonishing number of shoes. When I pointed out that he seemed to be trying to drown me out, he stopped talking and fell asleep.

As he gradually felt closer to me in a maternal transference, his anxiety at entering my office escalated as did the frequency of his making exciting discoveries and missing sessions. He declared with bravado that he would solve all his problems directly and leave the treatment, but as he lay sleeping beside the woman he had chosen for this purpose, he had nightmares that his father was attacking him with a knife. He gradually realized that his avoidance of the sessions was an avoidance of his castration anxiety, and that entering my office had the unconscious significance of vaginal penetration. He was panicked by the thought that his father would intrude into my consulting room and attack him. He reexperienced his sense of childhood inadequacy in the face of his father's power.

He was simultaneously afraid that I would trap him inside of me, so that he would not be able to get out. Associations to that worry led not only to his fantasy of a suffocating and uncontrollable mother but to his relating the comfort he derived from hiding out alone in his house with the blinds drawn, as though it were a cave, drinking sodas through a straw and seeing no one. He felt that his regressive defensive wish to be inside me as he wished once to be inside his mother was frightening as well as intensely humiliating. He preferred violent posturing, threats, and controlling me through excitation and interruption.

Controlling me in this way spared him not only the terror of penetrating a woman and finding himself his father's victim but of being alone, separated from his mother and yearning for and being vulnerable to her. If the thought of being in the power of a woman terrified him, so did terminating. I was his magic amulet, he declared; if I were not available to him, he imagined that he would be emasculated.

Mrs. Jane C

Mrs. Jane C also turned the analysis from a search for insight into a subtly enacted, enduring conflict solution in which insight became a desired conflict solution. A twenty-seven-year-old married musician and mother, she remembered latency masturbation fantasies of playing the clarinet to wild applause and excitedly described perverse activities involving urinating standing up. Both the effort to excite me and the sexual activities enumerated were associated with moments in which she believed that I had everything and she had nothing. Thus these efforts seemed to be an attempt to contain envious and destructive impulses. A heightening of Mrs. C's obsessive concerns about her body's being anything other than "straight and long" also accompanied the intensification of envious transference feelings.

She frequently dismissed her own associations, effectively withholding them. Often, moreover, she would reiterate her difficulties, evincing no memory of the unconscious meaning of her doing so, although just the previous day insight into those meanings had been the focus of the session. She would then react to a repetition of the previous day's discovery with great excitement, saying "I never realized that before." The excitement, repetition and palpable feeling of enhancement that accompanied it signaled that the interaction had important transference meaning. If, however, I sought to explore the reasons for her excitement rather than responding with comparable excitement to her sense of understanding and possessing new insight, she would feel worthless and convinced of my contempt.

Every insight was in this way turned into an occasion to exhibit an acquisition. The insight was then forgotten and the process of acquisition repeated. Every attempt on my part to analyze either the excitement or the whole pattern led to manifestly painful depression and suffering on her part. She was convinced that I was condemning what she had showed me as no good. Eventually she revealed that when she felt excited the excitement was accompanied by a conscious experience that she was exhibiting not only her unparalleled musical technique but her penis to me. When I did not show the responsive excitement she desired, she felt disappointed and deflated and the experience ceased to have the qualities of something real. Forgetting allowed her to repeat the sense that she had acquired and was showing me her penis.

Yet, even while experiencing the interaction as the actualization of her fantasy, Mrs. C was at the same time conscious that she didn't have a penis and was not going to acquire one, just as she also knew I was not contemptuous of her. This divided state of knowing and not knowing was also present in Dr. Paola A who knew and did not know that money was not the equivalence of masculinity and in Professor Morton B who knew and did not know that by replacing the sessions with homosexual encounters he was not going to work out the problems that led to his loneliness. Mrs. C spoke about this mental state of knowing and not knowing at the same time. I had pointed out to her in the course of an hour that out of the very envy she was talking about feeling she was stopping me from adding something that might be helpful to her. In a new tone that expressed mild amazement, yet also disapproval of herself, she said, "This has made the analysis much more difficult!" When I asked what she would have come for if she hadn't had a difficulty, she replied, "I never thought there was a problem for me to *work* on. I still don't at the same time that I do. I think I just have to hold out until you make me into what I want to be."

As her envy was addressed, Mrs. C recognized the great difficulty she had in holding onto the possibility that her understanding of anything that happened between us might be of interest to *both* of us because it was a product of *her* motivated interpretation. The growing ability to work *with* me marked the progress of the treatment. Nevertheless, for a very long time, insight was an opportunity to exhibit her instrument, and her reaction to my attempts to explore that exhibition was to experience me as depriving her of her acquisition. Forgetting was a means of repeating the experience.

Mr. Arnold D

In Mr. Arnold D's case, the relevant enactment was split off from the treatment to an extratransference relationship and supported by a fantasy of being a special patient. When that organization broke down, other omnipotent tokens became necessary and the analysis was interrupted. A writer from the South with severe work inhibitions and a general life paralysis, Mr. D suffered from impotence and had masturbated since childhood with a variety of perverse thoughts including imagining himself as a woman with a phallus. A picture of his mother as narcissistic, seductive, possessive, and extremely envious emerged. During the analysis, he began to recall her telling him stories about little boys who were castrated by strange men when they tried to be independent. In addition, Mr. D had felt ferociously rivalrous with an orphaned male cousin who lived with the family. When his cousin was killed by a motorcycle, Mr. D became immobilized by a terror of retaliation for hostile impulses related to that rivalry. The cousin's death became condensed in his mind with the castration story told him by his mother, and he handled both his knowledge about the female genital and its lack of a penis and his knowledge of his cousin's death by knowing and not knowing about them at the same time.

Mr. D had started a rather sadomasochistic relationship with a woman soon after the analysis began. The significance of the relationship and its particular sexual interaction, work showed, was that he was unconsciously bringing his cousin back to life. As long as the relationship continued, the analysis went smoothly. During the first three years work on destructive conflicts impeding separation and on competitive conflicts connected with castration anxiety and his cousin's death liberated him sufficiently for him to undertake a major career challenge. The potency symptom was also alleviated. When, in the fourth year of the analysis, he left his girlfriend, however, he brought the sadomasochistic behavior more directly into the transference.

In outrage occasioned by his now hearing an intervention as a slight, he described the assurance he had held since the beginning of the analysis that he was and had been progressing through its various stages as a model patient would. Even when he had been very angry at me, he had always imagined that his expression of anger made him a better patient.

He began to hold onto my interpretations by repeating them, struggling to understand them and to take them in. He worked them over intellectually. He would not understand and ask me to repeat. If I pointed out his behavior, he would hold onto that and work it over, or not understand and be stymied and request that I explain my intervention once again. Eventually associating to his behavior, he recalled latency fellatio experiences with a friend and thought about his cousin's smashed, dead body with great anxiety and then about his girlfriend. He recalled previous work in which he had realized he had made her into his male cousin to ward off the terror the recognition of the latter's death evoked in him and how he had believed as a child that women had penises. He felt terribly frightened when he thought that they did not, just as he felt frightened when he thought about his cousin being smashed up and dead. Underlining his insight and connecting it to his transference enactment, I pointed out that he was taking in my words as though he were taking in my penis in the same way he had wanted to suck on his cousin's penis to assure himself that his cousin was not mutilated, that girls were not without penises, and that he, himself, would not be smashed or castrated if he tried to be independent. He thought about one of his mother's castration stories and then began to repeat my interpretation and work it over. When I tried to point out what he was now doing to allay his terror, he repeated the behavior. Treating my interpretations in this way made him feel protected from his envious mother and supported from having to face the outside world. There motorcycles crashed and you could become pulp. At other anxious times he reported fantasies of sharing a penis with me so as to please me and of sharing his penis with his mother so as to mitigate the envy which he was afraid he would arouse if he succeeded.

Indeed, he had begun to use the analysis to divert his attention from looming challenges in reality linked with success. When I tried to point out this avoidance, however, he either worked over my words again or complained about my unsupportive attitude and about his fee. He began to overspend, acting as though he had unlimited financial supplies. When his deteriorating financial situation finally forced itself on him, he began to face his anxiety about "sticking out his neck" to complete a major piece of writing he needed to finish in order to advance in life. Although he began steps to complete it and faced the need to interrupt his treatment, he simultaneously began a relationship with an older woman.

Discussion of Cases

In each of these patients, transference action and content were related through disavowal. From the point of view of action, each of these patients turned the psychoanalytic enterprise into a stable transference enactment that supported a crucial disavowal of a portion of reality. By wiping out acquired insight, for instance, Dr. Paola A treated her analyst as she imagined men sadistically treated women while isolating insight into the significance of traumatic memories which made her aware of anxiety and depression associated with being female and alone. Her enactment also provided her, in fantasy, with a phallus equivalent that disavowed her vulnerable, female state. Mrs. C acquired insight, exhibited it, and forgot it in order to set the stage for acquiring and exhibiting it once again. In that way knowledge that she was without a penis could be disregarded. Professor B protected himself against his fear of his father and the latter's castration threats by duplicating in the transference the control he exercised in his homosexual encounters by exciting men. At the same time, he avoided his heterosexual wishes and the intense anxiety they engendered by avoiding entering my office as much as possible.

From the point of view of content, the reality that was disavowed had the significance of the absence of a penis in women. Professor B and Mr. D equated unpleasant reality such as the fact of a financial limit with the knowledge of the female genital. In the transference, they avoided knowledge of their avoidance and the castration anxiety linked to it by enacting reassuring homosexual interactions. Mrs. C and Dr. Paola A equated their female state with castration, disavowed it, and enacted a fantasy in which they magically acquired phallic equivalents. Mrs. C exhibited a penis in showing her insight.

To be sure, these patients' castration concern did not exist in isolation from other issues. It also represented earlier anxieties that had become integrated into it. By sadistically turning on me and annihilating insight, Dr. Paola A avoided facing a highly condensed set of anxieties that included retaliation for her envy and fear of object loss owing to her destructiveness and guilt over ills she believed she had inflicted in childhood. Professor B feared separation from a mother he experienced as engulfing as well as castration at the hands of his father; indeed, the latter intensified the former.

Each of the patients described used the analytic situation to counteract unwished for perception by creating out of the analytic interaction a circumscribed world in which the analyst provided a magical solution to those fears or depressive affects that would be stimulated by the recognition of the absence of a penis in women. Professor B turned the analyst into a magic amulet under his control. Mrs. C imbued insight with the significance of a phallus. Mr. D brought his dead cousin, whose death he equated with castration, back to life.

In each case, creation and re-creation were imbued with significant omnipotence and isolated so that the transference enactment was experienced as a circumscribed actuality even after its unconscious significance was understood. Mr. D continued to turn my interventions that he was turning my interventions into a homosexual interaction with his resurrected cousin into that interaction. Mrs. C recognized that she had to work on her problem herself *at the same time* that she believed that I would change her. These contradictions were not experienced as ego dystonic conflicts. The patients were unaware of the contradictions and their pervasiveness and strove valiantly to remain so.

Such contradiction is a sign of an ego organized by conflict solutions employing perverse defenses—that is, disavowal, splitting, and the creation of a fetish or its equivalent. When Freud (1927, 1938) described how the sight of the female genital with its lack of a penis made palpable and terrifying the possibility of castration, he specified that "a rift in the ego which never heals but increases as time goes on" (1938, p. 276) permitted instinctual satisfaction to be pursued at the same time that external danger is recognized. In the portion of the mind in which instinctual satisfaction was permitted, a disavowal of the absence of a penis in women took place. One can note derivatives of this conflict in Professor B's unwillingness to think about his depleted bank balance and his attempts not to hear my intervention that he did not want to look at it. Disavowal thus begins with a refusal to look or hear or remember or otherwise let register external perception.

Contiguity operates to provide a replacement for the missing penis not only when a fetish is formed but when a phallic equivalent will be used to allay anxiety and permit sexual excitement but not become implicated in sexual activity that leads to orgasm. As the observer averts his gaze, he substitutes whatever his eyes alight on for the thing that is not. The looking away also involves a narrowing of the field to be observed in order to eliminate everything but the substitute that by its presence denies the missing phallus. One analysand who watched videos featuring women's genitalia but insisted that the actual genitalia were blurred, looked at a piece of underwear, at a nipple, or at pubic hair. Only then could he become excited. This maneuver becomes the unconscious organizer for common derivative actions: Professor B's interrupting my attempt to confront him with his castration fear to tell a joke about a woman who bought many pairs of shoes, Mrs. C taking an insight out of its analytic context, treating it as the discovery of something new, and exhibiting it, an analysand's picking up of a tangential detail and concentrating on it at the expense of the whole or constantly sliding away from an anxiety situation to a tangential subject.

The result of this defensive activity is the well-recognized mode of cognitive thinking in which simultaneously a realistic attitude and one characterized by omnipotent thought coexist. In a rhythm of disavowal and the substitution of illusion, the latter replaces the former. Thus after insight into the fantasy quality of the transference enactment and its defensive significance, again and again these patients' belief in the enacted fantasy world was reinstated and the insight into its meaning was obliterated. Moral injunctions, another unpleasant aspect of the external world, are similarly disregarded (L. Grossman, 1993). As Chasseguet-Smirgel wrote, "Perversion appears as a rebellion against the universal law of the Oedipus Complex" (1984, p. 26).

In describing a transference perversion, I am extending perversion to derivative character manifestations (Arlow, 1971) and assuming it to be the longitudinal transference expression of an ego organized to permit the continuing of sexual activity in the face of the disturbing perception (or knowledge of the existence) of the female genital where the latter is taken as evidence of castration. Earlier anxieties influence this choice, and later conflicts become integrated according to its solution with the degree and type of interrelated oedipal and preoedipal conflict varying (Coen, 1992).

Transference Derivatives

Since analysis requires the patient and analyst to recognize and accept anxiety-provoking situations and unpleasant, even unpalatable truths, there exists a basic discontinuity between mutual collaboration and the operation of an ego that employs perverse defenses. Renik (1992) has excellently described the clinical result of persistent disavowal: "The patient does not persevere in the pursuit of truth in the face of unpleasurable affect. Such patients take the path of least resistance—and do the same again if confronted with the unpleasant fact that they have just taken the path of least resistance" (p. 551).

But if the operation of disavowal within a limited sector dispenses with a disagreeable truth, then the analysis cannot be seen in that sector as a mutual search for a truth that will be unpleasant but necessary to confront. Analysis must therefore become something else, and it is imbued with magic and turned into a circumscribed world unconsciously composed of interchangeable body parts and the sexualized relations between them (see Roustang, 1984; McDougall, 1985) in which the object engages with the subject in a way that obliterates sexual and other related (e.g., generational) differences (Chasseguet-Smirgel, 1984).[3] Dr. A, for instance, turned the tables, becoming male and hard-edged. It is also a metonymic world where part substitutes for the whole, or more specifically, whole objects are replaced by fetishes or their equivalents. Mrs. C fantasized winning me with her penis, but there was little distinction initially for her between acquiring a penis and possessing me in the sense of exercising omnipotent control. In one interchange in this fantasy world the object is experienced as providing or maintaining the existence of the penis so that separating from the object is synonymous with castration. Thus Professor B turned me into an amulet and equated termination with emasculation.

The creation of the fantasy world of the transference perversion roughly follows the pattern of displacement and narrowing of focus utilized in the creation of the fetish. In the clinical dimension of its creation, the patient

3. Roustang's (1984) work on Casanova's memoirs provides a remarkable description of this world.

diverts his attention and narrows his focus away from the analyst as a whole to a convenient and ordinarily neutral activity of the analyst—the giving of an interpretation, for example. In fantasy, the patient may turn that activity into the giving of a penis needed to ward off anxiety or into the confirmation of the presence of a penis, as well as turning it into the continuation of sexual activity that the fear or actuality of castration would otherwise have stopped. For Mrs. C, my interpreting was the equivalent of my giving her the penis she wanted. She could then excitedly exhibit it to me. Dr. A, on the other hand, maintained her belief in having a phallus by disabling me and the insights into her conflicted sense of being female that resulted from our work together. She used her disavowal of that work to put me in her place as the vulnerable female and sadistically attack me. Professor B used his ability to make significant connections to tantalize and control me, exhibiting himself sexually in fantasy to gain reassurance that his transference father would not castrate him. At the same time he disavowed his terror of entering my office, which he unconsciously equated with penetrating a vagina since being in my office confronted him with the female genital. The patient maintains the illusion that the fantasy is real through the analyst's necessary repetition of the chosen activity. Evidence of "excitement" on the part of the analyst, such as my interest in Professor B's insights, reinforces the disavowal of reality.

The contradictory thinking characteristic of the simultaneous disavowal and acceptance of the woman's lack of a penis is applied to the analyst. For the belief in the perverse transference fantasy world to be maintained, it must be accompanied by a partial disavowal of the fact that what the analyst provides is metaphoric. Thus the patient disavows the "as-if" or, as I shall refer to it, the "illusory" relation to the analyst in the circumscribed sphere of the perverse fantasy world. This disavowal coexists with a more apparently adaptable, reasoned approach to the analyst and the analysis—thus my patients' simultaneous seeing and not seeing their contradictory behavior I have already detailed.

Where patients find a way to create and maintain a perverse transference fantasy world, the motivation to perpetuate the transference compromise powerfully opposes wishes to terminate. Indeed, *termination becomes the transference equivalent of disturbing external perception.*

Of course, every patient to some extent avoids looking at painful conflicts, enacts a fantasy derivative in the transference in which he or she believes, has wishes gratified in it that he or she is loath to give up, transiently loses the as-if character of the transference; however, the sequestered and delimited illusory world that is maintained as real through a sexualized transference enactment is not something I would expect to encounter *with comparable delineation, persistence and concreteness* in a neurotic patient. The neurotic ego is more able to recognize and regulate action based on wishes for omnipotence. While I would not be surprised to find derivatives of these wishes, or their transient expressions, or find them as a phase in which a layer of narcissistic character defenses were worked through, I would in general anticipate a more flexible movement back and forth between fantasies and the recognition that fantasies that involve the alteration of reality cannot be permanently actualized. This relative flexibility is a reflection of defenses that do not so entirely interfere with the synthetic function of the ego, of anxieties less overwhelming, of destructiveness less unmodulated. On the other hand, these are not psychotic phenomena. The *sequestration* of the illusory world, its maintenance as an island untouched by rational considerations at the same time that the latter are left free to be applied in other areas of functioning, differentiates this material from a psychotic transference. Glover (1932) aptly formulated the perverse solution as a sacrifice of a small part of reality in order to preserve the greater part.

Since the existence of fantasy qua fantasy and the possibility of the patient coming to recognize it are a priori assumptions of the psychoanalytic process, the disavowal subtly undermines all analytic work and in so doing betrays a fundamental destructive motivation. While the disavowal represents a disavowal of the lack of a penis in women which defends against castration anxiety and/or depressive affect, castration anxiety is not by any means the only relevant anxiety. Other, developmentally earlier anxieties and depressive fantasies contribute to its intensity.

Psychoanalysis in any given case is far too complex an endeavor for univocality. To invoke a bedrock concept, as Freud (1937) did, repeats the problem under consideration in the attempted solution. The penis and its lack have specific meanings to each individual, especially in object relational contexts, and these are always also at issue (Grossman and Stewart, 1977). An underlying destructiveness particularly contributes both to a tenuous connection to primary objects, especially the maternal object, and to an instability in body image and sexual identity. Stoller (1975) fittingly called perversion "the erotic form of hatred." The intense destructiveness, instability of body image, and attendant tenuous object connections motivate the attempt to use the analyst to actualize a fantasy in which the analyst stabilizes the body image either by furnishing the missing part or by confirming its presence. The deep-seated hostile conflicts that manifest themselves in the undermining of the analytic work are precisely those that make the body image so unstable and the need for the object so compelling.

Although many aspects of the patients I have described fit Kohut's (1971, 1977) description of selfobject transference, selfobject transferences denote more circumscribed and specific transferences than the transference perversion. The latter delineates characteristics of a more general process of which selfobject transferences might be considered to form a part. Of course, including selfobject transferences under the rubric of the transference perversion requires the caveat that descriptive similarity not obscure differences in underlying conceptualization. The transference perversion is formulated as the longitudinal reflection of an ego organized around a particular and ongoing conflict solution. The underlying theory assumes that narcissism is always interrelated with conflicts over sexuality and aggression rather than a separate line of development and that the way the individual handles anxiety occasioned by his or her hostile and sexual impulses is primary, not secondary to the regulation of narcissistic supplies.

The conflict solutions that express themselves as a transference perversion grow out of pathology occupying a middle ground between neurosis and psychosis and are related to other useful clinical conceptions, from pathological dependency (Coen, 1992), to descriptions of the vertical splits in narcissistic personality disorders (Kohut, 1977), to patients characterized by conflicts of ambivalence (A. Kris, 1981), to what Kernberg (1976) has described as the middle level of character pathology. From a dynamic standpoint, patients within these interrelated groups have in common anal phase conflicts characterized by ambivalence, as well as related conflicts around separation and bisexuality. The anal stage ambivalence conflicts influence structure and conflict at all future stages. For instance, the failure of adequate libidinization of aggression influences the formation of structure with the most notable result being the lack of synthesis in the ego that Freud (1938) noted in relation to perverse organization. Object representations, similarly unsynthesized, are dominated respectively by the aggressive and libidinal drive derivatives so that the split resulting from the heightened ambivalence is perpetuated in superego as well as ego structure. Oedipal phase conflicts are engaged with this divided legacy as are all attempts to meet the subsequent exigencies of life. Relatedly, Chasseguet-Smirgel (1984) considers the perverse fantasy world to be the product of an anal regression.

The ego-altering perverse defenses I have described as common to the patients with a transference perversion do not, when pervasive, permit a sufficiently developed synthetic function to meet my criteria of transference neurosis. It is possible, of course, that with the resolution of the conflict and ensuing structural change in the direction of more synthetic capacities, a transference neurosis may develop. Certainly, the highest level perverse characters are better able to utilize insight and more rapidly to integrate it. Their transference evolution is less repetitive and more progressive; the undermining is more contained, symbolic, and amenable to transference examination. In their cases the categories of transference neurosis and perversion overlap, but that does not abrogate the existence of a separate transference perversion entity. At the other end of what must be seen as a continuum, in a transference psychosis, ego limitations prevent the relatively consistent discrimination of an internally derived component to perception. Thus, the ego does not distinguish between internal psychic reality and the external facts of the analytic situation. An interpretation becomes a sadistic penetration rather than only appearing so momentarily or only feeling *like* one.

The organization I have described as a transference perversion occupies a middle ground. On the one hand, the ego is sufficiently integrated to know and recognize reality. On the other, it is sufficiently divided simultaneously to entertain as real an omnipotent version of reality at odds with the truth. The patient shifts from the more regressed to the more advanced organization to maintain them both isolated from each other. The shifting lends the analysis its repetitive or circular character, which contrasts with the more progressive evolution characteristic of neurosis.

Technical Consequences of Delineating a Transference Perversion

Circularity should not be confused with a lack of therapeutic progress, however. It is rather part and parcel of the working through of the fundamental shifting from one organization to the other. More specifically, the sense of struggle involved reflects the engagement of the underlying and exceedingly important anal phase conflicts to which I have previously referred. Instead of measuring progress by change in content, although change and deepening of content also occur, more fundamental and characteristic is the increasing space for alliance and for self-observation that occurs simultaneously with the repetition of the undermining as the motivations for the latter are addressed.

In the most successful instances, patients become almost imperceptibly more able and willing to observe their contradictions, address their anxieties, take note of their disavowal and splitting, and explore what motivates those defenses. These changes go hand in hand with a modulation of destructiveness. When her need to exhibit insight was addressed, Mrs. C gradually felt less deflated and derived correspondingly more satisfaction from observing what she was doing with and to me. She became more aware of me as an individual and began to experience painful conflicts about reducing me to a thing out of hatred. Professor B over time grew more aware of the moments at which he sought to control me and could observe and explore the anxiety that drove him. In fact, recognition of the transference perversion as a distinct category from the transference neurosis may prove clinically useful *precisely because it helps the clinician focus on the defensive shifting of organizations and to approach through it the underlying anal conflicts.*

In the transference psychosis, the technical focus needs to be on discrimination of self and other, inner and outer, projection and introjection, that is, on the delineation of structure. In neurosis, when ego and superego are each well integrated, the central focus in analysis can usually be on whatever derivative content and attendant form the patient presents. This is the case whether analyst and patient together investigate ideas or the meaning of an action, a fantasy dominated by defensive measures, punishment, or wish. But when perverse defenses supported by an underlying ambivalence are operating to maintain a split of the type demonstrated by the patients I have discussed, an emphasis on what the patient presents, *without also attending to what he or she disavows and the way he or she does it,* will not be therapeutically effective. Thus I pursued with Professor B as far as possible the intervention he did not want to hear about the way he did not look. Too, the transference intervention to Dr. A that she seemed to be trying to make me feel as disregarded and helpless as she had felt as a child did more than address the phenomenon of her turning passive into active. It confronted her with a realm of childhood experience related to fantasies and anxieties about being female at which she also did not want to look. It required follow-up work on how she enacted in the transference to maintain her disavowal. This follow-up inevitably required the analysis of the hostility mobilized in wiping out the analysis and her analyst.

Since the patient maintains a defensive stability by shifting from the reality-oriented ego organization to the omnipotent and disavowing one, a technique is called for that addresses the transference manifestations of the *split* in the ego, the motivations for the split, the operation of the perverse defenses, and the resulting construction of the sequestered fantasy world characteristic of the transference perversion. Interventions need to focus consistently on the contradictions that the split in the ego defends the patient from knowing exist and the fantasies and mechanisms that maintain it.

Such a technique requires kindly and tactful, but nevertheless persistent, confrontation of the patient with that which he does not wish to look at. It runs counter to an approach derived from self psychology, for example, which emphasizes the patient's need to use the analyst to regulate his self-esteem rather than the need to help the patient see that his *necessary* use of the analyst *also* allows him to avoid disruptive anxiety it would be more helpful for him to confront.

It also, however, runs counter to models of classical analytic technique originally derived from the topographic theory, which emphasize the facilitation of regression and thus favor a rather passive analytic stance including free-floating listening (Arlow, 1987). If the analyst considers it "wrong" to introduce something the patient is avoiding because the patient has not mentioned it in the hour or because the patient's associations appear to be emerging freely as that judgment uses measures of quantity and fluency, it is easy to see how a patient of this type will be able to use the psychoanalytic treatment to please the analyst while continuing to avoid, thus maintaining the transference structure I have delineated.

It is *not* easy to maintain such a therapeutic focus without unwittingly enacting one aspect of the transference role to which the patient has assigned the analyst. Persistent confrontation, no matter how gentle, satisfies patients' masochistic wishes. Persistent patience in the face of the undermining of the analysis gratifies his or her sadistic wishes. Since the pathological goal of the patient is to continue the transference perversion not to use acquired insight to confront disturbing perceptions, the analyst is frequently prey to discouragement, frustration, exasperation, and thoughts of discontinuing the analysis. Regressively revived sadism or reactive masochism are obvious countertransference dangers that these patients easily incorporate into their sexualized maintenance of the illusory world. Professor B had a barometer exquisitely attuned to the level of exasperation he provoked in me and attempted to use it to control me.

It seems to me nevertheless essential to meet the patient's desperate attempts to turn the analysis into the sequestered fantasy world I have described with interventions that address those repetitive maneuvers and the anxieties and wishes that make them necessary. In struggling with the reactions evoked by their maneuvers, it helps to remind oneself that the very undermining of the analysis that is so discouraging and frustrating is actually a positive development: it is the transference embodiment of the patient's central conflict, and in vivo it awaits analysis.

Definitional Limits of the Transference Neurosis

I have attempted to undo the condensation that exists between *transference* as a verb and as a noun by distinguishing transferring as process from transference neurosis as one among several possible results—hence my attempt to describe alternative transference organizations. That is, I understand transferring to be the general, multifaceted, and shifting process within the patient in which the variable object representations of the analyst are constructed as a result of the analysis of previous compromise formations. Transference neurosis would be reserved for the result of that process as it moves progressively toward the core structuring pathogenic conflicts that gradually deploy themselves in the less defensive, more immediate, more crystallized form in an ego adequately integrated to permit neurotic-level functioning.

I have described the infantile neurosis recapitulated in a transference neurosis as an integrated solution to core organizing oedipal and preoedipal conflicts. The solution may be modified in latency or adolescence. Core conflicts emerge in the transference neurosis as combinations of structure and content and depend on individual life circumstances for their specifics.

Since oedipal conflict exists at a developmental apex at which earlier conflict is integrated and conflict solutions affecting structure (the formation of the superego) arrived at, oedipal conflict modified by preoedipal precursors will manifest itself as part of the content and structural result of the core organizing conflicts and their solutions. Structure and content are reciprocally and complexly interrelated. Both are components of a transference neurosis.

Technique that focuses on the here-and-now transference and considers it primarily a therapeutic object relationship tends to narrow transference connections to the present. This narrowing is not a problem in Kleinian thought because the original relation to the mother is already seen as transferential. But in a classically based conception of transference, the constructed object representations at the poles of the transference connection must also be taken into account. One of these is fixed in the past, in the representations of primary objects as these are mediated by fantasies, primarily unconscious (Boesky, 1983); the second is constructed as a function of the transference process according to the ego organization of the analysand and maintained as distinct from primary object representations where the ego structure of the analysand permits. Transferring as process, when guided by an integrated ego, results in the differentiated construction of an object representation of the analyst which is imbued with the fantasies concerned with primary objects, yet is distinct from the representations of primary objects. That construction constitutes one perspective on the evolving organization of a transference neurosis.

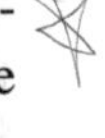

In the course of that evolution, shifting conflicts and compromises move progressively in the direction of transferential versions of more and more uncomfortable organizing conflicts and the fantasies and object representations involved in them. Necessarily requisite ego and superego functions include the deployment of signal anxiety, the relative taking of responsibility for thoughts and actions, the ability to synthesize conflict solutions, and the capacity to differentiate among object representations and between self and object representations. That does not mean that conflict will not disrupt these and other important functions, only that the ego and superego generally have these capacities, are not too prone to more generalized regressions, and do not lack a basic integration.

The relatively structured ego makes possible differentiation between the representations of the analyst and those of primary objects. Ongoing work increases that ability by increasing understanding of the propensity to confound past with present while it deepens the experience of the past in the present at the same time. The transferred similarities are thus perceived in the context of a growing awareness of difference. That increasingly concentrated amalgam constitutes what we might call the compound/complex compromise formation of the transference neurosis.

When the structure of the analysand includes an ego split characteristic of the fetishist Freud described, that split will be reflected in the organization of simultaneously contradictory sets of fantasies that compose the object representations of the analyst and before that the object representations of primary objects. As a function of that contradiction, a part of the transference illusion is sacrificed for the whole.

Where the psychic structure of the analysand is even more split and less cohesive, less synthesized object representations lead to less synthesized, more contradictory transferential object representations, a more chaotic transference picture, and a potentially greater sacrifice of transference illusion. Given the generally accompanying proclivity to rapid structural regression, the analysand may lose the ability to distinguish between the object representations of the analyst and those of primary objects. Mutual work necessary to understand transference processes thus is disrupted. Since the transference process can proceed along certain pathways only as far as established ego organization permits, the lack of differentiation between primary and transferential object representations may allow only an endless feedback loop to which only further structuralization can provide an alternative path. A paranoid transference in which the patient hears the analyst's interventions exclusively as murderous because he is convinced the analyst wishes him ill and is not able to recognize the analyst's good intentions in an example of such a loop.

The difference between primary and transference object representations as they are constructed, a factor we assume but usually relegate to the background, permits the necessary recognition of the illusory quality of the relation to the analyst. For a transference neurosis to evolve, an ego capacity to differentiate one object representation from another and a synthetic capacity of the ego to maintain those distinctions as noncontradictory within different fantasy elaborations are important and requisite functions.

We can then say that the process leading to a transference neurosis involves a transfer of the components of determinative unconscious conflicts originally from childhood and ensuing adaptive and maladaptive conflict solutions from primary object representations to the compound but noncontradictory constructs of the analyst. Simultaneously in the transference process noncontradictory relatively synthesized object representations of the analyst are constructed from the core unconscious fantasies involving primary object representations.

Where structure permits, a transferring process modulates into a delineated transference neurosis over time, partly by the working through of resistances. The object representations of the analyst as compounded and constructed by subjective forces and less driven observation do not instantaneously evolve. Since the level of conflict is not what defines the transference neurosis, narcissistic transferences are not themselves negative criteria. Rather, the degree to which a transference neurosis is possible depends on their function. When they occur within a developed psychic structure, their analysis theoretically will foster the further evolution of the transference process in the same way that any other work on transference resistance will. If the clinical picture consists of a more split or diffuse ego structure, however, other transference organizations are likely to evolve.

In view of these considerations, it makes sense to limit the transference neurosis and to remove its exclusive relation to cure in psychoanalysis rather than to enlarge the category until it includes every conceivable transference process. Transference perversion and transference psychosis would represent alternate paradigms comprising psychoanalytic processes characterized by movement toward greater ego and superego integration and structuralization and concomitant changes in object relations. In some cases these organizations might modulate into a transference neurosis. Whether all or only some could so transform themselves and whether relative success in outcome would be predicated on such a development are open questions. This formulation would assume that the infantile neurosis as a solution to conflict had occurred however fleetingly in childhood but was undermined by a subsequent regression. It is also possible, however, to postulate that a new process occurs during treatment in which infantile conflict is reintegrated in new compromises that have the functional equivalent of the infantile neurosis but are the creative products of new structure.

CHAPTER EIGHT

Enactment and Actualization

As noted in chapter 5, my respondents frequently emphasized a qualitative shift in the relationship between them and their patients, which they variously described as a shift toward greater intimacy, immediacy, and/or affective intensity. This regular observation of change can be ascribed to the working through of more defensively dominated layers of hierarchically organized fantasy—including those informing ego syntonic character defense—so that more uncomfortable and/or charged aspects of core conflicts emerge in transference configurations.

The observation of qualitative change in the patient was frequently accompanied by accounts of conflicts being simultaneously mobilized in the analyst. Several analysts, among them Dr. A (see chap. 3), Dr. N (this chapter, below), and Dr. R (this chapter, below), then went one step further and made the mobilization of their conflicts in the context of their profound affective involvement a definitive criterion of the transference neurosis itself.

Whether one can legitimately consider the mobilization of the analyst's conflicts a definitive criterion of the transference neurosis is questionable. I think it useful to make a distinction between the internal process of transference *in the patient* and the effect of that inner process and its behavioral consequences *on the analyst.* Given the necessary analytic progression in the patient toward more painfully felt and intensively experienced conflicts that are part of the transference neurosis, defensive compromises or resistances in the most inclusive least judgmental meaning of the term occur. One frequent version of such resistance involves enactment in the transference so as to actualize a childhood wish that either defended against the more conflictual wish being mobilized in the past and is being asked to do so in the transference present or is a disguised version of the repudiated wish itself. An enactment may utilize an aspect of the analyst's conduct of the analysis in such a way that the analyst either unwittingly collaborates in gratifying the patient while nonregressively carrying out the analytic task or unconsciously regresses to enacting (McLaughlin, 1991). Although the patient's enactments frequently elicit responses in the analyst, the response is not the patient's transference neurosis or, however frequent, a necessary concomitant of a transference neurosis. Analysis of the enactment—which first requires the analyst to be aware of all responses to it—may well undo a transient stalemate or facilitate and be a part of the analysis of the transference neurosis, however.

Recognized or not, transient unconsciously motivated enactment on the part of the analyst has always, in a sense, been part of analytic process. Although Dr. W, for example, was not advocating conscious manipulations or departing from his consciously neutral position, he noted that he had become aware of an unconscious adjustment to a remote and suspicious female patient that had its basis in a transient empathic identification. Recognition of the adjustment permitted analysis of the core factors motivating it.

Perhaps such unconscious adjustment, when not marred by countertransference conflict in the narrow sense, could be viewed from the wider perspective of the facilitation of the transference neurosis. The more thorough integration of the object representation of the analyst into the network of central organizing fantasies may arise not only through interpretations of defensively dominated fantasies and the unavoidable gratifications afforded by the psychoanalytic situation but also as a result of those gratifications made possible by the analyst's empathic identification with the patient and the subsequent unconscious gratifying microadjustments of his behavior. These may make specific ego syntonic character defenses less necessary and liberate energy for the struggle of analyzing them. This position would redefine such microadjustments as an inevitable and temporary mutually unconscious analytic event, the other side of conceptions of technique, and revise analytic neutrality to include the requirement that the analyst become aware of and analyze those transient and subtle adjustments and the unconscious wishes they gratify (see also Renik, 1993).

Such microadjustments correspond to what Sandler (1976) has called role-responsiveness. They involve temporary symbolic actualization of a wished-for object relationship. They are not a necessary part of the patient's transference neurosis, however. They are transferences of the analyst reacting synergistically with the patient's unconscious wishes and defenses. Nor should they be incorporated into conscious technique. In fact, the analyst's conscious thoughts about avoiding interpreting certain subjects need to be attended to as associations to the patient's conflicts and as evidence of the analyst's countertransferences.

Analysands, of course, do not require the unconscious contribution—

microscopic or not—of the analyst to enact. As any experienced analyst recognizes, patients may make use of the ordinary analytic interchange to actualize any wish including those that originally formed a part of the conflicts integrated into the infantile neurosis. Enactments that accompany the emergence of a transference neurosis and then, when brought to the analysand's attention, become part of the content being analyzed are often referred to under the heading of resistance to the transference neurosis. Dr. P, for instance, described a male patient who consistently "expressed a deep and nasty hatred" of his analyst only because he knew that his analyst "wouldn't hit him." At the same time, the analyst was "in the dark as to what was going on in the rest of his life." Although the expression of hatred might be viewed as an analytic advance, it actually was

> nonproductive because it didn't advance anything. There was no spin-off in the sense of increased ego capacities in other fields. The patient was generally nonassertive and continued to be nonassertive. . . . So what was that all about? It was all about the observable fact that an important figure from his childhood was absent from his analysis, over many years. And when I finally pointed out to him that he never talked about this person, he suddenly said, out of the blue, and surprised, himself, that he wanted that person all for himself!

New elements of the transference neurosis emerged into consciousness with intense affect when the silent actualization preventing its emergence was addressed. Of course, the resistance that concealed the transference neurosis was as much a part of that constellation as the concealed material. Dr. P made clear in his subsequent discussion the libidinal passion behind the patient's rebellious wish to possess the object all to himself and the oedipal nature of the partly hidden triangle.

The angry outbursts and unconscious withholding of material were thus a presentation of the transference neurosis as well as a resistance. The patient was possessing his loved object in fantasy by not talking about her in sessions. At the same time he was silently defying his rival by pretending to give the analyst what he, the patient, thought the analyst wanted to hear.

As enactment these wishes could not be worked with. The patient was trying to defeat the analyst by defeating the analysis. It is the analyst's task to help the patient transform such enacted wishes into mutually available content. Reciprocally, the patient's gradual ability and willingness to work on the content rather than continuing to enact is part and parcel of a transference neurosis. If the patient's behavior bores or annoys the analyst and he or she withdraws sadistically rather than interpreting the patient's enactment in a useful way, the transference neurosis will not be present in a form in which it can be approached. Although inevitable reactions to enactments occur in all analysts, not every analyst will withdraw or fail to notice the patient's omission.

It is in the nature of the analysis of conflict that the patient tries to acquire what he or she unconsciously wants (and wanted from a primary object) while the analyst attempts to analyze the wish that is covertly sought without unwittingly contributing to an enactment of it. The patient may then make use of the analyst's attempt to interpret the wish to actualize it. The following clinical material of my own was characterized by such a movement.

A young unmarried surgeon with intense, though unrecognized, libidinal transference wishes became increasingly passionate in the defensive insistence that he would never feel anything positive for me. "Never, never, never," he would declare, his voice rising, especially just before my vacations. At the same time, he made valiant attempts to elicit my admiration by detailing his latest accomplishments to me with pride and an expectation of praise. He experienced my interpretations of these attempts to win my admiration as cruel rebuffs. Each one fueled his passionate hatred. He took out his vengeance by enacting his defiance. Over and over he would forget my interpretations of his passionate involvement so that I was obliged to repeat them. The balance between us shifted without my initially recognizing it. In his fantasy, I had become a slave under his absolute control, one he wished to have as part of his vengeance. The defiance and the fantasy of having a female slave were a repetition of the way in which he had handled his oedipal defeat. Originally, my pointing out evidence of a contradiction between his professions of indifference and his actions was an interpretation he could hear, one that he reacted to defensively. My repetition of the interpretation, however, actualized his desire for revenge.

Thus, despite the received wisdom that psychoanalysts should not gratify a patient, especially where the crucial, intense, condensed organizing conflicts of the infantile neurosis are reanimated, it is sometimes hard to avoid gratifying a patient's wish even while interpreting it. Dr. N, discussing a case where the analyst's talking gratified the patient's negative oedipal wish (see below), insisted on the necessity of interpreting the actualization of the transference gratification:

> One of my unhelpful supervisors would have said, "Don't say anything to him. He wants you to talk too much. If you do say anything, make it very short." And how long should we do that? "A very long time. And gradually he will figure out for himself what he's trying to do." Of course that never happens. The bulk of my supervisors took that approach. Whenever there would be a recognition of gratification, the advice was "stop gratifying the transference"—as if you can in any way ever not gratify the transference.

Viewed from the perspective of the possibility of a silent actualization of transference wishes by the patient, the choice of interpretation acquires a byzantine complexity. In the following case, I struggled to find a way to remain relatively neutral in the face of gratifying either of the two alternatives dictated by the patient.

A young man began a session by saying that he had thought of asking a material favor, but since he'd recently discovered how much he wanted me to take care of him, he had decided not to ask. He realized, he continued, that the morning's forgetting that necessitated the favor was another in a long line of attempts to undermine himself. He had planned to use the morning to prepare for an event associated with the advancement of his career; now he would not be able to. In other areas of his life he regularly, in his mind at least, sacrificed himself, was not sufficiently rewarded, then felt aggrieved and victimized and, in his overt dissatisfaction, provoked people, further aggravating his situation and amplifying his sense of victimization. It was an effective and entrenched defensive position for him, but I had not considered until this moment how much his hard work in the analysis was its transference equivalent.

I asked him what was involved for him in not receiving the favor he had decided not to ask for. He described the inconvenience, the injury to his prospects, the loss of time, and the physical discomfort entailed and then went on to consider the deeper dimensions of his undermining himself: his guilt over the death in an accident in his childhood of a schoolmate, his belief that he had been responsible for it, his sense that he was always struggling with his guilt and was never free from his sense of responsibility for the death. While accurate, these latter associations had a "good patient" quality.

I considered the position he was placing me in transferentially: I could either accord him the favor or let him use the analytic situation to suffer. Overt action would gratify his wish to be an exception, whereas my abstinence would gratify his feminine, masochistic wishes, increasing his sense of entitlement. I asked the patient if he could think of any reason he could not *talk about requesting* the favor and analyze the situation with me at the same time. There was a silence. He reported that he was flooded with anxiety, could hardly think. What would he do to himself if remedying his morning's forgetting did not prevent him from the preparation that might advance his career? What would happen to him if he did not undermine himself but acted for himself? He would find himself alone in the world! Then he could be killed too! And look what I was doing to him! I was raising the possibility of his going out where I couldn't protect him! He was, in fact, angry that I couldn't protect him. He didn't want to act for himself or even contemplate a choice. In the subsequent work, it emerged that suffering in the belief that he was pleasing me permitted him to feel protected while he hid from his terror of being unprotected and from his rage toward his mother/analyst for being unable to protect him. The work revealed his difficulty in facing the psychic truth that neither his mother nor he was omnipotent.

Since a silent actualization often serves a resistance linked to childhood wishes from the infantile neurosis, it may manifest itself through the impression of a stalemate or, if never recognized and interpreted, become one. When it utilizes elements of the analytic setting including elements of the analyst's character (Baudry, 1991) and/or aspects of analytic technique itself, however, the analyst cannot always recognize that an important wish integral to the analysis of a transference neurosis is being enacted. Dr. N described a reanalysis in which the unresolved transference to the first analyst reappeared and the reasons for which it was not successfully negotiated were uncovered.

> The patient was a very excellent talker and a very attentive listener to my comments. I'd recently discovered he had a symptom in latency in which he needed to have his mother pat him on the back when he was in bed for a long period of time for him to fall asleep; if she didn't, he would demand that she comply. When his father attempted to interfere, which happened at least once, he got more upset. He was very close to his mother and not so close to his father.
>
> In the analysis the gratification of being soothed and patted was repeated when I spoke. If I spoke, I was very reassuring to him; I made him feel comforted, understood, admired, loved. That encouraged him to act in such a way as to unconsciously demand that I speak more and more. If I didn't speak, he became very impatient. He made pauses and breaks in his associations and left things unfinished and became more interesting at the end of the interview.
>
> These peculiar inconsistent hesitations, disruptions, and movements would create a tension in me to say something to him. When I would start to talk he would indicate that he was all alert to listen before I had even said anything.
>
> All this behavior was out of context with his personality. At first I didn't realize that they had anything to do with a transference neurosis. But I realized that he was not generally an eager anticipator of that kind. I became aware that there was a pressure on me to talk to him and to tell him and to elaborate. Once I picked up the fact that I spoke more elaborately in giving an interpretation than I usually do. I wondered "why am I doing this?" It became pretty clear to me that it was all built into this effort of his to use my voice as a way to soothe him and to relate to me as he had to his mother.
>
> That became a construction of mine in interpreting the transference,

and it led to material about an early period of his life that differentiated his expectation of me from his ordinary expectations of how I would appreciate him. For example, he presents information and associations and his work in a way that makes you feel interested. He expects to be appreciated because he's bright. But wishes for me to soothe and gratify him are not part of his conscious expectation of the way people should respond to him. I would distinguish ordinary expectations from this specific experience of gratification. This experience has to do with unconscious longings and with the tendency to repeat a gratification without realizing it.

The idea about his being gratified through my way of talking came up approximately a year ago. A lot of material has been worked through, which has put me in the position to show him the role of his resolution of the Oedipus complex in terms of his feminine identification, seeking gratification from a man in a disguised way.

It took a lot of work to get this idea where he could see it in terms of his own life and to recognize that this was an area of crucial difficulty with his first analyst. Indeed, the acting out of the negative Oedipus brought that analysis to a stalemate. The analyst gratified the patient's feminine identification by the way he made interpretations and was unable to interpret the ongoing gratification itself.

That analysis was marked by a significant difficulty. The analyst was always ten or fifteen minutes late, and the patient could not and did not demand any change in that behavior, even though he was inconvenienced by it very many times. A couple of months ago, he went back to the first analysis. In his mind, his leaving had nothing to do with his analyst's lateness. His wife was pregnant; he had reason to be worried because there was some suggestion of health problems. The day his wife went into labor, he discovered she would need a cesarean and he called his analyst up from the hospital to cancel. The analyst heard him describe the situation and said to him, "Well, have a nice day." And that was in his mind the end of the analysis. He felt that as a sarcastic, nasty, unsympathetic remark. It fit in with many other remarks that the analyst had made. But this one was decisive. He wanted something supportive and soothing and when it wasn't forthcoming, he didn't want to get anything from him anymore. That fit in with his attitude toward his father.

So in my mind I needed to interpret something about his feminine identification, and it took me a little time to bring it together. At the end of the interview, I said to myself, "Now I have to realize that he's not going to remember this because I have gratified him too much," the idea being that he would forget in order to get me to repeat the gratification. And yet there was no other way for me to have said what I said. So I had to pay close attention in the next session to see what's going to happen to this. And I did pay close attention in the next session, and indeed he forgot a good deal of what I had said; and I was then able to follow the first interpretation up with what I would view as an interpretation of the transference gratification that was more important than the content.

These connections with these early experiences had their effect, because it's clear that the feminine identification connects with the castration complex very specifically. He's a very timid soul who never even had a fight as a child. He's afraid he can be castrated and protects himself with his feminine identification and that has then to do with why he wouldn't stand up to the punctuality issue. The problem began to weave together, to locate itself in that period of time around the Oedipus complex.

I would consider what's happening in the analysis that determines this behavior to be the transference neurosis. But I can't just interpret the gratification or remain silent. I must interpret his reaction to my interpretation as well.

The signal of all of this to me is that it has an effect on the analyst, that when you are under the transference neurosis, you're under a very powerful emotional pressure either to frustrate or to gratify, and you have to be aware of that or you will never interpret it. The transference neurosis gets into you.

Sometimes unavoidable analytic actions may furnish the basis for a defensive actualization that keeps the analysis from progressing. Then, apparently mysteriously, an unconsciously motivated countertransference action that runs against all the analyst's ideals destabilizes the unnoticed actualization sufficiently to make its meaning clear. Although undesirable according to received wisdom, such an ego dystonic breach of acceptable analytic conduct with its suddenness and clear "sent from the unconscious" stamp can destabilize the unrecognized actualization that is preventing progress sufficiently to bring it to light. Dr. G described such an incident with a patient who constantly complained to his friends about how bad an analyst he had.[1]

A law student was in analysis with me for a long time. In the first phase, he expected to impress me and receive the benefits of my power and position. There were deep-seated passive, homosexual wishes. He wanted to borrow strength from an idealized and powerful male because he felt castrated. He'd identified with a mother he saw as inadequate, but he tried to do this at first by telling me all about his

1. This interview was taken down in longhand and subsequently elaborated.

infantile fantasies. He was emoting. It was feeling very stagy. He saw I wasn't responding. I tried to point out he was trying to impress me. He took that up in the same way. It was like writing on water.

In the second stage, if I didn't stoke him up, he saw me as attacking him. He quoted me out of context to all his friends to show how I tried to exploit him and how contemptuous I was of him. It was all wildly exaggerated. Each time, it got analyzed. His brother and father were lawyers. He'd always idealized them. Now he began to feel other things toward them—that his father helped him only in order to show off, for instance. With this hostile transference he was getting vengeance.

He made important gains. He was impotent, had avoided women. He started to be able to make love. But he got to a certain point in the analysis and he didn't move. He suffered because I did everything wrong according to him; he instructed me on how to do it right, criticized me to all his friends, and waited for the prince with the glass slipper. He felt castrated. To some extent this is punishment for being his mother's favorite. She told him, "No girl's good enough for my boy." In the transference he felt himself to be the favorite patient, difficult but especially talented and rewarding. I'm thinking, "Should I put a stop to this?" I'm frustrated, bored. It's becoming interminable.

One day I forgot his appointment. My countertransference. I apologized at the next session. He told me he knew he was irritating and boring, that it must be difficult listening to him. I realized he was not analyzing my faults, but was obviously trying to assume responsibility. He did not want to consider my lapse. He hadn't told anybody about this incident. His behavior was completely different from usual. This was a real lapse on my part. It made me realize he'd never believed his prior criticisms of me.

At the end of the hour, I spoke to him about the difference in his reaction. In the next hour he was scared stiff. He'd been up all night with intrusive thoughts; he was practically hallucinating in the hour. I was a giant snake. He had had a phobia for many years. He was occasionally afraid to go to sleep. He didn't like to kiss women if they put their tongues in his mouth. Now, I'm going to force my penis down his throat.

This led us to memories of his mother that were really repressed. She believed she was talking to dead people. She made wildly venomous remarks about friends she felt competitive with. He remembered when he was ten his mother described in detail an abortion she'd had before he was born, what the fetus looked like and how the doctor scraped her out. We could reconstruct his terror from childhood. She might destroy him. Her sense of reality and her self-control could not

> be trusted. If she didn't like him, she might attack him or get rid of him. He believed she might want to harm him out of vindictive penis envy. As a child, he'd constructed an image of a violent and terrifying phallic mother. He'd defended against remembering his terror of her by his wild exaggerations of how bad I was. When his defensive strategy didn't work, that terrifying phallic mother appeared in the transference. So that's the evolution of the transference neurosis.

Although he did not realize it, Dr. G's repeated analyses of his patient's accusations represented a reassurance that prevented a crucial conflict from becoming conscious. His reciprocal countertransference enactment, in contrast, reproduced the crucial strain trauma, the memory of which the patient had been repressing. By forgetting the appointment, the analyst acted unreliably, like the mother in the patient's repressed fantasy/memory complex. I shall return to this example later.

Responsive counterenactments on the analyst's part do not necessarily happen in such dramatic ways. They can manifest themselves by silence or overtalkativeness or maladroit wording or extra-analytically, in an action that nevertheless bears the unconscious stamp of the analyst's reaction to the patient's material. Dr. R, unable to think, took the therapeutically constructive action of going for a consultation. His account of his experience captured the subjective emotional cauldron of a countertransference response to a transference neurosis:

> The shift to a transference neurosis takes place, for me, largely within me. I find myself stirred in some way. I'm analyzing a man in his fourth year of treatment. There's been this interaction between us that has to do with latent homosexuality, competition, feeling and fearing and wishing for emasculation, and wishing to emasculate me. He has elements of a success neurosis. He has an older brother and a father both of whom he's afraid of outdistancing, afraid it would hurt their feelings or that he would lose their love. He also has a father hunger and longing. One of his early fantasies in treatment was that he was the sheep and I was the shepherd. I would lead him to greatness. He's never made much of himself. Underneath he had the fantasies that he was the Machiavellian prince, and I would be the Machiavellian tutor who would bring this out in him, and he would become a world beater, in both senses of the term, you know, destroying everything and everybody and also being very successful. He has trouble with his passive longings. He's terrified of homosexuality.
>
> I pointed out to him recently that he felt confused about whether he was a man or a woman; that this frightened him and was partly why homosexuality was such a terrible problem for him. It initiated a period in which he kept trying to put me into a feminine role. My inter-

pretations became ineffective. I couldn't understand what was going on. And what I did understand and what I said had a blunted impact. But the issue wasn't well represented in the content. It was more in the process, in this feeling defeated by him. And this went on for a couple of months, much longer than is my usual experience of being in doubt about what's going on.

I went for a consultation. We began to wonder whether he wasn't in a competitive castrating competition with me; what had been in the material as a passive-aggressive and anal control struggle had shifted to a struggle over phallic masculine issues. I went back to the material and all of a sudden it was clear that that was what was going on.

Now, I'd be loath to define this as a transference neurosis because what he talked about was the auditors coming to work, his struggles with his boss, what was happening with his girlfriend. All the content was directed outside of the treatment. So were his actions. He made a resolution to become more of a man. He decided that he's going to go back to an old girlfriend who really was stuck on him and whom he really liked, and try to see if they can't work it out and maybe marry. He does this in a rather flamboyant, impulsive way; but he does it. I don't say very much about it; I wonder about how much of it is defensive acting out against the homosexual transference; how much of it is a result of progress in the treatment.

After a couple of days, he brings in a dream that he is a woman giving birth to a baby, and the baby is a female baby. There's a woman in the dream that represents the girlfriend and a doctor. He's pissed at the doctor because the doctor knows that the baby he's delivering will be a girl. And hasn't told her. In his associations he makes clear that the doctor probably is connected to me; but more important than that, he's in a painful, humiliating position as the woman giving birth. And I'm not giving him what he wants—the information about whether it's a boy or a girl—maybe whether he's a boy or a girl?

Then he stops associating, begins to get angry, gets very tight and retentive, doesn't know why he's angry, tells me about it, that he feels an anger building, leaves the session, comes back the next day and is uncharacteristically silent. This man has been a very "good" patient for most of his patient life. He's almost never silent, but "he ain't marching" any further. We go on in silence and noncommunication. There's something about the session that follows the dream that recapitulates the dream with the roles reversed. I'm feeling helpless, I can't get anything out of him, instead of his feeling helpless and unable to get anything out of me. I'm the woman and he's the male doctor.

There are roots to this in his past. He used to play this game with his older brother. He used to walk around the house with a knowing smile on his face and his brother used to beat him up. All of this gets interpreted. He says virtually nothing to me for ten days. It was driving me out of my tree! I'm wondering, "should I sit him up? Is there some kind of catastrophe in the making?" I say that because (a) I'm wondering it, and (b) these are the kinds of thoughts that he engenders in me in this situation.

The point I'm trying to make is that if you wanted to find the transference neurosis, I think you have to go into the interior of the analyst rather than to the transcript of the session. What came out when he began talking to me was, I withhold from him, this is his chance to withhold from me. This man who sees himself as powerless gets a hold of something that he can shove down my throat. This really gets me. He's the dummy, I'm the intellectual; understanding is my prowess; and he cuts it off and takes pleasure in it. I'm helpless to do anything about it. So if someone twisted my arm and said, "What's a transference neurosis?" I would say, "That's a transference neurosis."

Some Considerations of Theory and Definition

For reasons that the preceding clinical material makes evident, many commentators today stress the analyst's participation in the psychoanalytic process (Gill, 1987). This emphasis has led to a telling formulation of the psychoanalytic process as a "vital interchange between two participants" in which "the examination of the patient's mind is realized within a matrix of a deeply buried pair of reciprocal self-inquiries" (Poland, 1993, pp. xii–xiii).

Certainly, interlocking transference processes lead to subjective states both in the analyst and in the patient, and these states have an effect on subsequent clinical developments. Despite criticisms to the contrary, the psychoanalytic process has never been a closed system (Grossman, 1992b). The effect on the analyst and his or her ability to deal with the transferences evoked by the patient's transferences inevitably have reverberating consequences for the ensuing process. I would argue, however, that the unconscious reciprocity between analyst and patient is of a different order from *transference as the process within the patient that leads to a transference neurosis*.

To condense the two categories is to confuse an assumption and an event, or in W. I. Grossman's terms, a principle and a circumstance (personal communication). The idea that transference is an internal process within the patient consisting of the patient's perception of the analyst in terms of central, partly unconscious conflicts toward important objects from the past was originally a parsimonious attempt to account for clinical data. It became, with time and repeated clinical experience, a theoretical assumption or principle. Variations in the manifest form in which that transference is expressed, as well as variations in the analyst's response to its expression, constitute events or circumstances. The fact that the analyst who is perceiving the actions and associations that he takes to imply the existence of transference is subject to biases of his own also constitutes a circumstance. Events or circumstances may alter the perception or formulation of a principle without the principle itself being altered in its essence.

The principle that is the conception of transference in modern Freudian thinking has as its basis a particular idea of how an object becomes a mental representation. Primary-object representations are seen as the result of a gradual and layered construction. They are fantasies gradually created by the child out of impulses, the defenses against them, and motivated perceptions of and experiences with materially real objects over time. Not necessarily verbal, they are hierarchically arranged around specific conflicts with predominantly defensive versions closest to consciousness. The object representations of the analyst are mediated by these multilayered, hierarchically arranged unconscious fantasies (Boesky, 1983).

The Kleinian conception of transference also exemplifies a principle, but one radically different from the classical concept assumed in these discussions of the transference neurosis. Since it is based on the underlying assumption of projective identification (M. Klein), it does include the patient's effect on the analyst in its definition and is of interest here as a comparison. For Klein "identification" meant a primitive form of knowing the other. "In so far as the mother contains the bad parts of the self she is not felt to be a separate individual but is felt to be the bad self" (1946, p. 102). Moreover, what is projected, practically from birth onward, is not only an impulse but an impulse in relation to an object or part object in the form of a "phantasy" (Klein's spelling and meaning; Isaacs, 1948). Phantasy, in this context, is the embodiment of impulse. Thus the tension of hunger is the phantasized bad object, which in projective identification is expelled and becomes the basis of knowledge of the other. The object representation of the mother begins in the translation of bodily tension into a bad object. The relationship to the mother is therefore to the projected bad object. *From the very beginning the relation to the mother is a transference.* Every subsequent relationship, then, every subsequent perception of an object, repeats this primitive, predetermined transference.[2]

2. If projective identification involves the connection between self and the object through the projection of unwanted subjective affect states by which the subject *knows* the other because it has located its own hatred in the other, knowing the other through one's own hatred in the other is indistinctly differentiated from controlling the other. Projective identification can, after all, be identified by the analyst only if it is success-

Since projective identification is assumed to constitute the original transference, conflicts that culminate in strong affects in the analyst or in mutual enactment tend to be related by theoretical assumption to the phase at which projective identification is stipulated to be a dominant phantasy. Moreover, the preverbal developmental level at which projective identification is assumed to dominate also influences the observer to select as evidence of transference the subjective, nonverbal, atypical affect or somatization the analyst recognizes in himself and attributes to the patient's projections. Although these data are clinically important and it is to the Kleinians' credit to have made other analysts more sensitive to them, a circular relation is established between what is identified as evidence and the clinical understanding of that evidence: strong or atypical affect in or enactment by the analyst is usually taken to be the result of the patient's projective identification.

From the standpoint of modern Freudian theory, where the principle underlying the concept of transference neither leads to an identical selection of clinical data nor accords them the same interpretation, the tendency to condense the interactive process of psychoanalysis with the internal process of transference and its possible transference neurotic result confuses more

---

ful, that is, if it has a real effect on the analyst. It is hard to see how this would not imply primitive phase-specific conflicts to which the attempted solution is to control the object *in reality* (Hayman, 1990). Segal, for instance, writes, "In projective identification parts of the self and internal objects are split off and projected into the external object, which then becomes possessed by, controlled and identified with the projected parts" (1973, p. 27). This ambiguity has long been recognized. Hayman (1990), for instance, described the objections of the independent group at the British Society during the controversial discussions: "There is certainly a lot of evidence that the inner world of many patients does indeed include unconscious phantasies of violently projecting distressing parts of their thoughts and feelings into their analysts.

"It is also undoubtedly a fact that analysts may be powerfully, even hypnotically, affected by the atmosphere that's around when analysands are affected by such projective processes. But whether this is directly caused by the patients' projections may be a different matter. Given that countertransference can register affects just when the analysand feels, believes or 'knows' that he's 'putting feelings into the analyst,' we might still question whether we consciously believe that that is what is actually happening. Do we intellectually credit that the primitive, unconscious delusion of the patient might be objectively true?" (pp. 79–80). Brierley observed that Kleinian "generalizations tend to be expressed in perceptual rather than in conceptual terms" (Hayman, 1986, p. 388). Although the exigencies of theoretical discussions of clinical work have probably pushed Kleinians toward an adjustment that has been incorporated and transmitted within their own oral tradition, Brierley's observation makes it clear why it is difficult if not impossible to distinguish between "phantasy" and actualization in projective identification.

than it clarifies. Thus, although reciprocal involvement today is recognized by many analysts as indispensable to change (Boesky, 1990, p. 573) and the transference neurosis in its older, more restricted meaning was once also perceived to be indispensable, it does not follow that the transference neurosis ought to be *defined* by the analyst's conflicts being reciprocally mobilized.

Gann (1984) advocated the criterion of symptom formation and suggested that the symptom formation of the historically conceived transference neurosis is the only alternative to leaving treatment or becoming aware of unacceptable transference wishes. Evolving analytic data of all kinds—screen memories, dreams, parapraxes—are transient conflict solutions (see also Renik, 1990), however. Progressive dynamic disequilibration in the direction of more and more uncomfortable core conflictual transference material, given the requisite ego organization, is to my mind a better criterion of transference neurotic evolution than a criterion based on symptom formation or on the reciprocal conflictual engagement of the analyst, even though such engagement frequently accompanies the transference neurosis as I have described it.

Rather than definitively ascribing to the patient's transference neurosis the power to mobilize the analyst's conflicts, I prefer to think of analyst and patient as two relatively self-contained core-conflictual units that intersect at points where conflict is congruent or complementary. The analyst offers him or herself to a transient identification with the patient. The identification is fueled by the analyst's empathy (Beres and Arlow, 1974), the latter based on a commonality of experience with the individuals we try to help, on the analyst's capacity to put himself imaginatively in the patient's place, *and* on the patient's capacity to involve and emotionally arouse. When conflict and defense are congruent, as they frequently are, transient identification may become less transient until and unless the analyst recognizes both his involvement and his personal reasons for it and reattains a state of mind that allows him to consider the patient's conflicts and needs more objectively.

To illustrate the separate contributions of analyst and patient in an ongoing transference neurosis struggle, one extremely personable patient has a rhythm of engaging me with her cooperation and willingness to work and then abruptly turning on me and threatening the continuation of the analysis. My subjective reaction is invariably a momentarily painful feeling of betrayal. The cycle enacts identification with and vengeance on a father who betrayed her love. The abruptness repeats the historical manner in which she was disappointed. My affect resembles her shock as a child, but in my frame of reference, affect is not evidence that she has projected that part of her into me. She may have a fantasy in which she has modified the object representation of her analyst by projecting into that representation her hostility, changing the here and now fantasy representation of me and thus her experience of being with me. She certainly *wishes* to turn the tables. In addition, at the moment of attack, I transiently identify with her disowned self-representation as betrayed, hurt, and humiliated by an oedipal defeat.

But, as I formulate the interaction, my affect comes from the same source as my ability to identify transiently with her and empathically to understand her, a similar-enough, developmentally expectable, oedipal conflict, which in this instance is obviously revived. My formulation requires distinctions between the primary object and the transference object in the patient as well as in the analyst. Further, it depends on two self-contained sets of conflicts, one in the patient, the other in the analyst. It is the similarity of the two sets of self-contained conflicts that permits the actualization in the analyst of a part of the patient's experience (see Sandler, 1987).

Like the theater spectator, the analyst opens himself or herself to the inner life of the patient by vicariously putting himself or herself in the patient's place in order to understand. This opening includes an opening to fantasies of omnipotently controlling the analyst such as are described in projective identification, as well as to many more fantasies and states of experience. Although the attempt certainly utilizes primitive processes of the kind Kleinians would describe as projective identification, this conscious attempt to understand the patient is also mediated by complex ego functions that I prefer also to account for.[3]

For the psychoanalytic process to facilitate the analysis of the transference neurosis, the analyst must be competent in the sense of being able to recognize his or her own reactions, understand them in terms of his or her own conflicts, locate them in terms of his or her own history, and be able to distinguish those reactions from the process occurring in the patient.[4] The increasing distillation and integration of core conflicts in a new organization incorporating the constructed object representations of the analyst, within the patient, is likely to reverberate with increasingly focused affective intensity in the analyst in a way that increases the latter's vulnerability to his or her own conflicts. This intensification increasingly demands the exercise of analytic competence. A very fine line exists between a more transient empathic identification and a less transient one. Thus, whether the patient is attempting to elicit an action from the analyst, or the analyst's transient identification has elicited conflicts in the analyst that enmesh him

3. Feldman (1992, personal communication) has pointed out that for Kleinians I am describing projective identification.

4. This competence is a psychoanalytic equivalent to what Culler (1980) has described as "competence" in a reader of literature.

or her in an unwitting action, such enactment is not an uncommon occurrence and may more than intermittently accompany a patient's transference neurosis.

The analyst's inner verbalizations as he or she listens to the patient are important derivatives stimulated by unconscious understanding of and reverberation with the patient's conflicts. Those conflicts generate not only affects and subjective states but a whole stream of silently verbalized ideas, hypotheses, and comments in our heads. All of these are empathically derived associations to the major unconscious fantasies, wishes, and conflicts the patient is conveying as he talks, their distance from a direct understanding of the material mediated by the defenses habitually summoned forth by the analyst when the latter's more acute conflicts are engaged. They are indicative of the presence of compromise formations in the analyst intermediate between enactment and clear understanding. That is, subjective *affect* is not the only clue to what is going on unverbalized by the patient. The verbalized thoughts that occur to us as we listen, no matter how random they seem, represent at least an idiosyncratic reaction to or a partial understanding of the unconscious fantasy that dominates the patient's associations. Optimally, these verbal signifiers of partially mobilized conflicts replace an analyst's action.

Often, however, the times when we need most to listen to ourselves are the hardest times to do so, as the following clinical material, in which I verbalized such an association, illustrates. After several associations about her work life, I heard a young married woman with two children mention something she had never mentioned before, a fear that I might move away. The thought immediately flashed through my mind that none of my patients had mentioned a widely publicized murder that had recently occurred in the next street. Instead of asking myself why that thought had come to me unbidden at this moment of the session, I acted. I remarked on the fact that the patient had not mentioned the murder and wondered if it might be connected to her fear that I would move away. She became very angry at me for interrupting her associations and trying to dictate what she talked about. As she lashed out, I found myself worrying about the technical propriety of having introduced a reality issue. Between her angry outbursts and my guilty obsessing, I heard her say that she had thought about the event a great deal, but not in connection with me. More angry attack on her part about my dictating the content of the session elicited increased worry about whether she was right in her criticisms on mine. All this time I had been silent. Noticing my discomfort and symptomatic thinking, I realized that a particular issue was making me more vulnerable than usual that day to guilt—but as a part of what kind of conflict? I asked myself. Just at that moment I heard my analysand in highest dudgeon say, "And I certainly can't imagine waiting in a dark alley and knifing you in the stomach!" It was a small step to interpret her transference wish, limpid through her negation, and to show her the defensive maneuvers she used to avoid knowing.

My *thought* about the murder was an association that already constituted an intuitive apprehension of my patient's central transference wish to murder me. My *conflict* over similar wishes prevented me from immediately realizing it. Moreover, my conflict lent itself to an identification in which I experienced the guilt my patient defended against acknowledging. My patient undoubtedly wished to project her guilt onto me as well. That was her own manner of resolving painful aggressive conflicts, but it was my corresponding internal conflict that made me feel uncomfortably guilty myself and temporarily paralyzed my ability to understand.

Where an analyst can empathically identify with his patient relatively unimpeded by conflict, his understanding is also liable to be more straightforward and less tortured than mine was in this instance. Where his own more mobile and profound conflicts are similar—and here the specific dynamic constellations different in every individual are relevant—he is liable to call on his characteristic defenses or character attitudes. This recourse opens the way to fulfilling a particular part in a wishful actualized object relationship, as victim or aggressor, for instance, to feeling anxiety or enacting or remaining silent or being vulnerable to an accusation that allows the patient to defend against guilt. Such an occurrence applies to the events associated with the deployment of a transference neurosis as well as to events associated with a less crystallized and object differentiated transference process.

Part of the analyst's response to a patient is, of course, to his or her manifest characteristics and actions. Just as some plays involve the spectator more intensely than others, patients who utilize character defenses such as seduction or provocation readily elicit emotional responses in others. To return to Dr. G's example at this point, one result of his patient's defense against the maternal transference was that he was both attacking and boring. Such manifest behavior is aggravating on its face (Olinick, 1993). How the analyst will handle that aggravation internally is a matter of the individual analyst's conflicts and character. But once the idea of a conflict-free sphere of the ego and with it the conflict-free analyst is discarded, we must think in terms of the degree to which the analyst's conflicts become involved or enacted and how that involvement can be put in the service of understanding the patient and freeing the patient's transferential expression of conflict for its analysis.

Distinguishing internal transference processes and their possible transference neurotic result from the interlocking transference processes in which they are embedded is, in practice, complex and uncertain. Some commentators, for instance, might hypothesize that Dr. G's patient fled to the past and to memories of his mother to avoid his fear that he had antagonized his analyst to the point of losing him. They would consider the recovery of memories principally a way of placating the analyst. That the memories emerged as a result of the analyst's lapse, however, was in any event part of the transference configuration of the phallic mother/analyst. The memories, moreover, changed and deepened the analyst's understanding of the transference resistance, and this change in understanding had beneficial consequences for the subsequent process.[5]

Renik (1993) has proposed that countertransferential action be considered an inevitable part of understanding and analyzing. It is conceivable, for example, that certain repressed traumatic events and the fantasies around them can emerge only after some equivalently experienced action by the analyst is subsequently placed in a context different from that of the original trauma through the analyst's postlapsarian conduct. This view would extend Dr. W's position about microadjustments to unconscious enactments noticeable to the patient. Dr. G's missing the session would thus be seen as an inevitable step in the analysis of the patient's conflict.

If, however, we return to the distinction between principle and circumstance and separate the idea of interaction as the result of two transferences from the internal transference process out of which a transference neurosis evolves, it is possible to see that what is inevitable for one analyst is not necessarily so for another. To speculate for a moment: Dr. G's patient had been broadcasting his analyst's imagined failings for some time. Perhaps sufficient evidence was available to reconstruct out of the patient's insistence on the analyst's failings some of the specifics of the strain trauma in which a primary object had left him unprotected and terrified. Such a reconstruction, by substituting the approximation of a past event for present transference action, might have preempted the need for the mutual creation of an equivalent trauma. The unconscious conflicts around the mother's frightening unreliability might then have emerged and been analyzed in a different form.

The here-and-now dimension of the transference neurosis is not, in any event, an end in itself. It is a way station to the discovery of past compromise formations and what originally composed them. The hope of an analysis is to modify those that continue to hold the analysand captive. I turn now to the relation between transference neurosis and the past revived in it.

5. This case is further discussed in chap. 9.

CHAPTER NINE

Remembering, Reconstruction, and Resolution

In its guise as the sine qua non of psychoanalytic treatment, a "pure culture," topographically defined transference neurosis—one extremely intense and consciously and completely centered on the analyst—can become a treatment goal in itself, so sought after that the role of the past is neglected and its interpretation postponed. Moreover, the analyst can become so identified with the patient's transference neurotic experience of the analytic present that he fails to understand that the present desires are resistances to remembering. As Dr. E commented:

> A hysterical patient is clearly involved in conflicted sexual feelings about the analyst, talks about them, very often with the additional feeling of anger at having those feelings frustrated. Sometimes the behavior is very florid because the feelings are out in the open. Younger analysts, especially, may get caught up in the patient's feelings and say: "Maybe the patient's right. This situation is one of inevitable frustration, and the patient just has to accept the impossibility of any kind of gratification of conscious sexual wishes." When that happens, he does not realize that a conscious transference experience of the patient is functioning as a resistance.

The realization that genetic interpretation can interfere with the intensity of the here-and-now experience has contributed in contemporary technique to an overreaction in which explicit genetic interpretation and reconstruction are minimized (Arlow, 1991; Curtis, 1983; Reed, 1993). Ferenczi, with his acute clinical sensibility, early perceived the intellectualization to which premature interpretation of the past could lead and emphasized that reexperience in the transference was essential. His disagreement with Freud, so enmeshed with his unanalyzed transference longings, set the terms of the current debate between encouraging intense transference reexperience, especially of trauma, on the one hand, and less affectively intense interpretation of the present in terms of the past, on the other (Grubrich-Simitis, 1986; Hoffer, 1991; Fogel, 1993).

But Ferenczi (1932) eventually had to confront the therapeutic limitations of the reexperience of trauma in the here-and-now analytic situation. In the following passage from his clinical diary he reflects on a patient who emerged from an altered state with no conviction about the trauma just reexperienced, so that she was doomed to endless experiential repetitions of the trauma and its subsequent forgetting in a way that has some similarity to the way the hysterical patient Dr. E mentioned above might have been reexperiencing childhood longings.

> It appears that patients cannot believe that an event really took place . . . if the analyst, as the sole witness of the events, persists in his cool, unemotional . . . intellectual attitude while the events are of a kind that must evoke, in anyone present, emotions of revulsion, anxiety, terror, vengeance, grief, and the urge to render immediate help. . . . One therefore has a choice: to take really seriously the *role* one assumes, of the benevolent and helpful observer, that is, actually to transport oneself with the patient into that period of the past (a practice Freud reproached me for, as not being permissible), with the result that we ourselves and the patient believe in its reality, that is, a present reality, which has not been momentarily transposed into the past. The objection to this approach would be: after all we do know that the whole episode, in so far as it is true, is not taking place now. Therefore we are dishonest if we allow the events to be acted out dramatically and even participate in the drama. But if we adopt this view, and contrive right from the beginning to present the events to the patient as memory images that are unreal in the present, he may well follow our line of thought but will remain on an intellectual level. . . . The patient prefers to doubt his own judgment rather than believe in our coldness. (Ferenczi, 1932, pp. 24–25)

Overidentified with his patient, Ferenczi failed to make crucial distinctions between fantasies about the analyst's abstinence and the abstinent position itself and thus confused the idea of a technical choice with the meaning the patient or analyst imputes to it. He also, however, was moving toward a formulation about the patient's need to reexperience a trauma in the presence of an object who can be differently experienced and perceived from the one who originally perpetrated, allowed, or was present during the trauma.

Freud's formulation of the transference neurosis as involving *new editions* of past conflicts also implies the role of the analyst as an object perceived and experienced as different from the primary objects if only by virtue of analytic functions such as presence, patience, and interpretation. Despite Freud's effort to concentrate his vision of therapeutic action exclusively on a transferential analyst, the trace of a present therapeutic analyst emerges in that formulation. It emerges, too, in Dr. E's just cited description of a hysterical resistance. One function of the therapeutic analyst, which is also a therapeutic function of the analyst, is to interpret the past as it is manifesting itself in the present, thereby creating a distinction between analyst and primary object.

Rather than two mutually exclusive positions in which transference experience is seen as an alternative to genetic interpretation and reconstruction, then, it is logical to consider two different sources playing into the transference neurosis, the reanimation of the past and its reexperience in the presence of an object who, though perceived according to and constructed from the fantasies that make up the primary object representations of the past, must also be perceived as different from them. The maintenance of these two transference poles, in fact, is necessary if a transference neurosis is to occur.

The Past in the Transference Present

As it was originally articulated, the concept of the infantile neurosis sought to specify the essence of what was mutatively recapitulated in the transference. That entity consisted in "some portion of infantile sexual life—of the Oedipus complex and its derivatives" (Freud, 1920a) and was additionally assumed to have once been a childhood symptomatic illness. The concept dovetailed with the idea that the transference neurosis, a new edition of the infantile neurosis, would itself involve symptom formation.

A different way of conceptualizing the past and its manifestation in the transference present, however, has evolved. Forgotten meanings or meanings attributed to forgotten childhood and adolescent events are organized into fantasy/memory complexes that continually affect the way the individual perceives the data of the external world. Since all perception of the external world is colored by those amalgams of fantasy and memory, pathology is a matter not of the presence of these specific fantasy/memory complexes or less awkwardly of these unconscious fantasies but of the strength, univocality, fixity, and persistence with which they direct perception under given conditions.

Unconscious fantasies are the expression of those childhood conflicts that arise out of wishes believed dangerous and unacceptable to life, limb, or loved one in interdigitation with the smaller and larger events of life, births, siblings, illness, the character of parents, rejections, injuries, chance observations, happenings, and coincidences. They express differently equilibrated compromise formations, some dominated by defense, some, particularly the danger situations (Freud, 1926a), by anxiety, still others by the repudiated wish itself. They are hierarchically arranged with the defensive versions generally closest to consciousness (Arlow, 1969).

Screen memories are particularly effective results of defensive fantasy elaboration. A relatively neutral memory related to a traumatic event by contiguity alone can replace the latter, following the pattern of fetish formation (Katan, 1969). An apparently traumatic event can conceal experiences that, though objectively rather benign, were experienced as intensely traumatic by the child. An actively hostile wish toward a newborn sibling can be screened by a memory of being unfairly chastised for trying to help. A primal scene observation evoking shock, betrayal, and a sense of inadequacy in a little boy can be displaced to a later time in a scene that stresses parental inadequacy. Memories, as Freud (1899) early pointed out, are amalgamated with fantasies and constructed.

The idea of the elaboration of childhood memory and conflict according to complex, hierarchically layered unconscious fantasies does not easily accommodate the original definition of the infantile neurosis. Since conflict solutions expressed as fantasies can modify ego structure and object relations and influence subsequent attempts at solution, the idea of the infantile neurosis being equated with oedipal conflict expressed in symptoms is simply too narrow in regard both to content and to form. Instead I have cited a definition of the infantile neurosis that emphasizes its manifestation as a structure in the mind, a central transformation of preoedipal and oedipal conflicts into a "more reality adapted, socially acceptable organization" (Tyson and Tyson, 1990, pp. 309–311). I bear in mind a reciprocity between structure and content with the possibility of the one implying the other at all times. A fantasy that expresses oedipal drive derivatives can simultaneously indicate narcissistic object relations. Thus the transference neurosis would no longer depend only on the developmental level indicated by the content of the conflict; instead the inevitable reflection of structure through which content emerged would need to be taken into account.

What emerges then in a transference neurosis present is more likely to be a compromise formation first dominated by a defense against organizing conflicts from various developmental stages toward one or more primary object representations. Sometimes, as in the following example, the whole analytic situation metamorphoses into a memory that is a central, organizing, defensively motivated screen. A determinedly undemonstrative young accountant was aggravated by any attempt to explore her transference feelings. She insisted that to be practical she concentrate her attention in the sessions on her troubling and ambivalent relationship with her considerably older boyfriend. When she was three years old, her mother had for two months become acutely ill. The event and surrounding experiences were preserved in a memory of being allowed to sit quietly at her mother's bedside for a limited time and then being forced to leave to attend a hated play group. Silently, as she continued to concentrate on her troubled relationship, derivatives revealed that the analytic session had become that bedside contact and the bell announcing the next patient's arrival had become the bus driver's summons to the play group. She never voluntarily mentioned her experience in the room with me or her discomfort with its interruption. Indeed, she would have preferred to experience the unacknowledged comfort derived from being with me by being "good" and working hard, and telling me of her troubles without becoming aware that the past had been reanimated.

My challenging her refusal to look at her transference feelings mobilized some of the anger held in check and helped her realize not only that the analytic session reproduced the bedside memory but, more fundamentally, that the memory screened conflicts. The memory depicted her mother as helpless and the child as good. Others were responsible for her being removed from that bedside. By seeing others as responsible, she would not be obliged to discover her rage at being abandoned by her mother in the latter's illness, nor would she discover her belief that the abandonment was punishment for making her mother sick; she would not see that she enacted vengeance on her analyst as she had in later childhood on her mother by a stubborn refusal to endow her ever again with importance; nor would she uncover her profound humiliation: something was wrong with her or she would not have made her mother sick. These fantasies of damaging her mother were also regressive versions of oedipal fantasies of competition. The screen memory that the analytic situation reproduced thus played a crucial defensive function in the transference neurosis as it had in the little girl's childhood conflicts. Among its many roles in those conflicts, it had warded off her intense guilt for imagined, vengeful, and competitive impulses toward her mother. Its transference neurosis reproduction played a similar defensive role toward me. Thus the past that might today be described as appearing in the transference neurosis present involves significant compromise formations organized as hierarchically layered fantasy/memory complexes.

Without articulating this change, many respondents tended to agree in practice. They expanded the content they believed was expressed in a transference neurosis to include preoedipal as well as oedipal and postoedipal conflicts. Many, like Dr. B more explicitly (see chap. 5), assumed a psychic structure capable of neurotic conflict. Dr. T (see chap. 4) compared the infantile neurosis in the original definition to a "genie out of a bottle, something that was preformed in the infantile period and then went underground into hibernation, and then comes forth in the analysis as though the intervening ten, twenty, or thirty years didn't occur"; she called that possibility "foolish and simplistic" and went on to question "whether one can always produce a discrete infantile neurosis underneath the transference neurosis." She thought in terms of a central cluster of repetitive conflicts.

The distinction between the level of conflict and the psychic structure through which conflict is expressed with the consequent broadening of the content comprising the transference neurosis is not meant to diminish the centrality of the Oedipus complex in a combination of its object relational and drive aspects as a major content of neurotic conflict. Without the consolidation of the superego, the ego could not easily take responsibility and regulate impulse in a way necessary for intrapsychic conflict. The formulation simply acknowledges that some conflicts have outcomes partly expressed as structure that may not be remobilized as content in a transference neurosis. The de facto expansion of the infantile neurosis of my respondents recognizes that if the most intense transference phase of an analysis consists in the uncovering and working through of unconscious conflicts occurring before or after the oedipal phase, given a requisite and integrated ego and superego, they are nevertheless part of that central constellation, related to the Oedipus complex in the individual's longitudinal development, either by contributing to the subsequent form of the Oedipus complex or by influencing the transformations of its conflict solutions.

Evidence from the literature supports this broadening. The contribution of preoedipal to oedipal is too well known to document. Greenacre (1956) discussed cases in which latency trauma organized and gave weight to earlier oedipal conflicts. She described a picture in which the earlier appearance in the clinical material and in the transference of the infantile oedipal neurosis defended against emergence of these organizing traumas of latency. These traumas were understood as evidence of "real" oedipal transgression. Until they could be reconstructed and the meaning attached to them understood and worked through, no amount of interpretation of the earlier oedipal conflict was effective. Jacobs (1987) cited adolescent contributions to the transference neurosis as well.

A striking and historically instructive instance of the central significance of adolescent conflict and the way it puts the original definition of the infantile neurosis in question occurs in Freud (1920b). In the treatment of the homosexual woman, he formulated the influence of an adolescent event on the rearrangement of childhood oedipal conflict solution. He incisively described a developmentally normal positive Oedipus complex in his patient revived in age-appropriate fashion in adolescence, only to be crushed by the birth of a brother. The adolescent girl, feeling humiliated and betrayed, reacted in vengeance, consciously abjuring men and looking instead to a (defensively) idealized older woman. Moreover, the transference Freud described bore unmistakable signs of the wish for vengeance against the analyst/father, while at the same time the dreams the patient reported to Freud evinced the wish for a baby from him. That is, there was evidence of an unconscious conflict toward the father manifested in the transference.

But the case challenged the overly schematic description of the transference neurosis as a new edition of a circumscribed symptomatic infantile neurosis. Freud may not have realized that his formulation about the adolescent revision of the earlier oedipal conflict solution required a modification in his definition of the infantile neurosis. How could cure be effected through the resolution of the infantile neurosis if the adolescent's reactive turning to a woman out of vengeance was not included in the definition of the infantile neurosis? Paradoxically, the discontinuation of the treatment maintained the theory of cure and the definition of the infantile neurosis.[1]

In an influential article written fifty years later, Tolpin (1970) also adhered to the narrow topographic definition of the infantile neurosis and restricted it to oedipal content. She contended that when oedipal conflicts are not resolved but repressed because of an inability to resolve them, the pathological oedipal complex "continues to exist and proliferate in the repressed enclave of the psyche, where it is no longer subject to modification by further experience" (pp. 277–278). This sequestered, proliferating pathological organization becomes the "central fixation point" for future regressions including those fostered by analysis. Tolpin argued that the developmentally normal attainment of the infantile neurosis precluded preoedipal pathology.

She did not, however, account for the preoedipal experiences that influence ego development in the direction of the pathological *repression* she described rather than the *resolution* she considered optimal. My own reading of the case she offered as an example of "purely" oedipal pathology is that preoedipal tolerance to the frustration of not being special did not develop and that this circumstance led to compromised ego functions, an aggrandized self-representation, and less than optimal libidinization of aggression. When the realization of oedipal defeat hit home, it did so with the force of a shock trauma. I do not think it clinically supported to isolate oedipal phase conflicts so completely from earlier ones and to conceptualize them alone as an infantile neurosis "proliferating" beyond the repression

1. Freud may have overlooked how his formulation could have modified his idea of the infantile neurosis in part because the narrow idea of the infantile neurosis as a symptomatic illness of childhood—an illness he did not understand his patient to have had—conveniently contributed to the rationalization of a possible countertransference. It is possible that he had a reaction issued in by the girl's father bringing her for a cure in a way similar to Dora's. On the evidence of his sparse clinical description, however, the analysis does not appear to have been unworkable.

barrier, while at the same time being incapable of modification. The persistent regression to what Tolpin refers to as a preoedipal fixation point does not preclude the possibility either that the phallic oedipal stage was attained and is present in the form of adequate psychic structure or that oedipal conflict plays a continuing and significant role while taking a more regressive form. The infantile neurosis is better conceived of in terms of its relation to the establishment of neurotic structure so that conflicts from whatever level may express an aspect of its content.

In contrast to Tolpin's formulation, Dr. T described an analysis in which childhood conflicts from several developmental levels coalesced in a transference neurosis that took the form of a characterological silence. Although many of the conflicts were preoedipal, oedipal conflicts were also expressed in regressive form:

> A young woman, sweet, cooperative, compliant, a phobic, timid, trying hard, inhibited, no easy access to emotions, a restrained and reserved style, small packages of emotion, presenting with an inability to form a lasting love relationship. The chief form of resistance for this patient is that she periodically goes silent on the couch, blocked, withholding, embarrassed. The resistance has to do with a narcissistic, very fragile mother, whose ability to keep her kids in her head was very, very limited.
>
> The relationship to me is respectful; massive reactions to separations, none of it conscious; no wish to think of me as anything but the furniture in the office; I'm out of sight, out of mind in the way she felt out of sight, out of mind with her mother. She made me feel what it was for her to feel that if she paused too long her mother would stop listening. This was a mother who was so distracted and so self-centered that if my patient didn't talk long enough, fast enough, or carefully enough, mother flaked out or changed the conversation.
>
> My silence means that her mother has stopped listening to her. It's very, very difficult for her to keep talking as though I'm still there. Knowing that, my tendency has been not to make her endure my silence as much as I might for somebody for whom silence can be a comfort or an opportunity. But two or three years in, the silences get longer and longer and more and more frequent, because along with everything else, there's more and more to withhold: there's been an increasing ability to form decent relationships, leave the mother's home, look for a real job, and enter the first, more reasonably grounded, related sexual relationship to a man.
>
> The transference neurosis with this patient manifests itself around the issue of silence with a manifest position of "I can't help it. I just don't have anything to say. I'm helpless. I can't do anything." Then she will tell me about what it's like when she's silent for twenty minutes.

And we deal with the issue of what she thinks I'm feeling or what she wants to make me feel.

During these silences, and as they get longer, I feel bored and frustrated and wonder more and more if analysis was a mistake. Finally I decide I've got to use my reactions as part of how we do it. Pregenital issues and separation for this woman are primary. One sibling was born after her so there are issues about what's been taken away and oedipally organized issues around older brothers. But the most prominent issue is with this mother, who was never there, who would forget to pick her up from school, who literally couldn't remember that she existed. That is how she made me feel. She couldn't remember that I existed in any consistent way. So the silences got more and more protracted; my ability to know what was going on in terms of the rest of her life was less; there was more and more depression; more and more hopelessness and helplessness.

I started wondering whether she was doing this sort of thing in the rest of her life. I suspected so. I had bits and pieces of it. Did I really know? No. I also had a feeling that this inhibition and restraint and withdrawal and this sadistic manifestation had to have an active antecedent somewhere. I knew genetically, historically, that this girl had been given to biting attacks and tantrums with her siblings in the nursery. But I couldn't find any of that actively in the analysis.

What I could do was use that knowledge to challenge the idea that this helpless, paralyzed person flooded with anxiety was all she was, to show her the degree to which this behavior was sadistic toward me, designed to keep me uncertain as to where I stood in the relationship. I had to show her that she needed to reproduce with me that core relationship with her mother, but with the roles reversed.

I made a series of statements to her about the fact that she was jeopardizing the analysis with the silence. That purposely censoring things, deciding she could keep things out of the analysis and have her analysis her way, and remaining silent on the couch for such long periods of time was the most diabolical thing she could do, that, in fact, she was going to undermine the analysis. I could be really smart in lots of ways, but I certainly couldn't be if I didn't have her words. And that it was really a tremendous concern to me. This was said in different ways over a long period of time, because it might have been insurmountable. I could listen to and understand and try to put together anything, but I required her to be there and I required her to tell me what was going on in her mind.

It had never occurred to her in that emotional way vis-à-vis me that there would come a point where her fantasies of failing would be realistic. The idea occurred to her that she was making it fail. That series of confrontations and discussions has accomplished several things. One, it has sparked some conflict about the adaptiveness of the ego attitude of permission to go silent and helpless. Patients have to bring willingness to fight against their own most basic tendencies. Gradually, despite her telling me how could I ask her to do what she couldn't do, there has been a real yielding. Even some episodic attempts to tell me about intense sexual feelings, about some activity with the boyfriend that had been withheld. Not surprisingly, what she withheld was masochistic behavior in which she submits to anal penetration and mutual anal penetration and to which there is even a pleasurable aspect, not just a victimized one. I think that is the most secret and most important component. But also, fewer reactions to separation, and more willingness to talk about how mean and spiteful and actively sadistic she is to her boyfriend.

Now, in the context of this watershed with me, I pointed out that I didn't think I was the only one who was always on the edge of my chair and never knew where I stood and never felt I could settle in, and never had any confidence that I had any kind of constant relatedness, that I meant anything to her; I'm sure she was managing to make everybody in her life feel that way, including the boyfriend. This is after much work, by the way, on separation and separateness. Because that had to come first. And there's been much confirmatory material now about what she was doing to him in that regard. The more active aspects of it, the biting, spiteful, actively aggressive child, is being relived more with the boyfriend than with me.

The silences have yielded. There's a different quality, right now, to the analytic productions and the nature of the alliance and to the analysis. I have no question that enormous aggression had to be bound every time this mother seemed to run from intimacy and to cut her off. The need to retaliate, to master the aggression by doing to other people what was done to her, organizes conflicts at every level, including oedipal.

Material has followed from the very prolonged tug-of-war with me—one, by the way, that took place in the most muted of tones includes a subtle eating disorder and increasing concerns about her body, her weight, and androgynous fantasies, and rage at the boyfriend who's immensely successful, and at the elder brothers who were preferred.

Dr. T went on to identify the patient's characterological "depression and withdrawal from any challenge" as the infantile neurosis: "She couldn't let herself learn. She almost became school-phobic. As a child, especially as a small child, she adapted to the mother's competitiveness, to feeling invisible, to having to find some way to be unique, for wishing to be a boy, by withdrawal and forfeiture." That compromise warded off the active manifestations of the patient's rage and sadism so that the latter appeared "only in the sibling relationships in the nursery and later in sexual play with her brothers" that was reproduced in promiscuous and dangerous behavior.

> I think that the best she could manage was a position in which she did not make demands on this mother, except in the most unconsciously indirect way. And the nondemandingness toward me is part and parcel of this analysis.
>
> This is a patient for whom the sense that I mean more to her than she to me and the absolute conviction that the other patients do it better is so concrete that at this point in the treatment I wonder whether the capacity for metaphor and as-if and observing ego is going out the window. This isn't a fantasy and a fear that the other patients do it better. This is an absolute, down-to-her-toes conviction. And a conviction that all the things I've pointed out about her not being able to sustain the process and keep talking confirms.
>
> This is the infantile neurosis. With this case, more than in others, I have a very clear idea of what this little girl was like at three and four. I have a sense of this child as a child who doesn't do well in school and waits. And nobody pays much attention. So does even worse in school and waits. And grew up feeling she couldn't do well in school, just as she couldn't free-associate. A child who didn't know she wanted it to be different, attempting constantly to live out fragments of that relationship to the other siblings in no kind of organized, cohesive way. As an adult, prior to the analysis, when she attempted to form a bond to men, her relationships were so organized by these conflicts that she couldn't tolerate intimacy except in the most sadomasochistic way. She became involved with incredibly inappropriate people, inviting assaults, picking up guys in bars. When she came into the analysis with me, she had moved back home.

What Dr. T calls the infantile neurosis, then, is a compromise formation that shows itself by characterological withdrawal and silence. Several conflicts from different developmental levels converge in this behavior: "I think that infantile neurosis included a merging wish with the mother, but somewhere along the line, mother becomes phallic for her. These conflicts were not only pregenital. There was an oedipal configuration that was very intense but was repudiated. How does it manifest itself with me? She has no competitive conflicts or feelings or fantasies about me. There's no competition. I won. All my other patients have won."

Remembering and Reconstruction

The forging of links between present and past occurs through remembering on the patient's part and reconstructing on the analyst's. Where the general analytic work of separating past from present sufficiently reinforces the adult ego, or where certain crucial fantasies concerning a primary object are sufficiently worked through in the transference, or from a variety of other interventions that cause shifts in the analysand's dynamic equilibrium, memories may voluntarily emerge in sessions without patients even being aware that they are newly remembering.

Sometimes the factors leading to the recovery of a memory can be clearly located. Dr. G's patient remembered his mother's frightening behavior (see chap. 8) only after his analyst had "lived up to" the patient's constant stream of accusations that he was a terrible analyst by forgetting the session. Dr. G had previously analyzed his patient's belief that his analyst was incompetent, unwittingly reassuring the patient that he was not in danger from a dangerous analyst/mother who would castrate him out of envy. This use of the analyst's act of analyzing was a defensive transference actualization on the model of the perverse character's practical joking and tall-tale telling (Arlow, 1971). That is, the patient insisted on the analyst's incompetence knowing that the analyst was not incompetent. In doing so, he disavowed frightening memories. He was saying, in effect, "My analyst is not incompetent, just as the memories I have of my mother acting in a terrifying and out of control way are not true." When his analyst "really" did something beyond what would rationally be expected of optimum analytic comportment, the patient could no longer hold his intense childhood castration anxiety in check. These intense feelings had been bound up with the repressed memories and fantasies about his mother and now emerged in the transference. But by distinguishing himself sufficiently from this frightening object representation by refusing to collude in denying his act, the analyst made it possible for his patient to feel safe enough to remember his mother's behavior.

The dynamic equilibrium of the patient does not always change sufficiently so that spontaneous remembering occurs. Where family behavior has included denial and substantial trauma to the patient has consequently been collectively denied, a patient's loyalty to primary objects will have significant hostility and a consequent inability to separate at its base. An inability to remember goes hand in hand with warding off the hostility that needs to be analyzed. Sometimes, shifts in dynamic equilibrium allow a proliferation of derivatives of organizing childhood fantasies or memories, and it is the analyst who must reconstruct a part of the fantasy/memory complex in order to allow the uncovering process to continue. The analyst is not only, in that case, fulfilling a requisite analytic function but may be experienced as fulfilling a childhood wish by doing what the parents failed to do. Such a therapeutic action may actually be necessary to allow the patient to differentiate the analytic situation from the past. Technical percepts that advocate the analysis of transference resistance as an unvarying preliminary risk failing such a patient.

As I have shown in detail (Reed, 1993), explicit memories can be reconstructed from the derivatives apparent in the patient's associations in conjunction with an ongoing transference context. That context must reproduce some aspect of the patient's relationship in fantasy or otherwise with objects significant to the fantasy or event to be reconstructed. As with any other form of interpretation, the procedure involves careful attention to the sequence and patterns of free associations. A specific reconstruction of this type frequently becomes necessary when a screen memory repetitively emerges in the patient's associations in place of the repressed memory and dynamic interpretations in the here-and-now transference do not lead to a deepening of the analysis (Arlow, 1991). Sometimes, important occurrences or the fantasies about them manifest themselves principally in sustained not readily explicable transference behavior that needs to be interpreted as an acting out of a warded-off memory. That interpretation involves the reconstruction of the memory.

Here is one such example: Although her suffering was overt, Ms. H believed she had not suffered enough because she had not adequately felt sad about the serious illness of an older sibling who had been her childhood protector and idol. After several years of productive analysis, however, she became unwilling to "go the extra mile" of suffering with someone as unsympathetic as I. For months she had attacked every one of my interventions, hearing them as either incomprehensible or contemptuous.

One day she reported a dream that clearly indicated, first, my transference position as her ill sibling and, second, her underlying wish to suffer *for* me. When told that she wanted to suffer and sacrifice for me as though I were her sibling who would then forgive her her health and mobility, she declared once again that what I said did not help. I just wasn't up to it, she added. I pointed out that she seemed to enjoy showing me up. "Absolutely," she replied. "I don't think you're any good." More attacks on my competence followed, interspersed with memories of fighting with, competing with, and envying her nevertheless understanding sibling before the latter's health deteriorated. Then she complained that a headache had started to bother her.

I linked her wish to suffer for me with avoiding guilt over the wish to show me up and vanquish me, and linked those transference feelings with the situation referred to in the previous memories: during Ms. H's early latency her sibling had been diagnosed with a chronic illness. But the illness did not affect their relative capacities for some time. She had felt ferociously competitive both before this reversal of fortune and after the knowledge of the diagnosis; she also felt favored and successful and as time went on, increasingly guilty about her competitive wishes and her own good health. She felt she had to suffer to be loved by her older sibling. "That's no help, either. What am I supposed to do with it?" she began and then interrupted herself to indicate she felt relieved.

It became clear, as the session developed, that while Ms. H had been complaining that my interpretations were no good, she had been wanting to show me up as inadequate, but also wishing and expecting that interpretations would be so understanding and loving that they would remove her transference wishes to put me down. These were occasioning too much guilt. She was contriving to sacrifice the analysis and remain "sick" out of that guilt. "That's crazy, to still be living in that," she said.

In the next session, however, Ms. H, suddenly angry, accused me of talking to her as though she were an idiot and a baby who couldn't do anything right, even tie her shoes. Her voice took on a childlike, contemptuous, teasing tone. The contiguity of the preceding associations concerning her sibling in the context illuminated by the previous day's work allowed me to reconstruct: when I spoke, Ms. H was hearing me as though I were her older sibling making fun of her. I continued that this sibling, consciously remembered as so protective, must have been enraged at being sick, envied her health and treated her the way she had been treating me and accusing me of treating her, with venomous contempt, scorn, and envy. Memories of being relentlessly teased, mocked in front of the neighborhood children, and beaten up by her sibling, all of which Ms. H had repressed, began to come back to her.

Normal sibling rivalry had been intensified to murderous rage by the older sibling's behavior. The ensuing guilt was intensified by the reality of the sibling's degenerating health. Repression of the sibling's cruel conduct and a defensive seeking for the sibling's absolution were the attempted ways of dealing with the relentless pressure of her unconscious guilt and rage. But the unconscious conflict emerged in the transference. Ms. H was stuck between wanting to suffer to gain my love and wanting to kill me. Although she did not remember her sibling's behavior, she experienced it in the transference present. In that present, she could use her conviction about my contemptuous attitude as a reason to punish herself by leaving the treatment. Since she used my interpretations to gratify her wish to suffer, repeated interpretations of her guilt did not facilitate her remembering her sibling's ill treatment of her. But clarifying her wish to suffer for me to receive love and absolution and avoid guilt changed the dynamic equilibrium, so that she could express the transference aggression more clearly and allow associations about her childhood relationship with her sibling to emerge in contiguity with the transference aggression. This contiguity made it possible to make a genetic interpretation about her guilt. What emerged next was a clearer demonstration that she heard the interpretations as though the analyst were a teasing, baiting, older sibling. It was then possible to reconstruct her sibling's belittling behavior.

One of the functions of reconstruction is to help the analysand distinguish between a perceived event (however subjectively received and registered) and the unconscious fantasy about it in which it has become enmeshed and which may secondarily lend it meaning. In the ongoing analytic process, that is no easy task. Dr. D offered a glimpse of the analyst's process of assessment as well as an example of an unusually close interdigitation of transference present and traumatic past:

> This patient is a college administrator of thirty-two who I've had in analysis for about three years now. We're beginning to be convinced this individual was sexually abused by father. This was unexpected. There were no memories before the analysis began. I have kept the idea in mind that this may actually have happened, or it may be that something else happened that was misinterpreted by the patient—perhaps being ill with a high fever and delusional, and father had to force oral medication down, which then retrospectively became reconstructed to being forced to perform fellatio. But we've been working with this over a considerable period of time. It's obvious that there was some trauma, because it's being relived on the couch, in terms of the affect of the experience. The patient regresses rather remarkably for a basically healthy individual, but very specifically, in little pockets. Memories come back almost with the clarity of screen memories, but they're very fragmented at this point. It's almost like putting together a puzzle; you get another little piece here and a little piece there.
>
> One of the very early memories that has come back recently is of having been in the bedroom with father and then being in the hallway, frightened and calling for mother, only mother's not there. Now, to give you a little bit of history: mother had a serious, chronic illness, but it was also complicated by what sounds like a hysterical reaction at times. And she would be frequently and unpredictably hospitalized. Sometimes she would go shopping, pass out in a store, and get taken to the emergency room. And so there's a lot of difficulty in terms of seeing mother as an unreliable person, someone who needed taking care of herself.
>
> But *this* memory is more specific, as if something had gone on in the bedroom with father, the patient had run out into the hall calling for mother, and she wasn't there. And there's a tremendous amount of fear, as this comes out.
>
> It so happened that the day after working on this memory in analy-

sis, there was an official event that included spouses at the college where the patient works and where I am on the consulting staff. My wife is known to a lot of the people at the college because she has been involved in some fund-raising activities, and she was expected to attend. She and the patient have met, but they've had very little to do with each other. It turned out that my wife didn't make it—there was a freak accident on the bridge that had blocked up all traffic coming over the river into the city for hours, only we didn't know that at the time.

This was a big affair, maybe five hundred people in the auditorium. But the patient wound up sitting a few rows behind me and noticed immediately that my wife wasn't there, that I was obviously alone, and panicked! Why was I there alone? Where was my wife? What had happened to her? It totally reproduced the situation in the memory, along with terrible anxiety. We didn't speak, just nodded as we were leaving, but I found out later that the patient had asked other people, trying to find out why my wife hadn't been there. And the next day in the session, we worked on understanding this reaction, and it furthered the whole transference relationship. But still at the end of the session the patient felt this intense panic, of still not knowing what had happened to my wife and of having to know she was all right! The fantasy that I had done something to my wife persisted, along with an agitated feeling that would not go away, until finally the next day the patient found out from mutual friends where my wife works and went by surreptitiously to see that she was there.

It wasn't just the relationship with a particular person from this early experience that was transferred, but the whole experience was replayed both in the transference with me and also in the situation outside that so closely reproduced the original experience.

I still have a question about what really happened. I don't have a question that something very traumatic happened that was experienced as if it had been sexual abuse. And I'm not sure that other kinds of things that get distorted can really produce that kind of intensity. It's an interesting question. You talked about narrative truth and all that sort of thing, and if it had been, say, an experience of being sick with a high fever and delirious, which was then later distorted, would that really produce the kind of stuff that comes back with such terror? I'm not sure that we can say that. This patient has been extremely frightened and unsettled while working on the couch. Just common sense would seem to say that something distorted and reconstructed later on should not carry the same intensity as a real experience that happened. But I don't know.

Given that Dr. D made no suggestion that sexual abuse had occurred and that the current hysterical climate around sexual abuse did not yet exist, knowledge that a major function of screen memory formation is defensive is one of the ways we can discriminate the likely representation of trauma from fantasy elaborations of a wish. Since a screen memory reduces the painful affects associated with the experience represented, it would be highly unusual to discover that these reluctantly emerging memories of childhood sexual abuse with their complex conflictual affective charge of rage, terror, humiliation, pain, guilt, and forbidden secret relationship would be used to screen an expectably less traumatic event. Indeed, several years after the interview, Dr. D reported to me that a history of repeated sexual abuse had been reconstructed and confirmed.

Resolution

In addition to the translation of the transference neurotic present into the conflictual past, the resolution of the transference neurosis also requires the realization that conflicts that the analysand experiences as played out within the analytic dyad are in fact internal conflicts. Dr. E described such a development:

> Some patients come in with rather tight obsessive-compulsive character defenses. During the course of the analysis, they have developed classical phobic symptoms. These symptoms represented an earlier phobia that had, historically, been transformed into the obsessional character. Through behavior and magical actions, the patient had then found ways of controlling the anxious phobic experience. In analysis the phobia was remobilized and appeared in the transference. The patient would have difficulty in coming to the session, for example. The requirement of attendance at the analytic sessions became the analyst's demands; the analyst became the superego demanding that the patient come and expose himself to the fear. With a little twist of the prism, this demand also became the analyst tempting the patient to engage in a forbidden activity. Eventually, the phobia was localized in the situation of being on the couch, coming in and getting on the couch, fearing some kind of comment or word that would be either judgmental or seductive.
>
> The patient felt that I was putting him in the situation where he would be tempted to talk about sexual things. At first, he said, "I have to get to this stuff; this is for my good." But then I became experienced as someone who was personally titillated and interested in his sexual life. If he did talk about it, I would either be seen as exploiting him for my own titillation or about to crack down on him in a condemning way and shame him for the very things that he had produced to please and

titillate me. There was a progressive transformation to different experiences that approached more and more closely the underlying conflict.

The important step was for him to see how he needed to have me in either role. He needed to disclaim his own sexual interest by making me the one who was seducing him. And he also had to see that he needed me to judge him as a way of keeping control over his feelings. He had to reclaim both his sexual impulses and his own projective conscience.

I conceptualize the final step, the relative resolution of the transference neurosis, as being a matter of the patient's being able to see, and experience in himself, that these were aspects of his own conflict that he had externalized onto me. I became both conscience and drive. He had to take this back and see that his own conscience was blaming him for what he wanted to do and integrate it with various genetic roots and crucial traumatic experiences. He became aware of himself as being the one who was responsible in an ego way, not a guilt way. It was *his* wish, *his* defenses, *his* superego, that had to be taken back into himself instead of projected onto me.

This example shows a progressive transformation of character into transference neurosis and a "relative resolution" of the transference neurosis. I say "relative resolution" because I certainly agree with those who say one doesn't give up, smash, or extirpate the infantile.

Dr. E's example of resolution focuses on the recognition and reclaiming of wishes toward delineated primary object representations. The recognition that projected wishes toward the analyst are one's own precedes the recognition that these wishes originated in childhood and were directed toward primary objects. The object of those wishes is also and simultaneously revealed to be an aspect of conscience. Childhood wish, object representation, identification, and structure formation meet in oedipal conflict resolution. The expansion of the content of the infantile neurosis should not obscure the fact that, regardless at what level the major conflicts of the transference neurosis occur, a reorganization of central unconscious compromise formations ultimately leads to a reorganization of oedipal conflict resolution as well.

Just as oedipal conflicts frequently incorporate those that precede them, a parallel movement occurs in the transference: the patient, more and more integrated, begins to exercise more consistently the psychic capacities that a less maladaptive resolution of oedipal conflict allows. Dr. P saw a clear crystallization of transference conflict into a transference neurosis as the result of a productive analysis:

The whole instinctive attitude of the analyst is toward clarification. Not dissection so much, but clarification. And unification. The mass of material in each session and over all sessions can be enormous. One cannot cope with that. As a physicist can't cope without clarification—of basics. And delineating the transference neurosis with this patient [see chap. 8] is an achievement of clarification, the final result of what started in the beginning of his saying to me, "Well, what would you like me to do?" And it also gives the patient the opportunity of making use of his own creativity, using the term in an ordinary sense. How is he going to make that decision? It's something that we cannot do. We've cleared the way. What his resources are is another matter.

I can't recall the exact instance, but with this patient, when I pointed out, how come I never hear about this certain person? and suddenly he said, "I want her all for myself!" there was a moment of crystallization in him. And so much fell into place then, with regard to this person. His hatred of his father, unrealized at the time, his intense unrealized sibling rivalry. Then from that he went on to what was a severe test for him, his grown daughter, who he finally conceded has a good figure! And went away from it, came back to it, and finally formulated the same thing. He wonders what kind of a sex life she has . . . and he wants her all to himself.

What remains for the patient is what I call creative work. To be able to take the chance of taking hold of his wife in the sexual act. Of meeting this professional issue that's now confronting him. Things are enough clarified for him to see his fear of doing them—which had been enmeshed in countless unclarifiable situations to which he responded primitively.

For its crystallization the transference neurosis utilizes ego and superego functions as they come to be liberated by better and more complete oedipal resolution than had been the case in the neurotic conflict solutions of childhood. This more efficient resolution of oedipal conflict is necessary for optimal structure building. As Loewald wrote:

For Freud the superego is the heir to the Oedipus complex. Introjections and identifications preceding the oedipal phase . . . go into the formation of the ego proper. The origins of the superego are to be found also . . . in those early identifications. . . . But the identifications that constitute the superego proper are the outcome of a relinquishment of oedipal objects: they are relinquished as external objects, even as fantasy objects, and are set up in the ego, by which process they become internal objects cathected by the id—a narcissistic cathexis. . . . I think it is correct to say that the early ["ego"] identifications take place during stages of development when inside and outside—ego and objects—are not clearly differentiated, which is to say that the stage where "objects" can be "cathected" is not yet

> reached or that a temporary regression from this stage has taken place. The later type of identifications, the superego identifications, . . . are identifications with differentiated objects of libidinal and aggressive cathexis—objects that themselves cathect in such ways. The later identifications thus can be based on the relinquishment of these objects. In actuality, of course, there is a continuum of stages between these two types and much overlap and intermingling of them. (1962, pp. 257–258)

Loewald goes on to discuss termination of an analysis in terms of the promotion of the experience of giving up an object that has been cathected and whose loss cannot be denied.

> Analysis, understood as the working out of the transference neurosis, changes the inner relationships which had constituted the patient's character by promoting the partial externalization of these internal relationships, thus making them available for recognition, exploration, and reintegration. By partial externalization, psychic structures in their inner organization are projected onto a plane of reality where they become three dimensional. . . . However, the analyst . . . is only a temporary external object. . . . The pressure of impending separation helps to accelerate this renewed internalization. . . .
>
> The goal [of an analysis] . . . is to resolve the transference neurosis, a revival of the infantile neurosis. The failure to resolve the Oedipus complex can be understood as a failure to achieve stable internalizations based on true relinquishment of the infantile incestuous object relations, leading to faulty superego formation. The resolution of the transference neurosis is thus intimately related to the achievement of true mourning by which relationships with external objects are set up in the ego system as internal relationships in the process of further ego differentiation. (pp. 260–262)

Resolution is relative, Dr. E noted, rather than absolute, as Freud believed when he wrote that in cure transferences would be annihilated. The unconscious fantasies and related memories that, in given contexts, once so dominated the individual's perception, persist in the unconscious. The individual knows of their presence but is no longer powerless to recognize their effects. Moreover, contexts that once elicited them automatically no longer do so with the same annihilating inevitability. Because resolution is relative, the transference neurosis, as recent studies have shown, can be revived (Pfeffer, 1961, 1963, 1993). Its revival undoubtedly contributes to the responses to patients that were described in the previous chapter. At best, however, its revived quality is more transient and the fantasies that constituted its nucleus are generally available to the more integrated ego for use in adaptive ways.

The gradual reclaiming of repudiated memories and wishes and the reordering of conflict solutions necessary for resolution of the transference neurosis go hand in hand with the gradual identification of the fantasies and memories from the past embedded in the transference neurosis present. Indeed, this synergy is the essence of structural change. As the individual becomes aware that he has created private systems of meaning for himself by organizing the contingencies of life into idiosyncratic, phase-specific, pleasure principle–bound, hierarchically layered fantasies, he also becomes aware of what events he has interpreted to fashion these fantasies, of the contexts in which, for him, specific rules of interpretation will likely predominate, and of the fact that these contexts repeat past situations, either erroneously construed by his less mature capacity to understand or powerlessly suffered in his childhood state (Reed, 1987).

The acquisition of this specific self-awareness involves ego functions that allow the analysand to notice his construction of present contexts in terms of the past. To turn for a moment to the second source of the transference neurosis, the contributions of the present, the analytic situation consists of two people embarked on a strange and taxing endeavor, one suffering and free-associating, the other attempting to help by intervening and understanding. Although designed to distinguish past from present, that mutual undertaking has a quotient of current experience that is not negligible. For a patient in that interaction to have bloodthirsty, sadistic, or incestuous transference wishes understood and to come to know that he will not be hated for having them or punished for telling them is to feel loved and accepted in the present. Such feelings foster positive wishes toward the analyst and the development of the new organization that is the transference neurosis. This organization facilitates the process of giving up active wishes toward primary objects for identification where appropriate.

Since the analyst is most different from the primary objects in his or her mutually agreed upon analyzing function, the identification with this function may be part of the resolution of the transference neurosis itself. That is, the ego functions that allow the patient to separate past from present for himself may be not solely a product of the patient's more thorough integration but be partly acquired by an identification with the interpreting function of the analyst.

Interpretations at moments of heightened transference affect are particularly important in fostering the distinction of past and present, of primary and transposed object representation. For the analysand, they originate from a dyadic partner whom the patient perceives to be under the domination of his unconscious fantasies without his initially knowing that his unconscious fantasies distort his perception. In the early stages of a treatment, when a patient cringes, unaware, on entering the consulting room and the analyst clarifies his fear, the intervention initiates awareness for that patient of the way his mind can construe neutral contexts as frightening. The observation and his understanding of it open a space between the experience and the mental set that creates the discordant perception.

The cumulative interpretations of what is transferred from the past to the here-and-now transference present by the figure perceived in terms of the latter is the means by which that space for observation is enlarged. In a roughly elaborated series of steps, not to be understood as entirely linear, (1) transference experience becomes (recognized) transference fantasy; (2) transference fantasy is recognized as originating within the analysand and ultimately deriving from childhood; (3) childhood fantasy or belief is recognized as the childhood construction of a particular event or events, their present construction deriving in part from the child's own wishes and fears; and (4) these childhood fantasy/memory complexes are recognized as aspects of the inner process of the analysand's mind interfering with perception.

To Dr. I's patient's discovery (see chap. 5) of the as-if aspect of the transference in her exclamation, "Oh! I made you into a witch" (step 1), we must add the progression, "That is the way I perceived my mother at the time my brother was born when I felt she had abandoned me and I was enraged and frightened. The terrifying witch was partly my rage at my mother, partly what I wanted to do to the baby out of envy and jealousy, and partly fears of retribution for those wishes" (steps 2 and 3); and "Whenever I have felt dependent on someone, I have seen the other person as bad and threatening as though it were always my mother preferring the baby to me and my inner reactions about that" (step 4).

Enlargement of the space available for interpretation, recognition, insight, and eventually self-analysis is, of course, a metaphor for the changes involving the ego and superego that are the outcome of the reorganization of the compromises of the infantile neurosis and of the resolution of the transference neurosis. When rage and aggression or sexual desire are owned rather than projected, when unconscious fantasies are realized and recognized as having their origin in childhood events not necessarily applicable to present circumstances, the individual no longer lives in thrall to rules of interpretation derived from the past.

inevitably disappointing approximation. Something essential is always sacrificed, clarity for complexity, polyvalence for specificity, guts for abstraction. To blame the word for our usage when another usage is possible is shortsighted. I think the concept of transference neurosis with its very important historical roots in Freud is a usefully evocative and clinically useful concept so long as we remove its exclusive connection to cure and consider it to have a double valence in which it designates both one kind of psychoanalytic process and a mutable, though individually determined, clinical entity shaped by the larger psychoanalytic process in which it is embedded.

Thus, for me, at least, *the transference neurosis can be conceived of as a mutable organization constituted simultaneously by the patient's affect-laden perception of the analyst as entwined with the core, organizing, unconscious fantasies (assumed to include relevant memories) from childhood and the gradual disengaging of the object representation of the analyst from those core fantasies.* These fantasies prominently feature constructed object representations and interrelations with and among them and are arranged hierarchically according to their historical function in the mental economy of the individual. They emerge in the transference with more clarity and affective intensity when more narcissistically protective, pain-reducing, distancing, defensive versions of these conflicts have been worked through and are no longer needed as frequently by the patient in interaction with the analyst. Thus the transference neurosis is characterized by a more intimate or intense therapeutic involvement than was previously the case. The libidinal quality implied by the word *intimate* permits the engagement within the dyad of intensely shameful and/or hostile wishes as well.

The evolution of a transference neurosis requires an ego and superego that allow the individual to discriminate to some extent inner and outer contributions to perception, to differentiate among object representations, to utilize signal anxiety as a response to impulse, to modulate affect, and to assume responsibility for thought and action, at least wherever intense conflicts do not present impediments. The concept of the transference neurosis as comprised of core organizing fantasy/memory complexes from childhood in interdigitation with an integrated ego and superego that permit internal conflict replaces the historical version in which it is seen as a new version of an oedipal, symptomatic infantile neurosis. The historic concept of the infantile neurosis is, in turn, replaced with one that emphasizes *integrated* conflict solutions reflected by adequate structure and functions. Preoedipal conflict and compromise determine whether a sufficiently integrated ego can meet the challenge of oedipal conflict so that sufficient synthesis can take place. The form and quality of the superego is likewise shaped by and dependent on preoedipal solutions to conflict, since the constructed parental object representations that compose it depend on the nature of compromises that precede and set patterns for oedipal solutions. A transference neurosis is shaped by an integrated and developed ego and superego. A transference perversion or psychosis reflecting a contradictory or more fragmented mental organization will evolve in the absence of synthesized conflict solutions.

This formulation leads to my distinction between transferring as an internal *process* and transference neurosis as one possible resulting *evolution*. The transferring process constitutes the figures of the analyst according to the central unconscious fantasy/memory complexes that regulate the patient's perception; but it depends on the organization of the mind to determine its course and form. Where adequate synthesis exists within preoedipal compromise formation and object representation so that oedipal compromises are relatively cohesive and a transference neurosis is possible, work on conflict reorganizes existing compromise formations away from distancing, protective, and self-enhancing configurations toward greater integration. This integration results in the liberation of capacities associated with more effective conflict resolution including more direct expression and experiencing of emotion about and toward the primary objects represented by the analyst. Thus, where adequate structure exists, the transferring process advances toward a transference neurosis organization.

Lest this formulation be considered a closed rather than an open and interactive system, it should be noted that an optimal transferring process also depends on the differentiation between the constructed representations of primary objects and the constructed object representation of the analyst. This second construction arises as a result not only of the patient's motivated perception but of the contributing actions and character of the analyst. This variable influences the individual shape, order, and character of a particular psychoanalytic process. In this sense the patient and analyst together may create resistances (Boesky, 1990), may fashion the most unreasoned analytic moments, and may arrive at particular insights. The perception of difference between the analyst and primary objects at times—but at different times depending on the patient/analyst pair—inevitably becomes difficult or transiently impossible even for the patient with adequate structure. Actualizations arising partly from the analyst's unconsciously motivated actions are also highly individualized, requiring specific intersection of individual conflicts in both analyst and patient. Points of intersection and thus manifest actualizations will differ from pair to pair.

Psychoanalytic and transferring processes are interdependent and complex. The transferring process transforms the core infantile conflict into a here-and-now organization as perceptually influential unconscious fantasies and related memories that organize the personality intertwine with the already subjectively constructed object representation of the analyst. The necessary analysis of resistance fosters the emergence of various results of this transferring process. It does so by gradually making conscious specific defensively motivated segments of the underlying core conflictual organization. Of course, these fantasy segments are not only defensive. A wish at one level reveals itself to function as a defense at the next. Thus a male patient's vengeful wish to murder his mother/analyst, when uncovered, next showed itself to be warding off painful ideas and feelings about masculine inadequacy and oedipal rejection. Analysis of wishful fantasies that prove from a wider perspective to be defensively motivated moves the process in the direction of greater immediacy and intimacy, to an experience of childhood conflict in the context of constructed object relations.

The psychoanalytic process thus designates a movement characterized by the distillation of central unconscious conflicts, with their concentration upon the constructed object representation of the analyst increasing in tandem with the growing integration of the psyche. Such distillation and integration is a sign of the functioning of higher-level ego capacities gradually liberated by shifts away from maladaptive compromise formations. From this point of view, where psychic organization permits, the psychoanalytic process results in a transference neurosis. But the transference neurosis is not a static entity. It is a mutable, multifaceted organization increasingly reflecting the essence of the complexly interlocking compromise formations that determine the functioning of the ego and superego.

A conscious, crystallized fantasy organization that has the analyst at its center for long periods of time is not a sine qua non of an analysis. It is possible to conceive of specific transferences (or the new organization itself) remaining predominantly preconscious facilitators at the same time that conscious work focuses more directly on infantile neurotic conflicts expressed through memories of primary objects (see chap. 3, Dr. A). The transference process is multifaceted. From one perspective it is a productive means of bringing unconscious conflict to light; from another, once the conflicts are revived, their transference to the analyst becomes a resistance to remembering the original conflicts with primary objects.

The intricate interplay of which the transference neurosis is the result in the context of the larger kaleidoscopic interweaving of the psychoanalytic process makes it difficult to reduce it to an operational role in the sense of something to be kept more or less continually in mind. Although the concept rarely plays such a role, this characteristic, a result of my more modern and complex definition, is not a sufficient reason for abandoning it. Among its uses are such necessary, if intermittent, operational functions as emphasizing the possible connection between certain core unconscious sexual and aggressive conflicts predominantly from childhood and the inexplicable sequential or alternating phenomena that might be currently unfolding around the analyst, that of accounting for the integration of specific transferences with unconscious conflicts, memories, and core fantasies, that of helping the analyst reorient herself so as to recognize that an apparent obstacle the patient is creating is a communication when seen from a wider perspective, and that of focusing the analyst on helping the patient work through defensive, distancing self-protectiveness.

The concept also usefully evokes the idea of a process moving toward an intensification and a distillation. My respondents' words—such as *cluster*, *complex molecule*, a *process of compaction*, *crystallization*—went hand in hand with such words as *immediacy, intensification,* and *intimacy.* These connections are empirical impressions arrived at in the crucible of clinical analytic experience. They require a concept. Whether this elusive phenomenon is a result of the analyst and the patient in interaction or of a process in the patient analogous to an organic one—or both as I believe—my respondents used *transference neurosis* to designate various multilayered transference cross sections inherent in the progression of an evolving analysis in which important here-and-now aspects of central childhood and adolescent unconscious conflicts were intensifying and becoming clearer. What needs designation, then, is the *precipitate of the well-progressing psychoanalytic process that ever becomes its subject matter.*

Always assuming adequate psychic structure, the transference neurosis can be conceived of as beginning with the patient's construction of the object representation of the analyst and continuing with the gradual uncovering of its manifold constituent parts. The construction informs the patient's current experience, shaping the form and content of his or her discourse, and becomes clearer and clearer either through here-and-now transference segments—enactments or verbal realizations—or directly, in the remembrance of the past. The young accountant who talked about her boyfriend but for whom her limited time in the consulting room talking to me became the duplication of her screen memory of her limited time at her mother's sickbed with all the unconscious fantasies that screen memory both expressed and defended against is emblematic.

Unspoken interactions may take shape through the form of the patient's behavior as well as through the form in which associations are presented. For instance, shifting conflict solutions that result from greater integration and create new more intense conflicts closer to original childhood ones may be indicated by a sudden paucity of associations (Glover, 1955), by subtle intensifications in characteristic behavior (Dr. E), or by particular patterns of displaced derivatives that may indicate the emergence of an unconscious fantasy involving the analyst and may be sensed by him before any further manifest sign appears in the material.

From a technical perspective, the deemphasis of the idea of an entirely conscious involvement with the analyst that must be constantly expressed by the patient reduces the analyst's temptation to ride the patient's conscious awareness of feelings for the analyst like Uncle Toby's hobby horse rather than allowing them to develop and ripen. Dr. P spoke to this technical concern when he telephoned me a few weeks after our interview: "Please tell them not to push it," he said. He meant to caution analysts against being so anxious about the patient having a transference neurosis that they insist on interpreting everything that manifestly occurs in the treatment as referring to the analyst. They should allow the organization to develop its form specific to the analysis and the patient, to ripen to a point where it could be addressed, indeed had to be because it had become a recognized resistance. He was anticipating the very problem Dr. Q tried to solve by avoiding the term.

One extreme of the insistence both Dr. Q and Dr. P were addressing was felicitously characterized by Dr. A as the "What about me?" style of intervention, especially where insistence on conscious transference feelings excludes crucial derivatives of core unconscious conflicts that emerge as the patient talks about his everyday life, his memories, his dreams, and nontransferential associations to them. Making the patient gradually aware of his transference, however, is often also cited as the way a more sustained transference neurosis is developed (e.g., Drs. B and R).

These are not necessarily contradictory technical stances. Derivatives beyond associations to the here-and-now transference are necessary to make a transference interpretation, and a complete transference interpretation technically includes a genetic component. In any event, differences in clinical situations require subtlety, not the rigid application of a principle enunciated for a separate purpose. Our greatest difficulties are less with theories than the way we use theory to rationalize countertransferences (chap. 2). Allowing transferences to ripen without beating them to death anticipates their eventual interpretation in concert with their genetic components. As patients become less guarded in revealing their inner experience to the analyst, they become more quickly aware of immediate experience and thus more able to communicate it. This awareness reciprocally facilitates the process of their evolving experience and its understanding, thus fostering the progression and distillation that are distinctive characteristics of the transference neurosis.

The proliferation of therapeutic paradigms has contributed to a confusing extension of the meaning of transference. It has been considered the total situation (Joseph, 1985), or as some interpersonalists hold, it is located exclusively in the interactions of patient and analyst. I prefer to think of an internal process with reactions ranging from global to specific. At one end of the spectrum we find attitudes and behavior toward the analyst that correspond to predictable fixed patterns of character. Character traits contain the history of an object relation (Baudry, 1984) and have attained an adaptive autonomy, so that they do not testify to the construction of the object representation of the analyst. As Drs. E and T emphasized, however, a more specific investment in the object representation of the analyst may manifest itself as an intensification of a character trait or in other subtle ways that may be difficult to distinguish from a characterological reaction on the basis of manifest appearance alone. When character traits manifest themselves as specific transferences, they often take the form of intensifications in action of the trait—that is, of very subtle enactments of transference wishes out of the patient's conscious awareness. They frequently utilize some unquestioned and easily overlooked detail of the analytic encounter.

With increasing specificity and breadth we find wishful fantasies that ward off more defended childhood and adolescent libidinal and aggressive wishes toward specifically constructed objects permeating the transference, and further along still less and less defensively distorted derivatives of those wishes toward specifically constructed objects. In all cases, the constructed objects reciprocally reflect aspects of the wish and defense as well. Increasing specificity brings with it increasingly delineated repetitive patterns that approach the core organizing constellations more and more closely.

Although Dr. E (chap. 6) described a character organization in which the core pathogenic conflict was sequestered by a maladaptive character structure that was relatively quickly recognizable and analyzable, it is more common to find the central unconscious conflicts diffused in derivative form throughout the character structure (Loewald, 1971). This observation has led some analysts to discard the transference neurosis concept and indiscriminately to designate character traits deployed toward the analyst as defense and specific transferences as transference. Often, they then find it necessary to distinguish between transference phases by such qualifications as "more important" or "deeper." That is, reliance on the term *transference* exclusively does not eliminate the need for distinctions that reflect clinical nuance.

The transference neurosis may take synchronic and longitudinal forms. The transference symptom with meaning on many developmental levels simultaneously is one synchronic form. Dr. W described another in which specific transferences coalesced into a larger multifaceted struggle (see chap. 5). In his description the analyst represented alternately and in rather rapid shifts the various primary objects involved in the organizing unconscious conflict. The funneling down inherent in the psychoanalytic process took the form of an integration of successive specific transferences into the central transference conflict in which the related unconscious fantasy/memory organization was available for interpretation. Dr. Q described yet another common synchronic picture in which central conflicts from a variety of developmental levels and with different primary objects coalesced in a central transference enactment. The longitudinal organization is a progressive sequence, a panorama of increasingly distilled and specific transference pictures (Greenacre, 1959; Blum, 1971). Analytic processes tend to combine synchronic and longitudinal organizations, although the question of sequence as opposed to alteration may also be partly a question of technique.

Organizing unconscious complexes are specific to each individual and infinitely varied according to the life circumstances out of which each of us has made his or her own meaning (Reed, 1987, 1993). Certain guidelines as to possible organization and developmental progression nevertheless exist among which oedipal conflict occupies a particular position. It stands at an integrative apex of significant developmental trends: psychosexual maturation (Freud, 1905), varied and modulated drive expression and inhibition, capacity for object relations, and the establishment of structure. Stressing the "compactness" of the transference neurosis, Dr. P indirectly equated the distillation characteristic of an evolving transference neurosis with the integrative capacity characteristic of the structure optimally accompanying oedipal conflict.

The expectation that the transference neurosis involves evidence of a progressive transference process that includes fantasy organizations stemming from the infantile Oedipus complex, as well as its precursors and significant reeditions, encourages the analyst to think of unconscious organization in terms of the interrelation of material from various phases and its dynamic interaction. For instance, a specific transference related to preoedipal fantasies can defend against a specific oedipal configuration. Moreover, it discourages defensive isolations that could conceivably arise if the concept of the transference neurosis were eliminated and the term *transference* used universally. Transferences in the latter case would risk being regarded as discrete entities rather than as entities interrelated by unconscious organization and various dynamic configurations.

The idea of transference neurosis as the product of a transference process in which the strands of specific organizing fantasy/memory complexes are unwoven and their constituent elements exposed to the light of rationality is related to the distillation and crystallization characteristic of the process. The concentration, distillation, and crystallization come about not only because the analyst's synthesizing functions interact synergistically with the patient's construction of the analyst and greater capacity to integrate unconscious material and thus to bring it forward but because analysis of specific transferences requires analyst and analysand to focus on the latter's private systems of automatic meaning that confine the patient to fixed patterns of affect, understanding, and behavior.

Organized unconscious fantasy/memory complexes are in fact systems that automatically and repetitively attribute fixed meaning. They have been constructed by the patient at moments involving terror, internal drive arousal, and/or unwished-for external perception. At these moments, for the individual only one meaning out of a plethora is possible. The unitary meaning fixes itself to a similar situation or contiguous object, to name only two possibilities, and persists with its unitary meaning and affect charge to influence current perception. Such private meanings dictate the rules by which the patient perceives the analyst. That is, they are the material out of which specific transferences are formed.

Work on these inflexible units facilitates integration of the experiences they isolate into the adult ego. The greater the integration made possible by the mutual work of analyst and analysand, the greater the patient's capacity becomes to integrate larger units of his system of meaning under his adult ego, removing the repetitive, fixed, autonomous invocation of univocal meaning in given circumstances. Perhaps the tendency of fixing on transference neurosis as a reification of unitary meaning, Dr. Q's and Dr. J's objection to the concept, is the corresponding countertransference reaction to this univocality, which my definition is attempting to circumvent.

There is a relation between the distillation of conflict into more interrelated specific transferences and the existence of developed ego functions. Just as, given an ego capacity to synthesize, oedipal conflict integrates preceding conflicts and fantasies within its more complex configurations, so unconscious fantasies attached to specific transferences become more complexly integrated with each other as they appear in oedipal configurations. The distilling and crystallizing characteristic of the analytic process as a whole depends on the patient's ego capacity, which when adequate permits the more complex integrations characteristic of the oedipal stage. That is why Dr. P spoke of certain borderline patients lacking the capacity for a transference neurosis and Dr. G spoke of the possibility of describing alternative evolutions that did not resolve into transference neuroses. For the evolution of specific transferences to complete itself in a transference neurosis, integration in oedipal conflict is necessary so that the more intricate system of isolated pathological meanings may be finally integrated into the adult ego as the latter are resolved. The major portion of the analytic work may reside in earlier phases, however, where a regression from oedipal conflict but not from the oedipal capacity occurs. Where the regression is structural and the distinction between the object representation of the analyst and that of constructed primary objects is obscured for long periods of time, we do better to consider the possibility of a transference psychosis.

The distillation of conflicted experience affectively intense enough to create such fixed meaning engages the analyst and is likely to reverberate with his or her own conflicts. It is probably responsible for the increased sense of subjective involvement described in chapters 5 and 8. When Bird (1972, p. 281) elegantly described the transference neurosis as "a new edition of the patient's original neurosis, but with me in it," he was referring to the subjective experience of the transference/countertransference matrix that occurs when fantasy/memory constellations relating to central aspects of the infantile neurosis are transferentially reanimated. I suspect that Freud was referring to the same experience with a negative sign in his last mention of the transference neurosis: "one must at least have struggled with the evil spirits to the best of one's strength" (1926b, p. 227). The power of these particular transference experiences is attested to not only by the analysts' insistence on the intensity of their subjective experience but by their accounts of their own enactments when they have failed to identify or understand the unconscious material stirred up in them.

The importance of the engagement by the transference process of these core fantasy/memory complexes cannot be overemphasized. All my respondents chose transference moments that touched aspects of such core organizing fantasy/memory complexes to illustrate their concept of transference neurosis. But these moments do not exist in isolation from the rest of the analytic process. They may be more important than other moments because the fantasy/memory complexes to which they are connected are so central, but they rely on the analyst's defense interpretations and derivative-gathering and synthesizing function to facilitate their emergence.

When they emerge, they bring to light material formerly repressed, disavowed, isolated, or otherwise defended against by the patient, which his increasing integration through the analytic process now renders less necessary. They are truly artifacts of the psychoanalytic process, facilitated by the analyst's identifying resistances and uncovering their wishful and defensive functions, at the boundary between the patient's increasing integration and the analyst's growing understanding of (and partially unconscious response to) the patient's material.

This exposition may strike some as too elusive and complex, but elusiveness and complexity are the fate of any attempt to put clinical experience into words. Knowledge of the transference neurosis and the skill to foster its emergence and recognize its frequently subtle development cannot be acquired by learning an academic definition. It is, rather, a knowing acquired through the growing pains of personal analysis, the further work of self-analysis, and the accompanying of patients through their analyses. Indeed, the definition of the transference neurosis is forged for each of us in the crucible of personal experience to such an extent that it is probably accurate to say that in every analysis the transference neurosis must be rediscovered and its meaning arrived at anew. That is, the definition of the transference neurosis is subjective and mutable; it depends, in each instance, on the two participants to that particular analysis, their interaction and the interaction of the various specters that compose their individual transferences.

In attempting to order the confusion, I have added my voice to those of my respondents and become one more subject. Such a development is inevitable. Whatever the position, there is no objectivity for a practicing analyst on the subject of transference neurosis. Transferences to teachers, supervisors, writers, one's analysts, the personal analytic experiences one has had, and the experiences one has had with patients all contribute to one's attitude toward the concept and one's understanding of it. Attitude and understanding inevitably then influence technique and the organizing and understanding of clinical material. It has also influenced my selections from the interviews. There is no unadorned, uninfluenced observation. Clinical data does not exist independently of a theoretical framework or independently of personal conflict and its resolution. It develops interdependently within the frames supplied by those other givens. The problem of an iatrogenic and possibly distorted transference neurosis with which Dr. T was concerned (see chap. 4) remains emblematic of the general problem of analytic category and its relation to subjective observation and existence.

References

Abend, S. (1979). Unconscious fantasy and theories of cure. *Psychoanal. Quart.* 27:579–596.

Alexander, F. (1948). *The Fundamentals of Psychoanalysis.* New York: Norton, 1963.

———. (1954). Psychoanalysis and psychotherapy. *J. Amer. Psychoanal. Assn.* 2:722–733.

Arlow, J. (1961). Ego psychology and the study of mythology. *J. Amer. Psychoanal. Assn.* 9:371–393.

———. (1963). The supervisory situation. *J. Amer. Psychoanal. Assn.* 11:576–594.

———. (1969). Fantasy, memory and reality testing. *Psychoanal. Quart.* 38:28–51.

———. (1971). Character perversion. In *Currents in Psychoanalysis*, ed. I. W. Marcus. New York: International Universities Press, pp. 317–336.

———. (1985). Some technical problems of countertransference. *Psychoanal. Quart.* 54:164–174.

———. (1987). The dynamics of interpretation. *Psychoanal. Quart.* 56:68–87.

———. (1991). Methodology and reconstruction. *Psychoanal. Quart.* 60:539–563.

Arlow, J., and C. Brenner. (1964). *Psychoanalytic Concepts and the Structural Theory.* New York: International Universities Press.

Bachrach, H. (1989). On specifying the scientific methodology of psychoanalysis. *Psychoanal. Inquiry* 9:282–304.

Barratt, B. (1984). *Psychic Reality and Psychoanalytic Knowing.* Hillsdale, N.J.: Analytic Press.

Baudry, F. (1984). Character: A concept in search of an identity. *J. Amer. Psychoanal. Assn.* 32:455–477.

———. (1991). Relevance of analyst's character, and attitudes to his work. *J. Amer. Psychoanal. Assn.* 39:917–938.

———. (1993). The personal dimension and management of the supervisory situation with a special note on the parallel process. *Psychoanal. Quart.* 62:588–614.

Beres, D., and J. Arlow. (1974). Fantasy and identification in empathy. *Psychoanal. Quart.* 43:26–50.

Bergmann, M. (1976). Notes on the history of psychoanalytic technique. In *The Evolution of Psychoanalytic Technique*, ed. M. Bergmann and F. Hartman. New York: Basic Books, pp. 17–40.

Bird, B. (1972). Notes on transference: Universal phenomenon and hardest part of the analysis. *J. Amer. Psychoanal. Assn.* 20:261–301.

Blum, H. (1971). On the conception and development of the transference neurosis. *J. Amer. Psychoanal. Assn.* 19:41–53.

———. (1983). The position and value of extratransference interpretation. *J. Amer. Psychoanal. Assn.* 31:587–618.

Boesky, D. (1983). The problem of mental representation in self and object theory. *Psychoanal. Quart.* 52:564–583.

———. (1990). The psychoanalytic process and its components. *Psychoanal. Quart.* 59:550–584.

Brenner, C. (1982). *The Mind in Conflict.* New York: International Universities Press.

———. (1992). Modern conflict theory: Or beyond the ego and the id. Paper delivered at the New York Psychoanalytic Institute, December 8.

Calef, V. (1971). On the current concept of the transference neurosis: Introduction. *J. Amer. Psychoanal. Assn.* 19:22–25.

Chasseguet-Smirgel, J. (1984). *Creativity and Perversion.* New York: Norton.

Coen, S. (1992). *The Misuse of Persons.* Hillsdale, N.J.: Analytic Press.

Cooper, A. (1987). The transference neurosis: A concept ready for retirement. *Psychoanal. Inquiry* 7:569–585.

Culler, J. (1980). Prolegomena to a theory of reading. In *The Reader in the Text: Essays on Audience and Interpretation,* ed. S. R. Sueiman and I. Crosman. Princeton, N.J.: Princeton University Press, 1980.

Curtis, H. C. (1983). Construction and reconstruction: An introduction. *Psychoanal. Inquiry* 3:183–189.

Dahl, H., H. Kachele, and H. Thoma, eds. (1988). *Psychoanalytic Process Research Strategies.* Berlin: Springer.

Dewald, P. (1990). Conceptualizations of the psychoanalytic process. *Psychoanal. Quart.* 59:693–711.

Dor, J. (1988). *L'A-scientificité de la psychanalyse.* 2 vols. Paris: Editions Universitaires.

Etchegoyen, R. H. (1991). *The Fundamentals of Psychoanalytic Technique,* trans. P. Pitchon. London and New York: Karnac Books.

Ferenczi, S. (1932). *The Clinical Diary of Sandor Ferenczi,* ed. J. Dupont; trans. M. Balint and N. Z. Jackson. Cambridge, Mass.: Harvard University Press, 1988.

Fogel, G. (1993). A transitional phase in our understanding of the psychoanalytic process: A new look at Ferenczi and Rank. *J. Amer. Psychoanal. Assn.* 41:585–602.

Fogel, G., and R. Glick. (1991). Postgraduate development: Rereading Freud, working theory through. *Psychoanal. Quart.* 60:396–425.

Freud, S. (1899). Screen memories. *S. E.* 3:303–322.

———. (1900). *The Interpretation of Dreams. S. E.* 4.

———. (1905a). *Three Essays on the Theory of Sexuality. S. E.* 7:135–245.

———. (1905b). Fragment of an analysis of a case of hysteria. *S. E.* 7:7–122; *G. W.* 5.

———. (1914). Remembering, repeating, and working-through. *S. E.* 12:146–156; *G. W.* 10.

———. (1917). *Introductory Lectures on Psychoanalysis.* Part III. *S. E.* 16:431–463; *G. W.* 11.

———. (1920a). *Beyond the Pleasure Principle. S. E.* 18:7–64.

———. (1920b). The psychogenesis of a case of homosexuality in a woman. *S. E.* 18:147–172.

———. (1923). *The Ego and the Id. S. E.* 19:3–66.

———. (1924). A note upon the "mystic writing-pad." *S. E.* 19:227–235.

———. (1926a). *Inhibitions, Symptoms, and Anxiety. S. E.* 19:77–174.

———. (1926b). *The Question of Lay Analysis. S. E.* 20:183–258.

———. (1927). Fetishism. *S. E.* 21.

———. (1933). *New Introductory Lectures on Psycho-Analysis. S. E.* 22:5–184.

———. (1937). Analysis terminable and interminable. *S. E.* 23:209–255.

———. (1938). The splitting of the ego in the process of defense. *S. E.* 23.

———. (1940). *An Outline of Psycho-Analysis. S. E.* 23:144–208.

Galatzer-Levy, R., H. Bachrach, A. Skolnikoff, and S. Waldron. (in preparation). *On the Efficacy of Psychoanalysis.* Ms.

Gann, E. (1984). Some theoretical and technical considerations concerning the emergence of a symptom of the transference neurosis: An empirical study. *J. Amer. Psychoanal. Assn.* 32:797–832.

Gediman, H., and F. Wolkenfeld. (1980). The parallelism phenomenon in psychoanalysis and in supervision: Its reconsideration as a triadic system. *Psychoanal. Quart.* 49:234–255.

Gill, M. (1954). Psychoanalysis and exploratory psychotherapy. *J. Amer. Psychoanal. Assn.* 2:771–797.

———. (1987). The analyst as participant. *Psychoanal. Inquiry* 7:249–260.

Glover, E. (1928). *The Technique of Psycho-Analysis: Supplement no. 3 to the International Journal of Psycho-Analysis.* London: Published for the Institute of Psycho-Analysis by Baillard, Tindall, and Cox.

———. (1932). The relation of perverse-formation to the development of reality-sense. In *On the Early Development of Mind.* New York: International Universities Press, 1956, pp. 216–234.

———. (1955). *The Technique of Psycho-Analysis.* New York: International Universities Press.

Goldberger, M., and D. Evans. (1985). On transference manifestations of male patients with female analysts. *Int. J. Psychoanal.* 66:295–309.

Goldberger, M., and D. E. Holmes. (1993). Transferences in male patients with female analysts: An update. *Psychoanal. Inquiry* 13:173–191.

Greenacre, P. (1956). Re-evaluation of the process of working through. In *Emotional Growth.* New York: International Universities Press, 2:641–650.

———. (1959). Certain technical problems in the transference relationship. *J. Amer. Psychoanal. Assn.* 7:484–502.

Greenson, R. (1967). *The Technique and Practice of Psychoanalysis I.* New York: International Universities Press.

Grossman, L. (1992). An example of "character perversion" in a woman. *Psychoanal. Quart.* 61:581–589.

———. (1993). The perverse attitude toward reality. *Psychoanal. Quart.* 62.

Grossman, W. I. (1986). Freud and Horney: A study of psychoanalytic models via analysis of a controversy. In *Psychoanalysis: The Science of Mental Conflict: Essays in Honor of Charles Brenner*, ed. H. Blum, A. Richards, and M. Willick, pp. 65–89. Hillsdale, N.J.: Analytic Press.

———. (1992a). Hierarchies, boundaries, and representation in mental organization. *J. Amer. Psychoanal. Assn.* 40:27–62.

———. (1992b). The analyzing instrument and the clinical uses of theory. Paper delivered at the Institute for Psychoanalytic Training and Research, October 30.

Grossman, W. I., and W. Stewart. (1977). Penis envy: From childhood wish to developmental metaphor. In *Female Psychology*, ed. H. Blum. New York: International Universities Press, pp. 193–212.

Grubrich-Simitis, I. (1986). Freud-Ferenczi letters: Relationship, psychoanalytic theory, technique. *Int. Rev. Psychoanal.* 13:259–278.

Grunbaum, A. (1984). *The Foundations of Psychoanalysis.* Berkeley: University of California Press.

Harley, M. (1971). The current status of transference neurosis in children. *J. Amer. Psychoanal. Assn.* 19:27–40.

Hartmann, H. (1939). *Ego Psychology and the Problem of Adaptation.* New York: International Universities Press.

———. (1950). Comments on the psychoanalytic theory of the ego. *Psychoanal. Study Child* 5:74–96.

Hartmann, H., E. Kris, and R. Loewenstein. (1946). Comments on the formation of psychic structure. *Psychoanal. Study Child* 2:11–38.

Hayman, A. (1986). On Marjorie Brierley. *Int. Rev. Psychoanal.* 13:383–392.

———. (1990). The inner world and the environment. *Int. Rev. Psychoanal.* 17:71–82.

Hoffer, A. (1991). The Freud-Ferenczi controversy: A living legacy. *Int. Rev. Psychoanal.* 18:465–472.

Isaacs, S. (1948). The nature and function of phantasy. *Int. J. Psychoanal.* 29:73–97.

Jacobs, T. (1987). Notes on the unknowable: Analytic secrets and the transference neurosis. *Psychoanal. Inquiry* 7:485–510.

Joseph, B. (1971). A clinical contribution to the analysis of a perversion. In *Psychic Equilibrium and Psychic Change: Selected Papers of Betty Joseph*, ed. E. Spillius and M. Feldman. London and New York: Tavistock/Routledge, 1989, pp. 51–66.

———. (1985 [1983]). Transference: The total situation. In *Psychic Equilibrium and Psychic Change: Selected Papers of Betty Joseph*, ed. E. Spillius and M. Feldman. London and New York: Tavistock/Routledge, 1989, pp. 51–67.

Katan, M. (1969). The link between Freud's work on aphasia, fetishism and constructions in analysis. *Int. J. Psychoanal.* 50:547–553.

Kepecs, J. (1966). Theories of transference neurosis. *Psychoanal. Quart.* 35:497–521.

Kern, J. (1987). Transference neurosis as a waking dream. *J. Amer. Psychoanal. Assn.* 35:337–366.

Kernberg, O. (1975). *Borderline Conditions and Pathological Narcissism.* Northvale, N.J.: Aronson.

———. (1976). *Object Relations Theory and Clinical Psychoanalysis.* New York: Aronson.

King, P., and R. Steiner, eds. (1991). *The Freud-Klein Controversies, 1941–45.* London and New York: Tavistock/Routledge.

Klein, M. (1946). Notes on some schizoid mechanisms. *Int. J. Psychoanal.* 27:99–110.

Kohut, H. (1971). *The Analysis of the Self.* New York: International Universities Press.

———. (1977). *The Restoration of the Self.* New York: International Universities Press.

Kris, A. (1981). The conflicts of ambivalence. *Psychoanal. Study Child* 39:213–234.

Kulish, N. M. (1986). Gender and transference: The screen of the phallic mother. *Int. Rev. Psychoanal.* 13:393–404.

Laplanche, J. (1987). *New Foundations for Psychoanalysis*, trans. David Macey. Oxford, England, and Cambridge, Mass.: Basil Blackwell, 1989.

Laplanche, J., and J.-B. Pontalis. (1973). *Vocabulaire de la psychanalyse.* Paris: P.U.F.

Lasky, R. (1989). Some determinants of the male analyst's capacity to identify with female patients. *Int. J. Psychoanal.* 70:405–418.

Le Guen, C. (1989). La psychanalyse: Une science? In *La psychanalyse une science?: VIIes recontres psychanalytiques d'Aix-en-Provence 1988,* par C. Le Guen, O. Flournoy, I. Stengers, and J. Guillaumin. Paris: Les Belles Lettres.

Levine, F. (1993). Unconscious fantasies and theories of technique. *Psychoanal. Inquiry* 13:326–342.

Loewald, H. (1951). The problem of defense and the neurotic interpretation of reality. In *Papers on Psychoanalysis*. New Haven: Yale University Press, 1980, pp. 21–32.

———. (1962). Internalization, separation, mourning, and the superego. In *Papers on Psychoanalysis*. New Haven: Yale University Press, 1980, pp. 257–276.

———. (1971). The transference neurosis: Comments on the concept and the phenomenon. *J. Amer. Psychoanal. Assn.* 19:54–66.

———. (1988). Psychoanalysis in search of nature: Thoughts on metapsychology, "metaphysics," projection. *Annual of Psychoanal.* 16:49–54.

London, N. (1987). In defense of the transference neurosis concept: A process and interactional definition. *Psychoanal. Inquiry* 7:465–483.

McDougall, J. (1985). *Theaters of the Mind.* New York: Basic Books.

———. (1986). Identification, neoneeds and neosexuality. *Int. J. Psychoanal.* 67:19–32.

McLaughlin, J. (1991). Clinical and theoretical aspects of enactment. *J. Amer. Psychoanal. Assn.* 39:595–614.

Meissner, W. W. (1989). A note on psychoanalytic facts. *Psychoanal. Inquiry* 9:193–219.

Menninger, K. (1958). *Theory of Psychoanalytic Technique.* New York: Harper and Row, 1964.

Milrod, D. (1993). Discussion of the report presented by L. Hoffman from the Kris Study Group on the Super Ego. New York Psychoanalytic Institute, February.

Nacht, S. (1957). Technical remarks on the handling of the transference neurosis. *Int. J. Psychoanal.* 38:196–203.

Oremland, J., K. H. Blacker, and H. F. Norman. (1975). Incompleteness in "successful" psychoanalyses: A follow-up study. *J. Amer. Psychoanal. Assn.* 23:819–844.

Pfeffer, A. (1961). Follow-up study of a satisfactory analysis. *J. Amer. Psychoanal. Assn.* 9:698–718.

———. (1963). The meaning of the analyst after the analysis. *J. Amer. Psychoanal. Assn.* 11:229–244.

———. (1993). After the analysis: Analyst as both old and new object. *J. Amer. Psychoanal. Assn.* 41:323–337.

Poland, W. (1993). Introduction. In *The Use of the Self*, by T. Jacobs. Hillsdale, N.J.: Analytic Press.

Quinn, S. (1987). *A Mind of Her Own: The Life of Karen Horney.* New York: Summit Books.

Rangell, L. (1954). Similarities and differences between psychoanalysis and exploratory psychotherapy. *J. Amer. Psychoanal. Assn.* 2:734–744.

———. (1963). Structural problems in intrapsychic conflict. *Psychoanal. Study Child* 18:103–138.

Raphling, D. L., and J. F. Chused. (1988). Transference across gender lines. *J. Amer. Psychoanal. Assn.* 36:77–104.

Reed, G. S. (1982). Toward a methodology for applying psychoanalysis to literature. *Psychoanal. Quart.* 51:19–42.

———. (1984). The antithetical meaning of the term "empathy" in psychoanalytic discourse. In *Empathy*, ed. J. Lichtenberg et al. Hillsdale, N.J.: Analytic Press, 1:7–24.

———. (1985). Psychoanalysis, psychoanalysis appropriated, psychoanalysis applied. *Psychoanal. Quart.* 54:234–269.

———. (1987). Rules of clinical understanding in classical psychoanalysis and in self psychology: A comparison. *J. Amer. Psychoanal. Assn.* 35:421–446.

———. (1988). Review of Mahoney, *Freud and the Rat Man. Psychoanal. Quart.* 59:238–241.

———. (1993). On the value of explicit reconstruction. *Psychoanal. Quart.*

Renik, O. (1990). The concept of transference neurosis and psychoanalytic methodology. *Int. J. Psychoanal.* 71:197–204.

———. (1992). The use of the analyst as a fetish. *Psychoanal. Quart.* 61:542–563.

———. (1993). Countertransference enactment and the psychoanalytic process. In *Psychic Structure and Psychic Change: Essays in Honor of Robert S. Wallerstein, M.D.*, ed. M. Horowitz, O. Kernberg, and E. Weinshel. Madison, Conn.: International Universities Press, pp. 135–158.

Rosenblatt, A. (1987). Epilogue: Transference neurosis: a phenomenon in search of a referent. *Psychoanal. Inquiry* 7:599–603.

Roustang, F. (1984). *The Quadrille of Gender: Casanova's Memoirs,* trans. Anne C. Vila. Stanford, Calif.: Stanford University Press, 1988.

Sandler, J. (1976). Countertransference and role-responsiveness. *Int. Rev. Psychoanal.* 3:43–48.

———. (1987). The concept of projective identification. In *Projection, Identification, Projective Identification,* ed. J. Sandler. Madison, Conn.: International Universities Press, pp. 13–26.

Segal, H. (1973). *Introduction to the Work of Melanie Klein.* London: Hogarth.

Shapiro, T. (1992). Discussion of Charles Brenner's paper, "Modern conflict theory: Or beyond the ego and the id." New York Psychoanalytic Institute, December 8.

Shaw, R. R. (1989). Hartmann on adaptation: Incomparable or incomprehensible legacy? *Psychoanal. Quart.* 58:592–611.

———. (1991) Panel: Concepts and controversies about transference neurosis. *J. Amer. Psychoanal. Assn.* 39:227–240.

Skolnikoff, A. (1993). The analyst's experience in the psychoanalytic situation: A continuum between objective and subjective reality. *Psychoanal. Inquiry* 13:296–309.

Stoller, R. (1975). *Perversion: The Erotic Form of Hatred.* New York: Pantheon.

Stone, L. (1967). Psychoanalytic situation and transference: Postscript to an earlier communication. In *Transference and Its Context.* New York: Jason Aronson, 1984.

Tolpin, M. (1970). Infantile neurosis: Metapsychological concept, paradigmatic case. *Psychoanal. Study Child,* 25:273–308.

Tyson, P. (1993). Neurosis in childhood and in psychoanalysis: A developmental reformulation. Paper presented at the spring meeting of the American Psychoanalytic Association, San Francisco, May 20.

Tyson, P., and R. Tyson. (1990). *Psychoanalytic Theories of Development: An Integration.* New Haven: Yale University Press.

Valenstein, A. (1993). Letter to author. September 3.

Weinshel, E. (1971). The transference neurosis: A survey of the literature. *J. Amer. Psychoanal. Assn.* 19:67–88.

———. (1990). Further observations on the psychoanalytic process. *Psychoanal. Quart.* 59:629–549.

Willick, M. S. (1989). Similarities and differences between psychoanalysis and psychoanalytic psychotherapy. Paper presented to a panel at the meeting of the American Psychoanalytic Association, December 16.

Wurmser, L. (1989). "Either-or": Some comments on Professor Grunbaum's critique of psychoanalysis. *Psychoanal. Inquiry* 9:220–248.

Index